09
9.

WITHDRAWN

THE NORMAN FATE
1100–1154

by the same author

THE SOCIAL STRUCTURE OF MEDIEVAL EAST ANGLIA
FEUDAL DOCUMENTS FROM THE ABBEY OF
BURY ST EDMUNDS
THE DOMESDAY MONARCHORUM OF
CHRIST CHURCH CANTERBURY
ENGLISH SCHOLARS
WILLIAM THE CONQUEROR
THE NORMAN ACHIEVEMENT

THE NORMAN FATE

1100-1154

David C. Douglas

Fellow of the British Academy
Emeritus Professor of History in the University of Bristol
Honorary Fellow of Keble College, Oxford.

UNIVERSITY OF CALIFORNIA PRESS
Berkeley and Los Angeles 1976

UNIVERSITY OF CALIFORNIA PRESS

Berkeley and Los Angeles, California

ISBN: 0-520-03027-3

Library of Congress Catalog Card Number: 75-13155

To
My Mother
In Loving Remembrance

CONTENTS

ILLUSTRATIONS

Acknowledgements and thanks are due to the Mansell Collection for plates 1, 2, 3, 4, 6a and 6b; and to Fillingham's Photography (courtesy of the Dean and Chapter of Durham Cathedral) for plate 5c. Plates 5a and 5b are from G. Zarnecki, English Romanesque Sculpture (Tirnati, 1951).

Map 1 was drawn by William Bromage. Maps 2 and 3 are redrawn by Neil Hyslop from Cambridge Medieval History, Vol. V, and reproduced by courtesy of Cambridge University Press. Map 4 is redrawn by Neil Hyslop from Edmund Curtis, Roger of Sicily and the Normans in Lower Italy 1016–1154 (Putnam & Co., 1912), and is reproduced by kind permission of The Bodley Head. Map 5 is from W. L. Warren, Henry II (Eyre Methuen, 1973).

The genealogical tables were drawn by Neil Hyslop.

ABBREVIATIONS

For most books and articles cited in the footnotes short titles have been employed and these are fully extended in the Select Bibliography, where further information is also given of the editions used. The following abbreviations have also been used in the notes.

Alex. Tel.	Alexander of Telese
Amer. Hist. Rev.	*American Historical Review*
A.S. Chron.	*Anglo-Saxon Chronicle*
Cambridge Med. Hist.	*Cambridge Medieval History*
Carmen	*Carmen de Hastingae Proelio*, ed. C. Morton and H. Muntz
Chalandon, Domination	F. Chalandon, *Histoire de la Domination Normande en Italie et en Sicile*, 2 vols (1917)
Collura	*Appendice al Regesto dei Diplomi di re Ruggero compilato da Erich Caspar*, ed. P. Collura
D.B.	Domesday Book, 2 vols, Record Commission (1783)
Eng. Hist. Rev.	*English Historical Review*
Falco Benev.	Falco of Benevento, *Chronicle*
Flor. Worc.	Florence of Worcester, *Chronicon ex Chronicis*
Gesta	*Gesta Francorum et aliorum Hierosolimitanorum*
Hefele-Leclerc	C. J. Hefele, *Histoire des Conciles*. French edition by H. Leclerc
Hen. Hunt.	Henry of Huntingdon, *Historia Anglorum*
Jaffé-Lowenfeld	*Regesta Pontificum Romanorum*, ed. P. Jaffé, 2nd edn by Lowenfeld, Wattenbach and others
Jamison, *Eugenius*	E. Jamison, *Admiral Eugenius of Sicily*
Jamison, *Apulia*	E. Jamison, *The Norman administration of Apulia and Capua* (British School at Rome)
Jamison, 'Sicilian Norman Kingdom'	E. Jamison, 'The Sicilian Norman Kingdom in the Minds of Anglo-Norman Contemporaries', British Academy *Proceedings*, XXXV, pp. 237–85
Kehr, *Urkunden*	K. A. Kehr, *Urkunden der Normannisch-Sicilischen Konige* (Innsbruck, 1902)

Malaterra	Geoffrey Malaterra, *Historia Sicula*
Ménager, *Emir*	L-R. Ménager, *Amiratus, l'Emirat et les origines de l'amiraute* (Paris, 1960)
Ménager, *Messina*	*Les Actes de S. Maria di Messina*, ed. L-R. Ménager (Palermo, 1953)
Mon. Ang.	W. Dugdale, *Monasticon Anglicanum*, new edn, 6 vols in 8 (1817–30)
Mon. Germ. Hist. SS.	*Monumenta Germaniae Historica: Scriptores*
Normanni	*Normanni (I) et la loro espansione in Europa* (Spoleto, 1959)
Ord. Vit.	Ordericus Vitalis, *Historia Ecclesiastica*. (Cited by volume and page from the edition by A. Le Prévost and L. Delisle, 5 vols [1838–55])
Pat. Lat.	*Patrologia Latina Cursus Completus*, ed. J. P. Migne
Pet. Diac.	Peter the Deacon, *Chronicon*
Re, *Cronisti*	*Cronisti e scrittori sincroni de la dominazione normanna nel regno di Puglia e Sicilia*, ed. G. del Re, 2 vols (Naples, 1868)
Rec. Hist. Croisades Occ.	*Recueil des Historiens des Croisades: Historiens Occidentaux*, 5 vols (1844–95)
Rec. Hist. Franc.	*Recueil des Historiens des Gaules et de La France*, 24 vols of varying dates
Round, *Cal. Documents*	*Calendar of Documents preserved in France*, ed. J. H. Round (1890)
R. Hist. Soc.	Royal Historical Society
Regesta Pontificum	*Regesta Pontificum Romanorum*, 8 vols (Berlin, 1911–61) (vol. VIII, with the sub-title *Italia Pontificia*, ed. P. F. Kehr)
Regesta Regum	*Regesta Regum Anglo-Normannorum*, ed. H. W. C. Davis and others, 3 vols
Röhricht, *Regesta*	*Regesta Regni Hierosolimitani*, ed. R. Röhricht, 2 vols (1893–1904)
Romuald	Romuald of Salerno, *Chronicon*
Studi Ruggeriani	*Atti del Convegno internationale di Studi Ruggeriani* (Palermo, 1955)
Watterich, *Vitae*	*Pontificum Romanorum . . . Vitae*, ed. J. M. Watterich, 2 vols (1862)
Will. Apul.	William of Apulia, *Gesta Roberti Wiscanti*

Will. Jum.	William of Jumièges, *Gesta Normannorum Ducum*, ed. J. Marx (1914)
Will. Malms.	William of Malmesbury. [His *Gesta Regum* is cited from the edition by W. Stubbs, 2 vols (1887, 1889); his *Historia Novella* from the edition by K. R. Potter (1955)]
Will. Tyre	William of Tyre, *Historia Rerum in partibus transmarinis gestarum*

PREFACE

The preparation of this book, which is a sequel to my study of *The Norman Achievement*, has placed me under obligations very similar to those which are recorded in its predecessor. Its publication, however, gives me the opportunity of expressing my abiding gratitude for all the sympathy and encouragement with which my friends have continued to sustain my work. Surely no scholar has ever been treated with greater generosity and kindness. The special debts I have incurred in connexion with the present book are, for the most part, recorded in the footnotes and in the bibliography. I am indebted also to my publishers for their continuing interest in my work, and in particular I wish to thank Ann Mansbridge for the meticulous skill she has devoted to the presentation of this volume. As for my wife and daughter, they know how much this book owes to them, and they know how grateful I am.

D.C.D.
Bristol, 1975

PART ONE
THE NORMAN KINGDOMS

PROLOGUE

I

The purpose of this study is to survey the historical process which during the earlier half of the twelfth century went to the making of Europe. Its particular aim is to assess the contribution made by the Normans to the political growth of Europe between 1100 and 1154. Of course, the selection of these dates is to some extent arbitrary, but these momentous years did mark a formative period in European history, and produced results which still endure. Thus the conditions of Christendom in 1154 might be vividly contrasted with that which prevailed some seventy years earlier. Then Europe was still politically divided, socially distraught, and economically undeveloped, whilst Christendom at large was confronted with hostile systems of morals and belief backed by political powers of truly formidable size and strength. But during the ensuing decades not only was the integrity of Christian Europe preserved, but the Latin West, having watched the establishment of powerful new kingdoms, was at the same time to acquire a new sense of cultural unity and a new access of political strength. These transitions were to affect the whole European future, and they occurred during the same years when there also began a new epoch in Norman history.

By 1100 the first period of Norman achievement[1] was over. The Normans had carried their relentless conquests northwards over England, southwards through southern Italy and Sicily, and eastwards over the Balkans as far as Syria and Antioch. But now what might be called the heroic age of Norman endeavour was passing, and the sequel would be less romantic, possibly less brutal and certainly more productive of enduring results. By 1100, when Henry I became king, the Norman conquest of England was assured, but the Anglo-Norman realm had still to be consolidated. Similarly, in the South,

[1] On this see D. C. Douglas, *The Norman Achievement* (1969).

though Roger the 'Great Count' had completed the conquest of Sicily before his death in 1101, much still remained to be done before the foundations of the Norman Sicilian kingdom could be securely laid. But after the reigns of King Henry I and King Roger the Great, it was evident that the realms they had ruled from London and Palermo had become under Norman government the wealthiest and not the least powerful of the kingdoms of Western Europe.

The changed nature of Norman enterprise during the earlier half of the twelfth century, and the common characteristics it then everywhere assumed from Scotland to Syria, were reflected in the character of the Norman rulers who were chiefly responsible for its success. In the Norman Principality of Antioch, which was one of the most notable products of Norman endeavour,[2] a comparison might be offered between the warrior Bohemund and Tancred, his more politic nephew and successor. But a more cogent distinction could be made between Henry I, the Norman ruler of England between 1100 and 1135, and his father William the Conqueror who had died in 1087. Henry preferred diplomacy to war, and coveted money more than military glory. Pitiless and extortionate, he owed his success to the trained administrators he 'raised from the dust to do his service'. In fact, the strength of the Anglo-Norman realm in his time and its increasing influence on Europe was to depend directly on its careful administration by an active bureaucracy which was itself closely under royal control. It was based also on the ceaseless accumulation of treasure by the king and its continuous expenditure in exchange for power.[3]

A similar transition during these years could be observed in the South. The conquest of Sicily by Roger the 'Great Count' deserves to rank as a feat of arms with the conquest of England by Duke William of Normandy. But it had been accomplished before the twelfth century began. And even more important perhaps was his recognition of what might be the future value to Norman power of the Greek and Moslem institutions and traditions which he found alive in the island he had conquered. This was in fact to be the basis of the spectacular and bizarre success of his famous son. Roger, styled the Great, first count, and after 1130 King, of Sicily was never noted for his prowess on the field of battle, but he enlarged his dominion; he created a kingdom; and he acquired a considerable overseas empire. Moreover his administration, based upon Norman authority but using Greek and Moslem expertise, would serve as a pattern for the future. Men such as Henry I and Roger the Great were the creatures of a new age. They were unlovable,

2 Below, chap. 10.   3 Below, chap. 1.

unscrupulous and hideously cruel. But there can be no question either of their outstanding ability or of their originality in the art of secular government. They were, furthermore, among the most influential rulers of their time, and their works would survive them.

The opening of a new phase in the Norman impact upon Europe may thus aptly be placed at the beginning of the twelfth century, and its conclusion be found about the year 1154. It is true that the full consequences of Norman action during this period would not be disclosed until later, but in 1154 Henry II from Anjou acquired and enlarged the empire which the Normans had established in the North, and in the same year there died Roger the Great, the first and the greatest of the Norman kings of Sicily. The political advance which had been made by the Normans by 1154 may thus for itself challenge attention. In place of what had been a congerie of French fiefs there had been formed an Anglo-Norman empire, expanded from the Tweed to the Pyrenees under Henry II, and including more of France than was ruled by the Capetian kings reigning from Paris. Similarly, in place of a number of Italian and Sicilian provinces under Byzantine, Lombard or Saracen government, there had been established a single Norman kingdom with its capital at Palermo, including not only all Sicily, but also almost all Italy south of Benevento – a dominion which extended from Termoli to Agrigento and from Capua to Syracuse.

There is little danger of exaggerating the magnitude of these transformations, but it deserves emphasis that they formed part of a single Norman endeavour which must be studied as a unity. Nor can its momentous and enduring consequences be appraised except by means of comparison between the Norman rulers of this period and the Norman kingdoms which they governed. Significantly, these great changes were effected during the same decades when the political and cultural structure of Europe was itself being transformed. It seems, therefore, pertinent to inquire whether there was not a connexion between the two movements.

II

An inquiry thus envisaged is, moreover, bound to have wider implications, inasmuch as it must record, and perhaps even modify, some of the contrasting interpretations of Western European growth in the Middle Ages which have from time to time gained currency among modern historians. The older notion of this period as representing for Western Europe a kind of wasteland between the twin peaks of classical culture has been long a-dying, and perhaps even now it is not wholly extinct. But it has been replaced by other more fruitful, but equally wide-ranging generalizations. Sometimes the dominant theme has been sought in the slow evolution of national states which led to a concentration on France, from which the Normans came, and England, which the Normans conquered. Other writers tended to search for a unifying principle in the development of law and secular government; and here too the effects of Norman rule might perhaps be discerned. But a more influential concept has been the notion that the major political development in the Middle Ages is to be found in the re-establishment and subsequent transformations of a Christianized Roman Empire, and in its unavailing struggles with the rival political power of the papacy.[4]

Doubtless there is some truth in some, or all, of these interpretations. But none of them would today be accepted without great qualification. A famous controversy[5] has for instance raised the question whether the expansion of Islam into the Mediterranean lands during the seventh and eighth centuries may not have severed Western Europe from its classical inheritance more effectively than did the barbarian invasions at the end of the Roman Empire. Again, the establishment of the Frankish empire in 800, though it embodied 'a tardy reminiscence of ancient Rome', is now more often regarded not as the beginning of a new movement but as the end of an old one. At all events, the empire of Charles the Great was soon to collapse. And it is, today, generally recognized that a distinct period in the making of Europe began towards the close of the eleventh century and displayed its characteristic features during the ensuing decades.[6]

The critical and individual importance of this period in European history may be found in the fact that during these years Western Europe was finally rescued from the threat of social and political disintegration, and started to enjoy the beginnings of a great revival. It is little wonder, therefore, that many causes have been suggested to explain this development which entailed such profound consequences for the future. In the first place, demographic and economic changes operating from about this time are being ever more

---

[4] Note the successive titles to the volumes of the *Cambridge Medieval History*: II 'Foundation of the Western Empire'; III 'Germany of the Western Empire'; V 'Contest of the Empire and Papacy'; VI 'Victory of the Papacy'.

[5] H. Pirenne, *Mohommed and Charlemagne* (1935). Cf. A. F. Havinghurst, *The Pirenne Thesis* (1939).

[6] See Marc Bloch, *Feudal Society*, pp. 55–72.

emphatically cited to account for the improved social stability, and the political growth, of Western Europe in this period.[7] Stress is now laid, for instance, on the increase in population which is said to have begun late in the preceding epoch. In 1100 the West had also recently seen notable improvements in communications. Better roads had been built, and more rivers bridged, while at the same time technical advances had been made in agricultural practice. As a result, more land had been brought under cultivation and life in the enlarged village communities of the West, which were now less isolated, became at the same time less precarious. Soon the growth of commerce would foster the nascent trading communities in the Western towns.

The economic consequences of these developments were widely spread. 'Western Europe,' we are told, 'emerged in the twelfth century as a single powerful and aggressive economic system.' And of that system the Norman kingdoms would form an essential part. Thus the continental connexion which dominated English government between 1100 and 1154 had widespread economic as well as political and cultural connotations. Indeed, what might perhaps be called a 'common market' began to stretch from Yorkshire through the industrial towns of Flanders and the Fairs of Champagne to the great cities of Italy and the ports on every shore of the Mediterranean. Such were the economic conditions of what has been described as 'England's first entry into Europe'.[8]

Moreover, the Mediterranean ports and the trade which plied between them were brought during these same years under ever-increasing influence from the Normans of the South. The best sea-route for merchants from Genoa and Pisa to the Adriatic and the Bosphorus, to Durazzo or Constantinople, lay through the Straits of Messina, which were after 1101 under firm Norman control. At the same time, all the commerce directed by sea from Spain or the harbours of Algeria or Tunisia towards Syria or Egypt, or towards the terminal points of the great Asiatic trade-routes, had to pass through the narrows of the Mediterranean which between 1100 and 1154 were coming more and more to be dominated by Christian fleets based upon Sicily which had recently been wrested by the Normans from Moslem rule. The importance of these conditions in promoting the unity and strength of Western Europe is not to be minimized.

Man, however, does not live by bread alone, and the course of European history during these critical decades is not to be explained solely or even

[7] R. W. Southern, *Medieval Humanism*, p. 140 and *passim*.   [8] *Loc. cit.*

5

chiefly by reference to economic forces. Of greater political significance perhaps was the notable reforming movement in the Western Church which can be associated with the successors of Pope Gregory VII.[9] Undoubtedly papal policy as directed by these men produced widespread changes in the whole pattern of ecclesiastical life in the West. But its political results are not even thus to be circumscribed. For nothing less was involved than the creation of Latin Christendom, not as a pious aspiration but as an operative, self-conscious, political and juristic entity. Should not the world be submitted to the Church and the Church to the papacy?

From some such idealized conception all the other major consequences of papal policy at this time were to be derived. Thus, for instance, was envisaged the sharp separation between priestly and lay orders within the Church, and the special duties and privileges which were ascribed to the former. Again, a new turn was given to the emphatic assertion of the 'freedom of the Church' from all secular influence and control. And above all there arose that exalted definition of the political rights and the sanctity of the papal office. The pope was to be 'supreme emperor', a 'monarch above the law who had been set up by God over all races and kingdoms, in as much as he was the divinely appointed guardian of the unity of the Church – the Body of Christ – the blessed company of all faithful people'.[10]

These notions were of course never fully put into practice, but they were none the less persistently influential during the earlier half of the twelfth century. The age of Henry I of England and of Roger the Great of Sicily was also the age of St Bernard, who proclaimed the papal policy with tireless reiteration during the whole of his influential life. The essence of the Church, he claimed, is its unity, and that unity is expressed in the supreme government of the pope who, as the 'Vicar of the Crucified', wields an authority which both in its sanctions and in its extent far transcends that of any other monarch.[11] It is against this background that the Norman impact upon Europe has to be considered, for the Normans not only made a contribution to the growing power of the papacy but they were also among the most effective opponents of many of its political claims.

Certainly, the issues which had thus been raised were far-reaching. Evidently the new assertions of ecclesiastical authority would bring the papacy into conflict with many secular rulers, and they would provoke not only a

[9] See in general A. Fliche, *La Réforme grégorienne*, 2 vols (1924, 1925). Cf. Douglas, 'Development of Medieval Europe', in Eyre, *European Civilization*, Vol. III (1935).
[10] E. W. Ullmann, *Papal Government* (1955), esp. chap. IX.   [11] *Ibid.*

clash among those charged with government, but also a cleavage, among Christians at large, between the demands of spiritual and temporal loyalties.[12] There was also the obvious danger that the new political claims of the papacy would provoke a growing separation between the Eastern and Western Churches, between the Western and Eastern Empires. And was it for a similar reason that Western Europe, now strengthened spiritually and materially, passed during this period from a defensive attitude towards the Moslem world and, in the Crusades, actually launched, again with Norman support, a counter-attack against Islam? These are wide questions, but it would certainly appear that most, if not all, of the factors which produced the social, ecclesiastical and political structure of Western Europe in the high Middle Ages can be seen actively at work between 1100 and 1154.

III

The crisis for Europe which was resolved during the earlier half of the twelfth century was in many ways unique in character, and it engendered acts and emotions which were in some respects peculiar to itself. Indeed, it will not always prove easy to enter into the mentality of that age of pilgrimages and strange penances, of true saintliness and bestial cruelty, of mundane preoccupations and of visionary fervour – an age in which the hardships and struggles of a social and ecclesiastical order, often under lethal stress, seemed to be matched by unending warfare between good and evil in the unseen world. Yet it is surprising how many of the problems of that distant time have recently become again of pressing significance. The modern world is no stranger to famine and plague. Men are still deeply concerned with the claims of secular governments to control the acts of individuals, and in the sphere of public affairs the part that England should play in the political life of Europe is still, as in 1100, a matter of urgent controversy. Nor should it be forgotten that while until the last decade of the eleventh century the relations between Christendom and Islam could be described in terms of a 'cold war', the Crusades, which were soon to come, were an outstanding example of that ideological warfare from which the present age has so lamentably suffered.

Indeed, a reconsideration of these distant happenings might even trench upon wider questions relating to that 'European civilization' of which we hear so much today. During the earlier half of the twelfth century Western

[12] Below, chap. 7.

7

Europe not only began to enjoy greater social stability, it was at the same time made more vividly aware of its Christian heritage. Correspondingly, a modern commentator can claim: 'The attempt to create a culture which would be European without being Christian . . . is now recognized as the main cause of the present crisis of European civilization.'[13] Be this as it may, it is evident that between 1100 and 1150 Western Europe became progressively more conscious of its own individuality, and that the peoples of the West began at the same time to develop a new pride in shared aspirations and a new sense of common purpose. It is in fact because of what took place during this momentous half-century that the West eventually took the lead in the promotion of the Christian culture characteristic of Europe. European civilization which in the past had owed so much to the East, and particularly to Byzantium, would henceforth seek its home in the Christian West where it would so flourish that in due course it would cover most of the world.

IV

The Norman contribution to the growth of Europe during these critical years thus deserves examination if only because it formed part of a development of such wide general importance. For the same reason that contribution cannot be considered in isolation, and its individual results must not be exaggerated. It can, for instance, be argued that during these decades the chief agent developing the medieval political system was the papacy, and at least until the death of the Emperor Henry IV in 1106 the strongest secular power in Western Europe was the Germanic Empire established east of the Rhine. Indeed, during the years which followed, not the least important political movement in Western Europe was perhaps the shift in the balance of power from Germany westward across the Rhine and southwards across the Alps.[14] Of this the growing strength of the Norman kingdoms might be regarded as both a consequence and a partial cause. But the rulers of Castille at this time, particularly Alphonzo VI and Alphonzo VII, were accorded the imperial title because of the signal services they rendered to the enlargement of Latin Christendom.[15] Evidently Norman enterprise must be considered as but one of the forces operating in the development of Europe between 1100 and 1154.

13 O. Halecki, *The Limits and Divisions of European History* (1950), p. 51.
14 Below, chap. 4.
15 'Chronica Adefonsi imperatoris' (*España Sagrada* XXI). Cf. G. Constable in *Traditio*, IX (1953), pp. 227 et sqq.

The European implications of Norman action during this formative period are not, however, to be ignored.[16] And their significance is further displayed if the three great Norman conquests – of England, of Italy and Sicily, and of Antioch – are regarded as forming part of a single movement of Norman progress resulting in the imposition of comparable ideas and institutions on widely separated lands and on notably distinct communities. In any case it would be idle to pretend that the Normans did not involve England more closely in the politics of Latin Europe, or that the Norman conquest of Sicily was without effect on Mediterranean trade or on the course of the Crusades. And the general Norman advance revealed by such comparisons undoubtedly entailed consequences for Europe as a whole. The growing power of the Norman kingdoms of England and Sicily inevitably increased the corporate strength of the West, and within those kingdoms new methods of government would be developed which would be widely imitated. The social structure of the Western world in the twelfth century was for instance based to a large extent on a feudal order which the Normans helped to create, and at the same time the Norman rulers in both the North and the South were to develop administrative techniques of such efficiency that others could not be indifferent to the example which they set. If Western Europe was in 1154 so very different from what it had been sixty years earlier, the transition must have owed at least something to those Normans who then imposed their will on so many lands.

The impress of the Normans on European growth must moreover be judged not only in relation to the power they acquired but also in connexion with the quality of the influence they professed to exercise. By 1100 the Normans had avowedly severed themselves from their Viking past, and had become vociferously Christian in their political propaganda and self-consciously French in their social ideas. Thus the Norman kings of the English could address their subjects in Normandy as *Franci*, and in the South Bohemund, the son of Robert Guiscard, protested that he and his followers were every bit as French as those warriors who had recently come from France over the Alps to Italy on their way to fight for the Cross in Syria.[17] Before his death in 1101, Roger the Great, Count of Sicily, Guiscard's brother, described himself in one of his charters as 'girt with the heavenly

---

[16] See above all the works of C. H. Haskins, especially *Norman Institutions* and *Normans in European History*. It is a pleasure to pay tribute once more to these remarkable books to which I and all other students of Norman history are so deeply indebted.
[17] Robert the Monk, II, c. 5.

sword and adorned with the helmet and spear of celestial hope'.[18] And when in 1130 his own son, Roger the Great, came to rule as king over a united Norman realm in the south, he claimed that his royalty, with all that it implied, had been bestowed on him by God Himself. Indeed, to appreciate the implication of this it is necessary to go no further than the lovely fresco in the Martorana at Palermo which displays the first Norman king of Sicily receiving his royal crown from the hands of Jesus Christ.

The full significance of such astonishing assertions merit mention inasmuch as they contributed both to the character and to the consequences of the Norman intrusion into European affairs at this time.[19] Throughout this period the Normans will be found continually exploiting the notion of the Holy War in their own interests and it was natural to them to assert their influence in promoting the crusades. The results of their policy in this respect would not prove negligible. The alteration in the balance of power in Europe effected by the Normans between 1100 and 1154 would for these reasons entail cultural and ecclesiastical as well as political results.[20] Correspondingly, the character of Western Europe in the Middle Ages would depend in large measure on its identification with Latin Christendom.

The influence exercised by the Normans on Europe during these fateful years must, none the less, be very cautiously appraised. For it would be easy to over-simplify a process which from its very nature was extremely complex. Care must be taken not to over-stress the relative importance of Norman enterprise by comparison with other contemporary developments in European affairs. It must, moreover, also be remembered that the Normans were themselves everywhere influenced in their turn by the contrasting traditions prevailing in the different countries over which they came to rule.[21] Nor was this all. The contribution of the Normans towards establishing the hegemony of the West undoubtedly calls for emphatic comment, but at the same time the Normans laid the foundations of the self-sufficient secular state of the future which would in due course challenge the political values prevailing in medieval Europe, and help thereby to disrupt the political unity of Christendom.[22]

It is in the light of these and similar wide general questions that the Norman impact upon Europe between 1100 and 1154 will here be surveyed. First it may be pertinent to note how the Norman kingdoms were stabilized, what were the similarities and differences between them, and why at this

18 Jaffé-Lowenfeld, No. 5460.

19 Below, pp. 31–47.

20 Below, chap. 4.   21 Below, chap. 8.

22 Below, pp. 214–17.

time they waxed in power.[23] Thus might it be possible to appreciate the place they came to occupy within the social and governmental structure of Europe in the age of Henry I of England and Roger the Great of Sicily.[24] Of equal significance is it to consider what effects Norman policy may have had on the relations between the temporal and spiritual powers of Europe during the Middle Ages,[25] and what was the Norman share in the initial success and final failure of the Crusades.[26] Here also might be revealed the Norman share both in fostering the political power of Latin Christendom and in contributing to its later disunion. Most important of all to ascertain, perhaps, is the part played by the Normans in promoting the pre-eminence of Western Europe, for on this not only the medieval achievement but also much of modern history would ultimately be based.[27] Assuredly the implications of Norman endeavour between 1100 and 1154 were both varied and extensive. For good or ill they impinged forcibly on the social and political life of Europe and modified its future destiny.

[23] Below, chap. 1.   [24] Below, chaps 2, 3 and 4   [25] Below, chaps 7 and 8.
[26] Below, chaps 9–11.   [27] Below, chap. 4 and *passim*.

Chapter 1
THE ANGLO-NORMAN REALM,
1100–1154

I

The Norman impact upon European growth during the earlier half of the twelfth century depended in the first instance on the firm establishment at that time of the two great Norman kingdoms. For of these one was in due course to dominate north-western Europe from southern Scotland to Gascony, while the other would exercise a decisive influence on Mediterranean politics from eastern Spain to western Syria. It would, of course, not be easy to delineate with any precision the period when this astonishing increase of power in Europe was attained. But the accomplishment can aptly be associated with the reign of Henry I in England and with Roger the Great, the most distinguished of the Norman kings of Sicily. Assuredly both Henry I and Roger the Great owed very much to the achievements of their outstanding fathers, William the Conqueror and Count Roger I. But in each case they preserved a political inheritance which was in danger of disintegrating, and in each case, by so doing, they enhanced the Norman influence on the making of Europe.

A study of this great period of Norman history, and of its consequences to Europe, may thus reasonably open with the accession in 1100 of Henry I from Normandy as king of the English, and the death in 1101 of Roger the 'Great Count' of Sicily. But if a comparative assessment is to be made of the influence exercised on Europe by Henry I and Roger the Great, full account must be taken of the distinct problems which confronted them, and the wide differences in the realms they ruled. Many changes had occurred in Europe between the accession of King Henry I and the achievement of Sicilian royalty by Roger in 1130. Nor is there any need to emphasize the obvious contrasts to be found between the Norman kingdoms in the North and the South. In the one case Saxon and Danish institutions and ideas needed to be developed by the Normans alongside those which they brought from south of the Channel. In the other the Normans were faced with mixed populations of Italian Lombard, Greek and Arabic stock, all of whom cherished their own traditions. In the sphere of administration, in particular,

12

such distinctions became immediately apparent. Under Henry I counts and *vicomtes* from Normandy or Maine might be seen serving in England as earls, or as sheriffs, presiding over the courts of the English shires. But there was nothing in Normandy or England to compare with that bizarre medley of counts, *vicomtes*, emirs, protonotaries, *strategoi* and *archons* which will be found in the South implementing the will of Roger the Great.[1]

Similar contrasts could indeed be found in connexion with almost all aspects of the social and cultural life of the two kingdoms. For example, England under Henry I saw the beginnings of an effloresence of Latin scholarship and romanesque art. But the court of Roger the Great became the centre of a brilliant and unique cosmopolitan culture to which Latin, Greek and Arab scholars and artists all made their individual contributions. It would, indeed, be futile to debate the rival excellencies of the scholarship and art which were developed under Norman patronage in the Norman kingdoms of the North and South, for both may surely command unstinted admiration. Neither the magnitude of the achievement nor the contrasts within it could be better illustrated than in the sphere of architecture. The wonders of Durham and Ely may be set beside the resplendant cathedral of Cefalú with its mosaics and the luminous Cappella Palatina at Palermo.

Despite such differences, there were many common features in the two great Norman realms, and in the motives which inspired their rulers, and it was perhaps natural that this should be so. Henry I was the son of the greatest of the Norman dukes, and his mother was a Flemish princess. It was inevitable, therefore, that he should be influenced by the particular enthusiasms which had promoted the rise of Normandy to a position of hegemony in northern France. By the time of Roger the Great these sentiments had certainly cooled, but though Roger never visited the Norman duchy, and though throughout his early life he was strongly influenced by his remarkable Italian mother, his father was none the less one of the architects of Norman power, and he would himself never forget that he was the grandson of Tancred of Hauteville. Thus both Roger and his biographers frequently sought to justify his acts, and particularly his assumption of royalty, by reference to his Norman predecessors.[2] Similarly, writers in the Norman North continued throughout the earlier half of the twelfth century to express their interest and pride in the exploits of their compatriots in the South.[3] Indeed, in

[1] See below, pp. 106 et sqq.
[2] See below, pp. 63, 64.
[3] Jamison, 'Sicilian Norman Kingdom'.

1138 – eight years after Roger had become king – a veteran Norman leader is reported to have raised the spirits of his followers on a Yorkshire battle-field by extolling the earlier Norman achievements in England, Apulia, Calabria and Sicily, all of which he proclaimed as parts of a single and a glorious enterprise.[4]

This community of sentiment enhances the significance of the surprising similarity to be found in contemporary accounts given of Henry I and Roger the Great by writers at different times and in widely separated parts of Europe. Indeed, it is little short of astonishing how close is the correlation between the early descriptions given by such as the Anglo-Saxon Chronicle, William of Malmesbury and Henry of Huntingdon on the one hand, and by writers such as Alexander of Telese, Falco of Benevento, Romuald of Salerno and Otto of Freising on the other. Something may perhaps here be due to deliberate copying, and something perhaps to a common convention, but when all qualifications have been made it is hard to escape the conclusion that these two Norman kings were held to share certain characteristics which separated them from most of their contemporaries. This is the more interesting inasmuch as both Henry I and Roger the Great faced similar problems, and solved them, at great hazard, by similar means. Both attained royalty only after difficulty and after surmounting a perilous opposition. Both made it a primary objective to establish a unified Norman realm consisting of many diverse provinces separated in each case by an arm of the sea. And it was their success in so doing, after prolonged warfare, that con-ditioned the impact they made upon the growth of Europe.

II

The accession of Henry I as king of the English in 1100 must be regarded as an event of European significance. It is natural – and it is appropriate – for the student of English history to select the year 1066 as the cardinal date in the expansion of Norman influence, but this can only be done with some qualification. As Domesday Book reveals, the Norman settlement in England had by no means been completed twenty years after the battle of Hastings, and in many other respects a similar situation might be revealed. As Sir Frank Stenton remarked: 'In the organization of Church and State, as in the vaguer sphere of social relations, the Conquest brought about an introduction of ideas which were to revolutionize English thought on public questions.

Ailred of Rievaulx, in *Chronicles of Stephen etc.*, ed. Hewlett, II, pp. 318, 319.

But the revolution itself belongs to a later age.'[5] Evidently the results to Britain of the Norman Conquest of England were not to be fulfilled until after the death of William the Conqueror. Its consequences to Europe would not be disclosed until the twelfth century.

In 1100, indeed, the work of William the Conqueror had itself been placed in peril. The Conqueror's basic achievement had been to create under a Norman duke who was also king of the English a conjoint Norman dominion stretching across the Channel and politically united under a single rule. The very powerful state which had thus been inaugurated would undoubtedly, if it survived, exercise an ever-increasing influence on European politics. But after the Conqueror's death, the unity of this realm was disrupted when his eldest son Robert, nicknamed Curthose, came to rule over Normandy with its dependencies while England passed to his third son William styled Rufus.[6] Such disunion, if it had persisted, might well have proved fatal to any extension of Norman influence in the North, and it had thus been of considerable interest to Europe as a whole when in 1096 Robert pawned his duchy to the king of the English in order to go on Crusade.[7] But of far wider importance were the events which followed the sudden and most mysterious death of William Rufus, allegedly by accident from an arrow shot from the bow of Walter Tirel, lord of Poix, in the New Forest on 2 August 1100.[8]

Whether Count Henry, the youngest of the Conqueror's sons, who was hunting in another part of the Forest at the time, was here privy to a murder can be endlessly debated.[9] What is certain is that the death of William Rufus came at a most opportune moment for him. For Robert Curthose was known to be already on his way back from the East, and by his marriage with the beautiful Sibyl of Conversano he had raised sufficient money to redeem his duchy from pawn.[10] But when he reached Normandy in September 1100, Rufus had been dead some six weeks, and Henry had acted with ruthless

---

[5] *Anglo-Saxon England* (1943), p. v.

[6] Whether this division was made at the Conqueror's request, as is suggested by Ord. Vit. (III, pp. 242–4) and 'The Monk of Caen' (Will. Jum., p. 45), or whether, as is more probable, in his despite, is fully discussed by J. Le Patourel in *Eng. Hist. Rev.* (1971), pp. 225–34.

[7] David, *Robert Curthose*, p. 91.

[8] A.S. Chron., 'E', s.a. 1100; Flor. Worc., s.a. 1100. See A. Freeman, *William Rufus*, II, App. 'SS'. The immense modern literature on the subject includes discussions on witchcraft, heresy and ritual murder (see H. R. Williamson, *The Arrow and the Sword* [1948]).

[9] See the erudite account in C. Brooke, *Saxon and Norman Kings* (1963), chap. XI.

[10] Ord. Vit., V, p. 88; Chalandon, *Domination*, I, p. 181; David, *op. cit.*, pp. 120–7.

speed to take advantage of his opportunity. Without waiting for the late king's burial, or even for a view of his brother's corpse, he hastened to seize the Treasury at Winchester, and on 5 August 1100, only three days after the death of William Rufus, he had himself crowned king of the English in Westminster Abbey by the bishop of London.[11] Thus when Robert arrived a month later to take possession of his Norman duchy, and to claim the English throne, he found himself faced by an established and anointed king.

None the less, Henry's situation at the beginning of his reign was extremely perilous, and it was characteristic of the astuteness he was later to display that he immediately sought to improve it by two acts which later were to prove of considerable importance. At the time of his coronation he issued a charter of liberties which would in due course do much to determine the ordered feudal arrangements of twelfth-century England.[12] Some three months later he married Edith-Matilda, whose mother was St Margaret, sister of Edgar Atheling, the last representative of the Anglo-Saxon royal house, and whose father was Malcolm III (Canmore), king of Scotland. In this way the Norman king was able to assert new rights over his subjects in England, and to make new pretensions to overlordship in Scotland. Even so, it was doubtful whether Henry could survive, and it was fortunate for the future of the Anglo-Norman state that Robert, who had taken possession of Normandy, delayed until July 1101 before invading England. And then he allowed himself to be brought to a settlement that saved his younger brother. By an agreement made at Alton, near Winchester, Robert gave up all claims to the throne of England while Henry relinquished nearly all his rights in Normandy.[13] Henry had in fact saved his English royalty at a high price. But it seemed as if the Norman power in northern Europe must again be divided.

For this reason the events of the next five years were to prove of crucial importance both to England and to northern Europe. They began with a rebellion[14] against the English king, sponsored by many Norman magnates on both sides of the Channel, and led by Robert of Bellême, head of the family of Montgomery and count of Ponthieu, who held no less than thirty-four castles in Normandy, the earldom of Shrewsbury, and control of the castles of Arundel, Blythe and Bridgenorth. For Henry successfully to with-

---

11 Freeman, *op. cit.*, II, pp. 345–50. Schramm, *English Coronation*, pp. 41, 42.
12 Douglas, *English Historical Documents*, II, No. 19.
13 David, *op. cit.*, pp. 134–6. Henry also agreed to make an annual payment to his brother.
14 Will. Malms., pp. 471–4.

stand this over-mighty ruffian was thus a considerable achievement. But the real significance of the suppression of the great Montgomery rebellion of 1102 was that it marked the final stage in the restoration of Anglo-Norman unity. For Henry was now able to take the initiative against Robert Curthose in Normandy.

Robert's authority in Normandy was in fact already declining, and Henry, by bribery and diplomacy as well as by military action, had created for himself a strong party in the duchy. Bayeux and Caen fell into his hands during these years, and at the same time he gained an assurance of neutrality both from the count of Flanders and from the king of France. Even the pope was brought to look favourably on his designs.[15] And so it was that in 1106 matters moved to a climax. Henry crossed over to Normandy with a large force, and after some desultory fighting he met Duke Robert at Tinchebrai, some twelve miles north of Domfront. The king's troops far outnumbered those of the duke, and after a battle which lasted only about an hour, Henry's victory was complete.[16] Most of Robert's greater supporters fell into his hands, and Robert himself was captured. Henry, moreover, was determined that his elder brother should never again disturb the political union between Normandy and England. Robert was therefore sent into close captivity where he remained for twenty-eight years.[17] Henceforth during the whole of Henry's reign there was no Norman ruler south of the Channel but the Norman king of the English. The unity of the Anglo-Norman realm had been restored, and its power would increase.

III

Henry's initial success must direct attention to this young man of thirty-two who was so steadily advancing towards a position of prominence in the European scene. Personally, however, Henry I must surely appear as not only one of the ablest, but also as one of the most repulsive among the kings who have reigned in England. This man, says one writer, 'was of middle stature, neither short nor tall; his hair was black and set back on his forehead; his eyes were mildly bright; his chest brawny; and his body well fleshed'.[18]

[15] David, *op. cit.*, pp. 155-7.
[16] H. W. C. Davis, in *Eng. Hist. Rev.*, XXIV (1909), pp. 728 et sqq.; (1910), pp. 295 et sqq.
[17] David, *op. cit.*, pp. 186-90. Did the duke, languishing at Cardiff, 'in sight of the Severn Sea', learn the Welsh language and leave behind him the vernacular poem which has been assigned to him?   [18] Will. Malms., p. 488.

His chief vices, adds another, were lust, avarice and cruelty,[19] and while he shared these with many of his contemporaries, his methods of indulging them were his own. It must be for the moralist to judge between the homosexuality that pervaded the court of William Rufus and the sexual adventures of Henry I, who acknowledged eight male and eleven female bastards. His avarice too was probably no greater than that of his father, but he was more subtle in the methods of extortion by which he accumulated a vast treasure. His cruelty was revolting. Though he cannot with certainty be convicted of fratricide, there is strong evidence that he connived at the murder of one brother, and he kept another in close confinement for nearly thirty years. He allowed two of his granddaughters to be blinded when they were hostages in his hands, and his punishments of malefactors were hideously savage. It was noted as an example of exceptional leniency on the king's part that when one of his household was accused of fraud he was not executed but blinded and mutilated. And in 1124/1125 when moneyers in England were suspected of issuing false coin, all those who could be found were castrated without further reference to their individual guilt or innocence. Again, in Leicestershire between 30 November and 25 December 1124 'there were more thieves hanged than ever before – forty-four men in that little time; and six men were blinded and castrated'.[20] Henry was of course not isolated in his brutality, but he was perhaps exceptional in the false geniality with which it was cloaked. 'He was facetious in proper season,' says William of Malmesbury, 'he was not personally pugnacious.'[21]

Assuredly he was a man to fear. But surprisingly he was also capable of inspiring affection in those he favoured, and he even achieved a measure of general popularity for the good order he caused to prevail. 'He came to be feared by the magnates,' says one chronicler, 'and beloved by the common people.' And another adds: 'He was a good man, and people were in great awe of him. No one dare injure another in his time. He made peace for man and beast.'[22] Possibly these eulogies were inspired in part by experience of the breakdown in public order which followed Henry's death. But they cannot be dismissed as mere rhetoric. And one early writer adds the very shrewd comment that this king 'preferred to gain his ends by persuasion rather than force'.[23] He was thus praised for his 'wisdom' and even – though quite

[19] Hen. Hunt., Bk VIII. Cf. Brooke, *op. cit.*, pp. 192–6.

[20] A.S. Chron., 'E', s.a. 1124, 1125.   [21] Will. Malms., p. 488.

[22] *Ibid.*, pp. 487, 488; A.S. Chron., 'E', s.a. 1135.

[23] Will. Malms., pp. 467, 468, 488.

erroneously – credited with erudition.[24] But it was in the adroit manipulation of men that he really excelled. He knew the power of the purse, and while coldly ruthless towards his enemies he was lavish in the rewards he bestowed on those he selected to do his will. It is therefore not surprising that the reign of this intensely able king will be found to be chiefly notable for his success in the development of administration.[25] His power was, moreover, fortified by his successful exploitation of the institutions of Anglo-Saxon England. Indeed, Henry's government was probably more efficient than anything that England had known since Roman times. As a consequence, the authority of the Anglo-Norman realm was strengthened, and its influence on Europe increased.

IV

In 1106 Henry possessed all the traditional rights both of a duke of Normandy and of a king of England, and it was his particular skill to combine these to his own advantage. For the same reason, he could assert his authority over many other lands. He was suzerain over Ponthieu and Boulogne, and he claimed to be overlord over Maine, Brittany and much of the Vexin. Often these claims would be disputed but frequently they were translated into practice. In 1106, for instance, Alan Fergant, duke of Brittany, fought under Henry at Tinchebrai, possibly as a vassal, and so also did Helias of La Flèche, count of Maine.[26] The interest of the interminable warfare which ravaged France during the ensuing years lies in the fact that it demonstrated the strength of Norman power against any opposition that might be brought against it. In Brittany, for example, the ruling house of Rennes made strenuous efforts to suppress the rival comital dynasty of Cornouilles which held large estates in the north of England,[27] and Count Helias of Maine strove with considerable success to free himself from Norman domination by placing his *comté* under Angevin protection.[28]

But Henry's chief enemy in France was always the French king. Louis VI naturally wished to separate Normandy once more from England, and he found himself possessed of a useful tool in William Clito, the son of Robert

---

[24] Cf. David, in Haskins, *Anniversary Essays* (1929), pp. 45–7.   [25] Below, pp. 103 et sqq.
[26] Lemarignier, *Hommage en Marche*, p. 121; Latouche, *Comté du Maine*, p. 52.
[27] La Borderie, *Hist. de Bretagne*, III, pp. 30–42; C. T. Clay, *Early Yorkshire Charters*, Vols IV and V.
[28] Latouche, *op. cit.*, pp. 45–57.

Curthose, who could be made the centre of all opposition in France to the Norman king of England. The success of Henry I against all these coalitions was thus very noteworthy, and in 1113 Louis was actually forced to recognize Henry as suzerain not only over Maine but also over Brittany and the Belléme lands in the Vexin. Nor was this all. Six years later, Louis was decisively beaten by the Normans in a pitched battle at Bremule.[29] It was a notable achievement and its results were to persist. In the years to come, Louis, still using the Clito as his tool, would continue his efforts to disrupt the Anglo-Norman realm.[30] But these were unavailing, and until the end of the reign of Henry I, the authority of the Norman king of England was dominant in the whole region of northern France from Boulogne to Vannes, from Cherbourg to Nantes.

The growing power of the Anglo-Norman realm under Henry I had already been signally recognized elsewhere in Europe. In 1110 – four years after Tinchebrai – Matilda, the daughter of the Norman king, then aged nine, had been betrothed to the emperor Henry V and ceremoniously sent over to Germany to be trained there for the imperial station for which she was destined.[31] In 1114 the marriage took place with the maximum of pomp at a time when the emperor was reaching the climax of his career. Both parties had much to gain from the alliance, particularly in respect of the relations with the papacy, and there are some reasons for believing that the initiative may in the first instance have come from Germany. There is no doubt, however, that the prestige of the Anglo-Norman monarchy, which was of comparatively recent establishment, gained very much from the match. Henry I was later proud to emphasize the imperial status that had been acquired by his daughter.[32] Matilda for her part continued to style herself empress even when she had made her second marriage with the count of Anjou, and after the death of her father she contended for his inheritance as 'Empress and Queen of the English'.[33]

Much of Henry's success in Europe was due to the fact that he was able to mobilize the resources of England to promote Norman policy everywhere. In particular he could utilize for this purpose what was the most highly deve-

---

[29] Luchaire, *Louis VI*, Nos 158, 258; Ord. Vit., IV, pp. 355–66; Hen. Hunt., pp. 241–2.
[30] Luchaire, *Louis VI*, Nos 334, 369, 384, 404.
[31] On the implications of this marriage see K. Leyser, 'England and the Empire in the early twelfth century', R. Hist. Soc. *Trans.* 5, Vol. X, pp. 61 et sqq.
[32] Will. Jum., p. 304 (a continuation by Robert of Torigny). Cf. Leyser, *op. cit.*, p. 67.
[33] *Regesta Regum*, III, No. 343 of 1141.

loped taxational system in the contemporary Western world. The 'felds' which had been levied under Edward the Confessor and exacted with even greater vigour by William the Conqueror, represented, as Domesday Book was to record, an advanced system of direct taxation. This was now fully at the command of Henry I, and was to prove one of the chief agencies of his progress. It is significant, for example, that a very heavy tax levied upon England provided the exceptionally large dowry which Matilda took with her to Germany.[34] But far more important were the opportunities thus given to the Norman king to make abundant use of mercenaries in his French campaigns.[35] Everywhere, in fact, the Normans were to employ large numbers of mercenaries in their wars. And mercenaries could only be used on this lavish scale by rulers with very large financial resources at their disposal. It was indeed to become a cardinal condition of the growth of Norman influence between 1100 and 1154 that the richest princes in Western Europe were the Norman rulers of Sicily with all the wealth of Palermo at their disposal and the Norman kings of England with their well-filled treasury at Winchester.

And if English mercenaries helped Henry I in France, so also did his continental power assist him in extending his dominion over Britain. As early as 1102, at the time of the forfeiture of the Montgomery lands, Henry evidently considered himself as overlord over the whole of Wales,[36] and he had good reason for so doing. The extension of his authority into Wales was to be aptly illustrated in 1114 when a king of Powys served as a vassal of Henry I in France. A similar situation was also developing in Scotland.[37] Three successive Scottish kings – Edgar, Alexander II and David I – acknowledged Henry I as their overlord, and were themselves dependent upon Norman support. In 1092 it had been with Norman assistance that Edgar had overthrown Donald Bane with his Celtic followers, and in 1114 Alexander II could be seen in the service of his overlord during Henry I's Welsh wars. The consequences to Scotland of this Norman penetration were to be profound, and the process greatly fortified the power of the Norman king. After 1120 Henry would encounter new and formidable difficulties, but he

[34] A.S. Chron., 'E', s.a. 1110.
[35] J. C. Prestwich, 'War and Finance in the Anglo-Norman State', R. Hist. Soc. *Trans.* 5, Vol. XIV (1954), pp. 19–44.
[36] Lloyd, *Wales*, II, *passim*.
[37] Ritchie, *Normans in Scotland*, chaps III and IV.

would always be able to maintain his position as the ruler of a united Anglo-Norman realm which had become dominant over most of Britain and over much of Northern France.

V

The consolidation of the Anglo-Norman dominion in the time of Henry I, and the influence it came to exercise in Europe, was due not only to the Norman king but also to the aristocracy by which he was surrounded. It was, in fact, a small group of some fifty or sixty great families which ensured the social cohesion of Henry's disparate kingdom. This aristocracy was of course predominantly Norman, but in earlier years there had also been a considerable influx into Britain from Flanders and Brittany. In Henry I's time this development was reflected particularly in the establishment of a great Breton family in the Yorkshire honour of Richmond, and there were many other similar examples.[38] In Scotland the house of Stewart derived from the neighbourhood of Dol, while the house of Douglas was probably of Flemish origin.[39] It is thus remarkable that there never developed any Flemish or Breton variations in the feudal structure of Norman England, as the families which came to dominate that structure were closely knit together by intermarriage. Henry I had introduced among them a new element from the Cotentin where he had long been lord, and by 1106 they had become conscious of their common interests, and conscious also that they shared those interests with their king. There was of course always rivalry among them, and always the danger of disturbance from over-mighty individuals. But modern scholarship has decisively rejected the older Whig notion that the dominant theme of Anglo-Norman history was a constant opposition between 'Crown' and 'Baronage'. More accurately, it could be visualized as the hazardous reorganization of English political life by an exceedingly able group of men with the king at their head.

In respect of the Norman contribution to European politics at this time, the same re-appraisal needs to be made. These interconnected families, small in number and exceedingly powerful, continued to hold landed wealth on both sides of the Channel, and their power was ever increasing. During these years, for example, Wales saw the advance of Philip of Briouze in Radnor,

38 C. T. Clay, *Early Yorkshire Charters*, Vols IV and V.
39 J. H. Round, *Peerage and Family History*, pp. 115–17; Ritchie, *op. cit.*, p. 233; Maxwell, *History of the House of Douglas*, I, pp. 3–5.

Bernard of Neufmarché in Brecknock and Robert FitzHamon in Cardiff.[40] In Scotland, too, there now appeared prominently for the first time such families as those of Bruce, Somerville, Avenel and Soules, all of whom can be traced to their origins in Normandy.[41] It would thus have been highly detrimental to the interests of this Anglo-Norman aristocracy for Normandy and England to be politically separated. They might – and they did – dispute over what person should rule the realm, but generally speaking they were agreed that there should be one, and only one ruler of this conjoint dominion. It was thus for severely practical reasons that they sustained the unity of Henry I's realm, and thereby enhanced its influence on Europe.

Their power in this respect, and the manner in which it was developed, deserves more detailed illustration than it generally receives. The Beaumont family might be cited as an example,[42] for Robert, son of Roger of Beaumont, inherited his father's large estates in the valley of the Risle, and by the beginning of the twelfth century he had become one of the largest landowners in England. Later he became count of Meulan and earl of Leicester, and was to survive until 1114. Meanwhile, his younger brother, Henry, acquired wide lands in the southern Midlands, and King Henry gave him also the peninsula of Gower in Glamorgan. But he retained in Normandy the barony of Annebecq, and in due course became earl of Warwick. The political significance of the complex of power which is thus disclosed is further enhanced when it is found that one of the undertenants of this earl of Warwick was a certain Anschetill of Harcourt who is frequently mentioned in the records during the period 1115–19 and who was still living in 1130.[43] This man was a younger brother of William, lord of Harcourt, a small lordship near Brionne,[44] and also brother to Richard, who was an undertenant of the family of Briouze in Sussex.[45] Yet another brother was to have a notable career in the Anglo-Norman Church. Thus it was that a family which had not as yet

[40] Lloyd, *Wales*, II, pp. 374, 375.

[41] G. W. S. Barrow, 'Les familles normandes d'Ecosse', *Annales de Normandie* (1955), pp. 295–317.

[42] *Complete Peerage*, VII (Leicester) and XII (Warwick), and the authorities there copiously cited.

[43] *Mon. Ang.*, VI, pp. 1326, 1327; *Red Book of the Exchequer*, p. 325, Pipe Roll of 1131 (for Leicestershire).

[44] Ord. Vit., IV, p. 45; Loyd, *Anglo-Norman Families*, p. 51; *Cart. Beaumont-le-Roger*, ed. Deville, p. 32.

[45] *Red Book*, Pipe Roll of 1131, pp. 71, 72, 89; Salter, *Oxford Charters*, No. 38; Lees, *Records of the Templars*, p. xlvii.

attained the status of tenants-in-chief of the king was already spreading its influence over Normandy and England.

The expanding power of the house of Clare is another example.[46] Richard of Clare, son of Gilbert of Brionne, the count, not only inherited his father's wide lands in Normandy but before his death about 1090 added to them the honour of Tonbridge in Kent and many manors in Essex and Suffolk. His brother Baldwin, lord of Meules, near Lisieux, became at the same time sheriff of Exeter, and the progress of the house continued into the next generation. Of Richard's sons, one, Gilbert, took over his father's Kentish and East Anglian lands, and also became lord of Cardigan, whilst another son, Walter, acquired the lordship of Gwent, and was the founder of Tintern Abbey. Gilbert's son, also named Richard, was in 1138 made earl of Pembroke. Similarly, the family of Lacy[47] during these years acquired the honours of Weobley in Herefordshire, Pontefract in Yorkshire, while retaining their lands in Normandy. And in the case of the Ferrars, Henry, lord of Ferrières-Sainte-Honourine, was established in Staffordshire by 1086. Of his sons, one succeeded to his Norman lands and was taken prisoner at Tinchebrai, whilst another became lord of Tutbury in Staffordshire and was made earl of Derby as a reward for his prowess at the battle of the Standard in 1138.[48]

VI

Family records such as these have far more than a merely genealogical interest. They illustrate better than any generalizations the political role played by this powerful and restricted Norman aristocracy in sustaining the unity of the Anglo-Norman realm, and explain the success of Henry's policy in preserving intact his conjoint dominion so that in due course it might be transmitted in its totality to his successor. That policy was in fact to be notably displayed in 1115 and 1116 when he made his barons both in Normandy and England recognize his legitimate son William as sole heir to all his dominions. The significance of that event was immediately appreciated by contemporaries. The Anglo-Saxon Chronicle mentioned the oath taken in Normandy, and one of Henry's charters was actually dated by reference to it. Similarly, publicity was given to the oath that was sworn in

[46] Round, *Feudal England*, pp. 458–80.
[47] W. E. Wightman, *Lacy Family* (1966).
[48] D.B., I, *passim*; Ord. Vit., IV, p. 231; V, pp. 111–12.

England to the man who had been 'designated as heir to the kingdom'.[49] For these reasons the tragic death by drowning of William, together with his half-brother Robert and their roistering companions in the wreck of the *White Ship* off Barfleur in 1120, [50]must be regarded as perhaps the most serious reverse ever sustained by Henry I. All Europe was likewise concerned. For it was of vital interest to Western Christendom that the coherence or disintegration of the Norman dominion in the North might now be called in question through a disputed succession.

The crisis thus foreshadowed would in due course involve England in civil war, and place in peril the political union of Normandy and England which was essential to the maintenance of social order by the Norman monarchy. Indeed, its main interests for England lay in its demonstration of the character of Norman administration under strong kings, and the disasters which might follow its collapse.[51] The same developments would also entail the formation in France of new and formidable feudal groupings, and would impinge on the future destiny of royal Capetian dynasty. Nor would this prolonged crisis be resolved until the empire which the Normans had created was restored in an enlarged form under new direction and with such power that it might aspire to the political domination of the whole of the West.

It is in fact these major questions which alone can lend interest to the petty wars and the intricate diplomacy by which Henry I attempted to repair the disaster of 1120. He could not afford to ignore the threat, since his most obvious successor was now William Clito, the son of Robert of Curthose and the protégé of the French king. At once, therefore, Henry married again in the hope of an heir,[52] and when no heir was forthcoming he seized the opportunity offered him by the death of the Emperor Henry V in 1125 which left his daughter Matilda a widow. Without delay he forced a representative group of his barons to recognize Matilda as his successor both in Normandy and England.[53] Then, before the year was out, he arranged for Matilda to be betrothed to Geoffrey, son and heir of Fulk V, count of Anjou, thus disrupting the Angevin alliance with the French king.[54] It was a bold coup to which Louis replied in 1127 by investing the Clito with the county

[49] A.S. Chron., 'E', s.a. 1115; Round, *Documents*, No. 904; Eadmer, *Hist. Novorum*, pp. 237, 290; *Regesta Regum*, II, No. 1204.

[50] Will. Malms., pp. 496–9; Warren, *Henry II*, p. 3.   [51] A.S. Chron, s.a. 1137.

[52] A.S. Chron., 'E', s.a. 1121. His bride was Adela, daughter of Count Godfrey VII of Louvain.

[53] Round, *Geoffrey de Mandeville*, pp. 31, 32.

[54] Ord. Vit., IV, p. 498.

of Flanders.[55] In the next year, however, a chance arrow put an end to Clito's career, and Henry's position was further strengthened when in 1133 a son was born to Geoffrey and Matilda – Henry, the future ruler of the whole Norman empire.

Such were the events which helped to condition the upheaval which immediately took place on the death of Henry I in Normandy on December 1135. A considerable section of the Norman baronage found it possible to repudiate their sworn allegiance to Matilda, who was disliked both for her sex and for her arrogance, and also for her connexion with Anjou, the traditional enemy of Normandy.[56] These magnates therefore transferred their support to Stephen, grandson of William the Conqueror and brother to the reigning count of Blois, whom they found personally acceptable and who already had great possessions both in France and England. And Stephen himself was quick to take advantage of the situation, acting with a ruthless speed worthy of his Norman predecessors. He was at Boulogne when he heard of Henry's death, but he crossed the Channel immediately and hastened to London where he induced the citizens to acclaim him as king. Then he moved at once to Winchester where he seized the Treasury. After this he passed back to London in order to persuade the archbishop of Canterbury to crown him.[57] Thus on 21 December 1135, some twenty days after the death of Henry I, Stephen of Blois was consecrated king in Westminster Abbey, and the coronation was specifically held to apply both to Normandy and England.[58] A disruption of the dominion ruled by Henry I had thus been averted, and the court which Stephen held with great magnificence at Oxford at Easter 1136 was attended not only by an exceptionally large number of magnates from both sides of the Channel but by the archbishop of Rouen and four out of the six bishops in Normandy.[59] The unity of the Anglo-Norman realm had been spectacularly re-asserted at a time of confusion and stress.

VII

The succession to that united realm had, however, by no means been assured by the events of 1135–6. North of the Channel, Matilda's rights were soon

[55] Luchaire, *Louis VI*, No. 379.

[56] It was even suggested that the oath to Matilda had been set aside by the dying king (*Gesta Stephani*, p. 7).

[57] R. H. C. Davis, *Stephen*, pp. 17–18; Cronne, *Stephen*, pp. 19–20.

[58] In 'Angliam et Normanniam', *Gesta Stephani*, p. 8.

[59] Round, *Geoffrey de Mandeville*, App. 'C'; *Regesta Regum*, III, No. 271.

to be vigorously championed by magnates who either recalled their oath to the empress or who feared the changes that might follow Stephen's ascendancy.[60] This strong party included King David of Scotland, Earl Robert of Glouces- ter, one of Henry I's bastards, and Brian 'FitzCount', the illegitimate son of Alan Fergant, ruler of Brittany. But more vital was the support that Matilda through her husband would receive from Anjou. For Angevin power was moving to a climax under Count Geoffrey, who between 1129 and 1151 was not only lord of his own *comté* of Anjou, but master also of Maine and of most of Tourraine. And now through his marriage this ambitious man could claim rights not only to England but more immediately and practically in Normandy, which he promptly attacked.[61]

Stephen too was possessed of large resources both in France and England. He had been brought up at the court of Henry I, whose favourite nephew he was, and his accumulation of wealth had been spectacular. Before 1113 he had received the lands and dignities of the count of Mortain who had been captured at Tinchebrai. Then he obtained no less than 250 manors of the honour of Eye in Suffolk which had been forfeited by Robert Malet; and he was also given lands in Lancashire and Yorkshire out of which he later endowed the abbey of Furness.[62] Most important of all was his acquisition by marriage of the *comté* of Boulogne.[63] And he could count on most influential backing from members of his own family. His younger brother Henry had been made bishop of Winchester in 1125, and his elder brother, Count Theobald IV, was at this time bringing the fortunes of the great house of Blois to their peak.[64] The question of the succession to Henry I therefore concerned France scarcely less than England. While the details of the warfare waged after 1138[65] both in France and England between the grandson and the granddaughter of William the Conqueror do not concern this study, the unity of that struggle deserves emphasis. In 1136 Stephen had to bear off an attack by the king of Scotland on behalf of the empress, whilst about the same time Matilda, with her husband and the earl of Gloucester, was ravaging Normandy. In March 1137 Stephen therefore

---

[60] A new class of 'disinherited' had in fact been created – 'the men whom Henry I had set up and whom Stephen had pulled down'.

[61] Powicke, *Loss of Normandy*, pp. 8–22; Chartrou, *Anjou*, pp. 36–58.

[62] Round, *Peerage and Family History*, pp. 166–8; Davis, *Stephen*, pp. 7–8.

[63] Stephen's marriage to Matilda, heiress to the *comté* of Boulogne, took place in 1125 at the instigation of Henry I.

[64] Luchaire, *Louis VI*, pp. lxxxviii–xciii.   [65] Cronne, *Stephen*, pp. 26, 27.

passed over to Normandy in an attempt to repel their invasion,[66] but early in 1138 he had hastily to return in order to quell the disorders which in his absence had erupted in England. The notable victory won by his supporters over the Scottish king in August 1138 at the Battle of the Standard in Yorkshire[67] may itself, for all its glamour, be regarded as essentially an episode in a warfare which was being waged on both sides of the Channel. Perhaps indeed it was only Stephen's command of the sea-route by Boulogne which prevented the empress and the earl of Gloucester from coordinating their efforts with those of King David in 1138, but in the next year they were both back in England and established at Bristol. Thereafter desultory warfare ensued, which was to reach its English climax in 1141 with the defeat and capture of the king at the battle of Lincoln (2 February) and the subsequent repulse of the empress from London and her own defeat at Winchester when the earl of Gloucester was taken prisoner and exchanged for the captive king. This chaotic warfare in England was inconclusive, but in Normandy a more decisive result was being obtained, for there the progress of Matilda's husband, the count of Anjou, was constant.[68] In 1141 he got possession of Falaise and Lisieux, and the next year he occupied the Avranchin and the Cotentin. He extended his authority steadily over the whole duchy, and in 1144 he entered Rouen in triumph to be installed as duke by the archbishop in his cathedral and to be thereafter confirmed in his duchy by Louis VII of France.[69]

The conquest of Normandy by Count Geoffrey was in fact the turning point in the struggle between Anjou and Blois for control of the Anglo-Norman realm. Not only was Angevin strength thereby increased, but for the first time since 1106 there was a political separation between Normandy and England, a matter of vital concern to the Anglo-Norman baronage, many of whom held lands on both sides of the Channel. As it became clear that Stephen could neither regain Normandy nor establish full control in England, many of the magnates gradually became convinced that their interests would best be served if the duke of Normandy became also king of England, an aspect appreciated by Geoffrey himself. Already in 1144 he regarded himself in Normandy as sponsor for the rights of his wife, and in 1150 he formally handed over the duchy to her son Henry, who was then aged seventeen.[70]

[66] Will. Malms., *Historia Novella*, ed. Potter (1955), p. 21.

[67] Ailred of Rievaulx, *Chronicles of Stephen*, II, pp. 318 et sqq.

[68] Haskins, *Norman Institutions*, pp. 127–51; Delisle, *Actes Henri II*, I, pp. 135, 136.

[69] Haskins, *Norman Institutions*, p. 130.   [70] Delisle, *op. cit.*, pp. 121–4.

From this time the cause of the empress was to be led less by her than by her son. He had several times been in England and had received a knighthood from the king of Scots. But now he could take more effective action, and his new effort was based upon Normandy.[71] In March 1152 he received a new accession of strength when he obtained in marriage Eleanor, heiress of the duchy of Aquitaine, whose marriage to the king of France had recently been annulled.[72] The future seemed to be in his hands. His father had died in 1151, and now the magnates of Normandy and England were constrained to arrange a peace which would in due course assure his triumph. There were of course compromises in the arrangements then made. Stephen was recognized as ruler of England, but the king acknowledged Henry with some qualifications as his heir.[73] Thus after Stephen's death on 25 October 1154, Henry duke of Normandy and count of Anjou, count also of Touraine and, through his wife, duke of Aquitaine, succeeded to the Anglo-Norman realm which in this way had been enlarged and reunited.

The so-called 'Angevin empire' to which King Henry succeeded on his coronation on 21 December 1154 was essentially the Anglo-Norman realm which had been founded by William the Conqueror and consolidated by Henry I. On these foundations had been erected a vast imperial state which stretched from the Tweed to the frontiers of Spain, which included most of France, and whose authority was extended over Wales, Brittany and much of Ireland and Scotland. Moreover, this imperial realm was regarded by Henry II, as it had been by Henry I, as a unity. It is thus misleading to intrude notions derived from modern nationalism into the policy of these kings, or to criticize them for spending so much of their time outside England.[74] They acted naturally and profitably in this manner in order to defend the totality of their inheritance. They were not national figures. They were European rulers. And as such they were among the most powerful monarchs of their age.

Thus was the Anglo-Norman realm exalted to a dominant position in the political structure of the West. And it is only by reference to the manner in which its integrity had been sustained, and its power increased, that its contribution to the Norman impact on Europe between 1100 and 1154 can be assessed. But its influence cannot in this respect be considered in isolation.

---

[71] Delisle, *op. cit.*, p. 123. [72] W. L. Warren, *Henry II*, pp. 42–5.
[73] Davis, *Stephen*, chap. X.
[74] See the very notable passage by Haskins (*Normans in European History*, pp. 84–9). The teaching of the master on this matter could hardly have been more convincingly expressed.

The Anglo-Norman realm which was inherited at last by Henry II was not the only Norman state to be firmly established during these decades. During the same period there was created in the South that other Norman kingdom comprising southern Italy and Sicily which was to exercise a controlling influence on Mediterranean politics. Ten months before the coronation of Henry II in London there died at Palermo Roger the Great, the first and the most distinguished king of the Norman realm of Sicily.

Chapter 2

THE ADVENT OF ROGER THE GREAT,
1101–1129

I

It was in the summer of 1085 that Robert Guiscard, the terrible Norman duke of Apulia, set out eastward to direct his sons in a last attempt on the Empire of Byzantium. He reached the island of Cephallonia at a time of torrid heat, and found himself stricken with fever. On 17 July, five days after landing, he died in the extreme north of the island on the peninsula of Athir,[1] and just as his astonishing career had excited the imagination of contemporaries so also were the circumstances of his death to be widely debated.[2] It seems, however, that his second wife, the Lombard Sigelgaita, and at least one of his sons, were with him at the last, and a later account states that many other Norman notables surrounded their dying leader.[3] Specially named among these were Robert of Loritello, the grandson of Tancred of Hauteville; Geoffrey of Conversano, the father of the beautiful Sibyl who was later to marry Robert duke of Normandy; William of Grandmesnil, son of the powerful Hugh of Leicester, and nephew of Robert the first Norman abbot of the great monastery of St Eufemia on the Calabrian coast; and Odo 'the good marquis', the father of that Tancred who was one day to be prince of Antioch.[4] It was indeed a representative Norman gathering that watched the passing of Robert Guiscard, and there must have been many in that company who wondered what the future would bring.

On the news of the death of Robert Guiscard, it was said that Greece, freed from her enemy, rejoiced in peace; Calabria and Apulia were convulsed.[5] He had been the chief agent in effecting the Norman conquests

[1] Anna Comnena, VI, c. 6; Will. Apul., V, vv. 295, 325–7; *Annales Barenses*, s.a. 1085; Chalandon, *Domination*, I, p. 282. Some scholars (e.g. Yeatman, *Bohemund the First*) believe that Guiscard died not in Cephallonia but at Cassiope in Corfu. But see M. Mathieu (ed.), *Guillaume de Pouille*, pp. 334, 335, and the authorities there cited.

[2] The most fantastic of the many stories is that he was poisoned by Sigelgaita, who tried also to poison Bohemund (Ord. Vit., III, p. 82). This need not be taken seriously. For the macabre story of the manner in which the body of Guiscard was brought home to be buried at Otranto, see Anna Comnena, VI, c. 6; *Chron. Breve. Norm.*, s.a. 1085.

[3] Ord. Vit., III, pp. 182–8.   [4] See below, pp. 183–93.   [5] Malaterra, III, c. 41.

in the South, and after his death the dominions which the Normans had won began speedily to fall into disunion and disorder. Thus Roger Borsa his son by Sigelgaita, became titular duke of Apulia,[6] but his rule was promptly challenged by his half-brother Bohemund of Taranto, who made himself master of all the territory between Conversano and Brindisi. Capua too fell into chaos, and for a time actually expelled its Norman rulers, whilst in 1094 Amalfi declared itself independent.[7] But further to the south a very different development was beginning with the rapid advance of Guiscard's youngest brother Roger, soon to be known as the 'Great Count'.[8] In 1085 this Roger was already master of most of Calabria. By 1091 he had completed the conquest of the whole of Sicily with his spectacular capture of Syracuse.[9] And in 1094 he led the expedition which recovered Capua for the duke of Apulia, who in turn was becoming ever more dependent upon the support of his uncle in Sicily. Thus before the death of the Great Count on 22 June 1101,[10] the pattern of Norman power in the central Mediterranean had been transformed. Apulia and Capua had waned in importance. The dominance of Norman Sicily over Norman Italy was clearly foreshadowed, and perhaps even (though more dimly) the eventual establishment of a single Norman dominion in the South.

Certainly, Roger the 'Great Count' had left a notable political legacy to his successors, and the later achievement of the first Norman king of Sicily would owe much to what had been accomplished by his father. None the less, it must at first have seemed doubtful whether that inheritance could be seized. The family which the 'Great Count' had been given by his three successive wives had consisted mainly of girls, and in 1101 his only surviving legitimate sons were two young children. There was Simon, who was then aged seven, and Roger, some two years younger.[11] Roger had been born on 22 December 1095.[12] In 1105 he was to succeed his father as Count Roger II. In 1127, after strenuous fighting, he was to become duke of Apulia, and lord over all its dependencies, including Capua. And finally in 1130 he

---

6 *Cod. Dipl. Barese*, I, Nos 18, 19, 20, 30, 43; Malaterra, III, c. 42.

7 Pet. Diac., IV, c. 10.   8 See Douglas, *The Norman Achievement*, especially chap. III.

9 Malaterra, Bk IV, *passim*. Modern scholars have disagreed about the chronology of these events. I here follow Amari (*Musulmani*, Vol. III) and Pontieri (Malaterra, pp. 85, 104).

10 Ann. Bari (Lupus), s.a. 1101. The date is given in the Necrology of Montecassino.

11 Caspar, *Roger II*, Reg. 'A'.

12 Citations in Caspar, *op. cit.*, Reg. 'B'. Later legend suggested that St Bruno came out of his hermitage near Squillace to baptize the child (*Acta Sanctorum*, 6 October), but there is no sure evidence to support this charming story.

achieved royalty as king of Sicily, and extended his rule over all the Norman dominions in the South. Posterity was to acclaim him as 'Roger the Great'.

II

In 1101, however, few would have cared to forecast such a career. For the fate of Simon and Roger must then have seemed very precarious. They were the sons of Adelaide, the third of the wives of the 'Great Count', and on her there thus descended at once a responsibility that was both heavy and hazardous, for the surrounding situation was full of menace. The Norman conquest of Sicily had only recently been completed, and on the Italian mainland the Norman power had disastrously degenerated since 1085. It was therefore in circumstances of considerable peril that in 1101 Adelaide undertook the regency on behalf of her elder son. And conditions were made the more difficult when it became apparent that Simon, whose birth had been hailed by such lyric enthusiasm by Malaterra,[13] was growing up as a very sickly boy. He was in fact to die on 13 September 1105,[14] leaving his rights in Sicily and Calabria to Roger, the future king, and to the care of his courageous mother. The figure of Adelaide, countess of Sicily and later queen of Jerusalem, must therefore attract considerable attention.[15] She was the daughter of a baron in the north of Italy, the Marquis Manfred who was a younger son of Boniface 'del Vasto', lord of Savona near Genoa. And through her husband Roger I and her son Roger II she became wife and mother to two of the most remarkable rulers of medieval Europe. She was moreover to make her own contribution to the survival of their work.

Her career was thus indeed noteworthy. But before it ended Adelaide was made victim of one of the most sordid intrigues of the age. In 1113 Baldwin I, king of Jerusalem, sought her in marriage.[16] He had already been twice married, but he lacked legitimate issue, and one of his wives had died[17] whilst the other had been discarded.[18] Moreover, Baldwin needed

---

[13] Malaterra, IV, c. 19.

[14] Necrology of Palermo. Cf. Chalandon, *Domination*, I, p. 358.

[15] On Adelaide, see in particular E. Pontieri, in *Studi Ruggeriani* (1955), pp. 327–435.

[16] Albert of Aix, XII, cc. 13, 14; William of Tyre, XI, c. 21.

[17] Godehildis, daughter of Ralph of Tosny. She died at Marash in 1096.

[18] She was the daughter of Thatoul, the Armenian governor of Marash, who offered with her an enormous dowry which in fact was never paid. Nor was the lady herself wholly satisfactory. She was alleged to have bestowed her favours on the Moslem sailors who brought her to her wedding, and her later conduct in Jerusalem invited similar comment. At last, Baldwin,

money, and Adelaide, as the widow of the 'Great Count', was one of the richest heiresses in Europe. For her part, Adelaide is said to have coveted a royal title, even though the court at Jerusalem can have offered few attractions after the splendours of Palermo. Perhaps, too, she may even at this juncture have been mainly concerned with the interests of her son for whom she had already done so much. For she accepted Baldwin's offer only on the express condition that if the union should prove childless the kingdom of Jerusalem should pass to Roger of Sicily,[19] and it is at least possible that in 1113 Adelaide may have been privately aware that she could never have another child.[20] In any case, the terms for the match were solemnly accepted. Baldwin's envoys in Sicily agreed to them on oath, and these oaths were later renewed at Jerusalem in the presence of the king, the patriarch Arnulf, and the chief man of the realm.[21] In the course of the summer of 1113, therefore, Adelaide sailed to her wedding in Palestine with a splendid retinue.

Either for physical or other reasons, however, the marriage proved both sterile and unhappy; and Baldwin, having secured the dowry from Sicily, was soon ready to invite ecclesiastical excuses for repudiating his Sicilian wife. Arnulf, the patriarch of Jerusalem, who had done much to promote the match, obtained from Pope Pascal II instructions to pronounce it invalid on the grounds that Baldwin's second wife was still living (though disreputably) at Constantinople.[22] Adelaide was thus cast off. Naturally she was highly indignant, and, 'sad and sorrowing' both at the affront and at the futile waste of her wealth, she prepared to return to her own land. Humiliated, but not disgraced, she reached Sicily in August 1116, and forthwith retired to the convent of Patti near Tindaris where she ended her eventful life on 16 April 1118.[23]

---

having no further financial interest in her, dismissed her to the convent of St Anne in Jerusalem. But in due course she escaped to Constantinople where the gaieties of a great city gave more scope to her particular talents. These scandals, and others like them, are fully reported by Guibert of Nogent and William of Tyre.

19 E. Pontieri, in *Studi Ruggeriani*, p. 423.

20 William of Malmesbury (p. 451) remarks that Baldwin repudiated her not long after taking her to his bed: 'aiunt incommodo tactam quo ejus genitalis cancer morbus incurabilis exederit'. Whatever may have been the exact nature of the complaint, Adelaide must have known about it before she left Sicily. On the other hand, William of Malmesbury's 'they say' may suggest that he was here repeating malicious gossip.

21 Will. Tyre, XI, c. 21.

22 Letter of Pascal, *Pat. Lat.*, vol. 103, col. 405, Albert of Aix, XII, c. 34.

23 Will. Tyre, XI, c. 29; Necrology of Palermo; Caspar, *op. cit.*, Reg. 36a.

The historical importance of the career of Adelaide lies, however, in those years between 1101 and 1112 when she ruled Sicily and Calabria on behalf of her two young sons. Her regency is only sparsely illustrated by contemporary evidence, but she must have been faced immediately with the menace of feudal disorder once the control of the 'Great Count' had been removed, and the threat was certainly increased by the anarchy which was inexorably spreading through southern Italy during the first decade of the twelfth century. Prince Richard of Capua, for example, could only regain possession of his own capital city at this time with the greatest difficulty,[24] and after 1104 his war with his brother Robert reduced the whole large region round Gaeta to chaos. There, in 1103, the Lombard Landulf had been deposed after heavy fighting by the Norman William of Blosseville, who was in turn soon replaced by another Norman, Richard 'de Aquila', who styled himself 'consul and duke'. But in 1105 the men of Gaeta were negotiating a treaty without reference to any ruler at all.[25]

In Apulia conditions were even worse. The principality of Capua was socially unified through its Lombard traditions, but by contrast, Apulia was divided between provinces in the north where Lombard traditions were dominant, and a wide region in the south which had long been subjected to Greek influence. The struggle between the two nephews of Adelaide, Roger Borsa, the duke whose power was in the north, and Bohemund of Taranto in the south, thus contributed to the further dismemberment of a duchy which was already socially divided, and by 1101 there was a complete breakdown of political authority. In 1100 a revolt at Canosa, for instance, illustrated the inability of Duke Roger Borsa to control the cities, whilst the rebellion of Henry count of Monte-Saint Angelo between 1105 and 1107 illustrated the virtual independence which had been gained by the great feudatories.[26] It is noteworthy that in 1106 Roger Borsa was not even consulted on the question of the succession to Prince Richard II of Capua who was nominally his vassal.[27] Nor was he able to intervene in any way in the affairs of his rival half-brother Bohemund during the latter's spectacular journeys through Italy and Western Europe in 1106 and 1107 before returning to the East. Even more significant, magnates, such as the counts of Monte-Saint Angelo and Conversano were at this time beginning to date their

---

[24] *Ann. Benev.*, s.a. 1101; *Liber Pontificalis*, II, pp. 258–67.
[25] *Codex Diplomaticus Caietanus*, II, pp. 159, 169, 177, 183.
[26] Chalandon, *Domination*, II, pp. 308, 309.
[27] Romuald of Salerno, s.a. 1106.

official acts by reference to the regnal years of the emperor of Constantinople, and without any allusion to the Norman duke of Apulia.[28]

In view of the widespread decadence of Norman power in Italy it is remarkable that no general anarchy in Sicily and Calabria followed the death of the 'Great Count' in 1101. Some revolts undoubtedly took place, since many years later the inhabitants of Castel Focero petitioned Adelaide's son to repair buildings which had been destroyed when his mother 'scattered her enemies like chaff before the wind'.[29] But the fact that the succession of the infant sons of Count Roger I was effected without calamity must surely be attributed in the first instance to his own strong government and to the stable conditions he had made to prevail in the dominions he had ruled. The achievement of Roger the Great was facilitated by the work of his father, and made possible by the successful regency of his dauntless mother.

III

It was the achievement of Adelaide to bridge the perilous gap between the constructive Sicilian rule of her remarkable husband and that of her still more remarkable son. In so doing she made her own contribution to the Norman impact upon Europe. Of course in this task she was dependent on the power that had been built by the Great Count and still more perhaps on the notable ministers mainly of Greek origin, who had been established at his court.[30] Prominent among these was a certain Eugenius, who as early as 1092 was styled notary and who was later to be designated as archon and emir.[31] He prospered sufficiently to become a notable benefactor of the Basilian monastery of St Michael the Archangel near Troina[32] and he was the ancestor of a notable administrative family which later in the twelfth century exercised great power at the Sicilian court.[33] He was, moreover, representative of a fairly large number of Greek officials on whom Adelaide

28 Chalandon, *Domination*, I, p. 308.

29 Caspar, *op. cit.*, p. 28. The *Historia Sicula* of the so-called *Anonymus Vaticanus* also alludes vaguely to such troubles which are perhaps reflected in some of the charters of the period (Cusa, *op. cit.*, pp. 313, 334, 471). Ordericus Vitalis (V, pp. 33–5) tells a story of Adelaide appealing for help to Robert, the son of Robert I duke of Burgundy. But this tale is unconfirmed and should probably be treated with scepticism.

30 Douglas, *Norman Achievement*, pp. 183–207.

31 Pirro, *Sicilia Sacra*, ed. Mongitore, II, pp. 1016–17; Cusa, *Diplomi Greci*, p. 400; Ménager, *Emir*, p. 27; Jamison, *Eugenius*, pp. 35–48.

32 Jamison, *Eugenius*, p. 35.   33 *Ibid., passim.*

could call for support. There was, for instance, Bon, who attests charters between 1090 and 1107 with the style of Syndic or Protonotary[34] and there was also Nicholas 'of Mesa', a chamberlain who was influential shortly after 1100.[35] Most important of all, however, was the famous emir Christodoulos, who was to make so deep an impression on the Norman realm.[36] Possibly his first appearance at the Sicilian court can be detected in a charter which was allegedly given to the abbey of S. Maria of Marsala in 1097 or 1098,[37] and thereafter he appeared in a long series of charters until 1129.[38]

The full importance of the Greek element at the Sicilian court was not to be demonstrated until later, when Roger the Great developed his own special type of administration which was to exercise so great an influence on the European future. But already in the early years of the twelfth century such men must have been to some degree responsible for sustaining the government of Adelaide, and the contribution they made to the survival of the Norman state at a time of peril is not to be minimized. So strong did their influence appear to contemporaries that many of them received high titles of honour from the Eastern emperor himself.[39] At the same time it was natural for Adelaide to depend on the prelates who had recently owed their appointments to the Great Count. Men such as Robert bishop of Messina, Roger bishop of Syracuse, who was a Norman, Gerland bishop of Agrigento, who came from France, and Anscher, who was a Breton in the Norman monastery of S. Eufemia in Calabria,[40] might be expected to support the continuation of Norman rule of Sicily.

None the less, Adelaide can herself claim much personal credit for the preservation at this time of the Norman dominance in Sicily and Calabria. Indeed, the consistency of her administration in this respect could be further illustrated from her own charters. Already in October 1101, when her husband had been dead only three months, a diploma granted to Gregory abbot at San Filippo at Fragalá[41] in the diocese of Messina, displays Adelaide as official ruler of Sicily in association with her son Simon and his brother Roger. Again, in 1107 after the death of Simon, Adelaide, in company with the young Roger, granted to the abbey of St Bartholomew in Lipari the tithe of Jews living at Termini Immerese.[42] Similarly, in 1110 Adelaide and

---

[34] Caspar, *op. cit.*, pp. 631–5.
[35] Ménager, *Emir*, p. 39 n. 1.
[36] *Ibid.*, pp. 28–38.
[37] *Ibid.*, No. 3.
[38] *Ibid.*, Nos 4, 6, 7, 8, 13, 18.
[39] *Ibid.*, pp. 41–3.
[40] Caspar, *op. cit.*, pp. 583 et sqq.; Jordan, in *Moyen Age*, XXIII and XXIV; Ménager, *Messina*, p. 44 n. 1.
[41] Cusa, *Diplomi Greci*, p. 294.
[42] White, *Norman Monasticism*, No. XII, p. 250; Ménager, *Emir*, No. 4.

Roger, this time acting together, gave to the bishopric of Squillace the church of S. Maria de Rochella,[43] and at about the same time they issued a diploma in favour of the abbey of S. Eufemia in Calabria.[44] Signs of the coming change were, however, now beginning to appear. As early as 1107 it was as count of Calabria and Sicily that Roger confirmed a 'gift of villeins to the Church of S. Angelo de Raith', and in January 1112 it was with the same title that he joined his mother, 'Adelaide the Countess', in a gift to the monastery of S. Opolo at Mileto.[45] But six months later – in June 1112 – Roger appears with his mother in a benefaction to Palermo as Roger, 'jam Miles, jam Comes'.[46] He has come of age; he is a knight; he is count. The regency of his mother is evidently about to end.

Thus had earlier traditions been sustained. But already there could perhaps be detected an indication of a new development. Adelaide came from the north of Italy. Except through her husband she had few personal contacts with Norman Apulia or Norman Calabria. After her marriage, therefore, and still more during her widowhood, her interests were centred on Sicily. It is thus not surprising that, during her regency, Mileto, which the Great Count always regarded as his capital, and where his body had been brought for burial, rapidly declined in importance.[47] Adelaide and his sons seem to have made Messina (which was the centre of Count Roger I's Sicilian administration) their principal residence, and it was from Messina that the majority of the comital charters in the time of Adelaide were dated.[48] Towards the end of her regency, however, there were indications of a change. The charter of January 1112 for S. Opolo was issued at Messina. But the famous diploma which Adelaide and her son Roger gave to Palermo cathedral in June of that year was issued 'when they were sitting in the hall of the archbishop at Palermo surrounded by their clerks and their barons and their knights'.[49]

The transition is notable. It would be rash to see here the record of an inauguration ceremony,[50] but Palermo with its splendour, its wealth and its teeming population was clearly in Adelaide's time exercising its irresistible attraction as the natural capital of Norman Sicily. The change

[43] Caspar, *op. cit.*, Reg. 13.
[44] K. A. Kehr, *Urkunden*, No. 3, p. 413; Caspar, *op. cit.*, Reg. 12.
[45] Ménager, *Messina*, No. 2, p. 49.   [46] Ménager, *Emir*, No. 10.
[47] Lenormant, *Grande Grèce*, III, pp. 280–5.
[48] Cusa, *Diplomi Greci*, p. 324; cf. Kehr, *Urkunden*, No. 3.
[49] Ménager, *Emir*, No. 10.   [50] Amari, *Musulmani*, III, p. 355.

from Messina was in fact inevitable. But it was none the less influential. In 1112 Messina was predominantly Greek and predominantly Christian. The permission given to Moslems to live in Messina seems to have been limited to a comparatively small group who were employed as servants. Palermo, on the other hand, which had for so long been a great Moslem metropolis, was still overwhelmingly Islamic both in population and character. It is thus significant that the young Roger the Great at the very beginning of his independent rule as count should be discovered at the age of seventeen enthroned among his magnates at Palermo.

IV

Little is known of the history of the young Count Roger II during the early years of his independent reign, but such charters as survive display him holding his courts peaceably, and with regularity, in the various parts of his dominions. Thus in 1114 and 1115 he was at Mileto and in other cities in Calabria whilst in 1116 he had returned to Sicily and held his courts both at Palermo and at Messina.[51] In 1117, at Messina, it was at a court of which any young ruler might be proud that the count, at the request of Hugh abbot of Holy Trinity Venosa, exempted from secular service the Greek monasteries situated in the dependency of S. Martino di Calabria.[52] This ordered progress at such a time deserves special note, for it may be emphatically contrasted with the terrible conditions prevailing elsewhere in Norman Italy.

Across the northern frontier of his Calabrian dominions the young Count Roger could watch anarchy inexorably spreading over the Norman lands. Early in February 1111 there died both Roger Borsa and his life-long opponent Bohemund of Taranto, titular prince of Antioch.[53] It was moreover an additional misfortune that neither of these rulers left an heir of adult age to sustain his interests in Apulia. The sole surviving son of Roger Borsa was William, who was still a boy, but who was accorded the title of duke and the rights which his father claimed in Calabria and Sicily as the successor of Robert Guiscard. Since, however, Bohemund's heir of the same name was also in 1111 a minor, it was left for the widows of Roger Borsa and Bohemund I, Alaine from Flanders and Constance of France, to act as regents for their young sons.[54] As a result, the earlier rivalries which had

[51] Chalandon, *Domination*, I, pp. 363–4.
[52] Ménager, *Emir*, No. 12; Caspar, *op. cit.*, Reg. 35.
[53] Roger on 22 February; Bohemund on 6 March (Necrologies of Montecassino and Molesme).
[54] Chalandon, *Domination*, I, p. 317.

torn Apulia were now exaggerated by two women who were both incapable of controlling the magnates who owed them a nominal allegiance. The unhappy duchy thus lapsed further into chaos, and Norman Apulia during these years became overshadowed by Norman Capua, though even there the power of the Norman ruler was precarious.

It was also characteristic of this period that the cities of Norman Italy should have begun to take advantage of the struggles between the great provincial families in order to promote their own independence. Thus at Benevento a faction of Lombard citizens was arrayed against a Norman coalition headed by Robert II prince of Capua, Jordan count of Ariano and Rainulf count of Alife, while away to the south, at Taranto, in Bohemund's country, a similar situation developed.[55] But the anarchy of the time could perhaps best be illustrated in the terrible history of Bari during these years. After 1111 Constance, now styling herself 'daughter of the King of France',[56] attempted to regain possession of the city, and two factions made their appearance. The one aimed at complete independence and the other, headed by Archbishop Riso and a certain Grimoald, relied on the support of Constance, and Tancred count of Conversano. In 1117 Grimoald arranged for the murder of the archbishop and threw Constance into prison,[57] thereafter declaring himself 'Prince of Bari', and it is symptomatic of the degeneration of the time that after 1118 he was recognized as such. In this way Bari, whose capture had marked a vital stage in the Norman conquests in the South, passed for a time completely out of Norman control.

The squalid warfare that ravaged Norman Italy at this period inevitably influenced wider developments of European importance, for when the anarchy was reaching its climax there was played out (also mainly in Italy) the concluding act in the struggle between pope and emperor over the investiture of prelates. Only a few weeks before the deaths of Roger Borsa and Bohemund I, Pope Paschal II had been made prisoner in Rome by the emperor Henry V, and the ensuing conflict between them was to continue until a compromise solution was at length found in the Concordat of Worms in 1122.[58] The fierce rivalries in Norman Italy at this time cannot therefore be dissociated from the greater issues which were vexing Christendom. Many magnates from Apulia, for instance, joined with the papal party in Rome in welcoming the proposal made by the Eastern emperor Alexis I that his son John should become emperor in the West, 'according to the

55 Jamison, *Apulia*, p. 230.
57 Chalandon, *Domination*, I, pp. 318, 319.
56 *Cod. Dipl. Barese*, V, No. 64.
58 Jamison, *Apulia*, p. 228.

usage formerly prevailing among Christians'.[59] The scheme was of course impractical. But there were many in Apulia, it would seem, who considered that the province which Robert Guiscard had wrested from Byzantium should turn again towards the East. Alexis himself appears to have been conscious of the advantages he might gain from such sentiments, and he was ready to exploit them to the extent of bestowing Eastern titles on Apulian notables.[60]

In these circumstances papal policy was itself between 1111 and 1121 inevitably directed towards the Norman South. In 1111 Paschal had lacked the support which his predecessors had received both from Robert Guiscard and from the princes of Capua, but during the ensuing conflict with the empire it was to the South that the popes usually fled when they were ejected from Rome. As a result they clearly had an interest in restoring order to the Norman states from which they might seek effective support. Thus in 1113 Paschal II intervened personally in the wars raging round Benevento,[61] and in the next year he held a council at Ceprano where he sought to restore peace to Gaeta, and where he also invested the young William both with the duchy to Apulia and with the overlordship of Sicily.[62] In 1115 the same pope was at Troia where he enjoined the magnates of Apulia to respect and extend the Truce of God by refraining from private war for the space of three years.[63] And the same policy was continued by Paschal's immediate successors. Calixtus II in 1120 strove to restore peace to distracted Bari, and it was owing to her personal intervention that the long-suffering Constance of France was released at last from captivity.[64]

The papacy could, however, expect little reciprocal assistance from Apulia during the reign of Duke William, for the new duke was not the man to check the anarchy ravaging his duchy. He was, we are told, a young man 'of medium height, good looking and very pleasant to everyone, pious and gentle and much beloved by those with whom he moved'.[65] Duke William in fact courted and won a facile popularity. The people of Benevento publicly lamented his early death.[66] But during his rule chaos inexorably spread over Apulia, and the waning authority of the duke was confined to a restricted region round Salerno. Thus when the emperor Henry V returned to Italy in 1117 and expelled Paschal II from Rome it was with the prince of Capua, and not with the duke of Apulia, that the pope took refuge,[67] and

[59] 'Secundum morem antiquorum fidelium' (*Pet. Diac.*).   [60] Ménager, *Emir*, p. 43.

[61] Falco Benev., s.a. 1113.   [62] *Ibid.*, s.a. 1114.   [63] *Ibid.*, s.a. 1115.

[64] Watterich, *Vitae*, p. 114.   [65] Romuald, s.a. 1127.   [66] Falco Benev., s.a. 1127.

[67] Pet. Diac., IV, c. 64.

it was Prince Robert of Capua and not Duke William of Apulia who supplied the troops which in 1118 escorted Pope Gelasius II into his capital after his election.[68]

The helplessness of Duke William was in fact already becoming clear, and Count Roger in the South soon became strong enough to take advantage of the situation in order to extend his own power in southern Italy. By 1121 he was intervening actively in the affairs of distracted Apulia. William had already placed his share of Calabria in pledge to the count of Sicily, and in 1122 he was forced to appeal in abject terms for Roger's assistance against his own rebellious vassals. The help was given but the price was high. Roger compelled the duke to cede the whole of Calabria absolutely and in perpetuity, and to give up his remaining rights in Messina and Palermo,[69] and this was only part of a larger plan. It was apparent that William would be childless and it is alleged that in 1122 in return for a large sum of money the duke made the count his heir.[70] Whether this was so or not is doubtful, for there is another story that when Bohemund II left for the East in 1126 William entered into an agreement with him that they would each leave their lands to the other.[71] At all events, when William duke of Apulia, the pope's vassal, died without issue on 25 July 1127,[72] a crisis immediately developed which involved all the powers in southern Italy. Capua, Apulia, Calabria, Sicily, the feudal baronage and the insurgent cities were alike implicated, and the papacy itself was inextricably concerned. Here too might be the opportunity for a ruler with inherited wealth, with power and with ruthless ambition. Count Roger II seized it. He was just over thirty years of age, and he now entered upon the fierce struggle which was to last with few interruptions for the next twelve years.

His first act was to assert his plausible but disputed claims to Apulia, and within a month of Duke William's death he appeared with seven ships and a small force in the Bay of Salerno. The men of the city, however, refused to receive him and even killed one of the envoys he had sent to demand their submission. A strong party in the city led by Archbishop Romuald was, however, anxious to accept him as duke, and Count Rainulf of Alife, Roger's brother-in-law and later his most bitter enemy, was also ready to support him on certain conditions. The citizens of Salerno thus submitted with the stipulation that the castle in the city should remain in their own

---

[68] *Liber Pontificalis*, II, p. 313. [69] Ménager, *Emir*, p. 24.

[70] Romuald, s.a. 1122. Cf. Chalandon, *Domination*, I, p. 380.

[71] Will. Tyre, XIII, c. 21. [72] Chalandon, *Domination*, I, p. 385 n. 2.

hands.[73] Amalfi followed suit; and Roger pressed on to force the submission of Melfi, Troia and Montescaglioso.[74] Honorius II, therefore, acutely aware how dangerous might be the union of all southern Italy under the count of Sicily, immediately excommunicated Roger, and refused him the duchy of Apulia. Further, in order to repel the intruder, he organized a coalition led by Jordan II prince of Capua, and including all the discontented elements in Apulia such as Grimoald of Bari and Tancred count of Conversano.[75] The alliance, however, soon broke up. Jordan of Capua died in December, and the campaign was conducted on the papal side with singular incompetence. Thus Roger, who had crossed over from Sicily with a large mercenary force, soon found himself master of the situation and on 23 August 1128, outside Benevento, Honorius was forced to withdraw the sentence of excommunication and to invest the count of Sicily with the duchy of Apulia. This he did by means of the presentation of a banner, and he also confirmed to Roger the homage of Robert, the newly established prince of Capua. In return, Roger proffered his liege homage to the pope and promised neither to invade the principality of Capua nor to allow anyone to disturb the papal rule of Benevento.[76]

It was now left to Roger to exploit his victory. He entered Apulia in 1127 with a force estimated at more than nine thousand men, most of them Saracen mercenaries. After campaigns of singular brutality involving Brindisi, Siponto, Montalto and Troia he advanced towards Bari itself, which surrendered to its new duke in August.[77] Grimoald of Bari and the family of Conversano submitted in their turn, and Roger confirmed his triumph at a great council held at Melfi in the autumn.[78] He had in fact reconstituted the duchy of Apulia as it was in the time of Robert Guiscard. All Bohemund's former territories from Brindisi to Taranto were now restored to the ducal demesne, and the authority of Roger of Sicily as duke stretched over the whole of Apulia and was recognized by the papacy.

V

At the beginning of 1130 Roger, now ruler or suzerain of all the Norman lands in the South, was evidently approaching a position when his dominions might be united into a realm, and when he himself might perhaps acquire

[73] Jamison, *Apulia*, pp. 221–2. [74] Chalandon, *Domination*, I, pp. 388, 389.
[75] Falco Benev., s.a. 1127. [76] Falco Benev., s.a. 1128; Pet. Diac., IV, c. 96.
[77] Alex Tel., I, c. 17, 18. [78] Alex Tel., I, c. 21.

the status of a king. The stage had thus been set for the final act of the drama. But the conditions in which it was to be played were determined in large measure by events in Rome over which Roger had at first little control.[79] On 14 February 1130 Pope Honorius II died at Rome and, even before he was buried, violent dissension broke out respecting his successor. Two elections took place in different quarters of the city. At one of them, held under the protection of the family of Frangipani, a minority group among the cardinals unanimously elected Cardinal Gregory of Sant Angelo, who took the title of Innocent II. At the other, a larger number of cardinals, many of whom were of advanced age, chose Peter, son of Pierleoni I (Petrus Leonis), and he assumed the style of Anacletus II. Which of these two elections was the more grossly illegal was not at first clear, but it was finally Innocent II who came to be recognized as the legitimate pope. This, however, did not take place until after a schism which lasted many years and which brought discord to the courts and most of the bishoprics and monasteries of Western Christendom. The issues involved in that double election at Rome in February 1130 far transcended the rivalry of two Roman families. They were sorely to perplex Europe until 1138, and they still divide scholars today.[80]

The family from which Anacletus came had already played a strange and influential part in papal history. His great-grandfather was a Jew named Baruch, who after his conversion to Christianity took the name of Benedict.[81] He was succeeded as head of the house by his son Leo, whose brother reigned in Rome in 1118 as 'Pope Gregory VI', and whose wife may have been aunt to Hildebrand, later Pope Gregory VII.[82] Leo was in turn succeeded by Pierleoni I (Petrus Leonis), who was the father of Anacletus. The family was notorious for its great wealth (doubtless derived from money-lending) and it appears to have retained its Jewish filiations. But it became zealously Christian in its religious professions, and the great popes of the reforming period from Alexander II to Paschal II undoubtedly owed much to its support.[83] It is understandable, therefore, that Anacletus should in

79 Cf. Gregorovius, *Rome*, IV, pp. 412–16.

80 Compare, for instance, the persuasive account given by H. Bloch in 'The Schism of Anacletus and the Glanfeuil forgeries', *Traditio*, VIII (1952), pp. 159–264, with those given by P. F. Palumbo, 'Lo Schisma del MDXXX', *Misc. del Deputazione romana di Storia Patria* (1942), by A. Fliche in *Hist. de L'Eglise*, IX (1946), pp. 42–75, and by Knowles and Obolensky in *The Christian Centuries*, II (1968), pp. 84–103.   81 See below, Table VI.

82 For the family, see H. Bloch, *op. cit.*, p. 163, and R. L. Poole, *Studies in Chronology and History*, pp. 207 et sqq. A family connexion between Anacletus and Hildebrand was first suggested by Dr Poole.   83 H. Bloch, *op. cit.*, pp. 164, 165, 178–80.

1130 have received the backing of many Roman ecclesiastics, particularly those of the older generation. But about Anacletus himself it is difficult to pronounce judgement. Doubtless he had his faults, and being wealthy as well as ambitious he probably, like others in such a position, used bribes to advance his cause. But the portraits painted of him by his enemies during the schism lack any verisimilitude. Before 1130 he had had a distinguished and not dishonourable career in the Church, and it is hard to believe that after his election as pope he indulged in the wildest sexual irregularities including incest with his sister Tropea.[84] This venomous propaganda might indeed have been disregarded here (even though it was unfortunately fostered by St Bernard) save for the fact that the conflict between Anacletus and Innocent became an essential factor in the establishment of the Norman kingdom of Sicily.

At first it seemed that the cause of Anacletus would prevail. Both Rome and Italy gave him general support, and elsewhere he obtained early recognition from important ecclesiastics such as Adalbert archbishop of Bremen and the prelates of Scotland. At Rome, moreover, his faction, after much street fighting, obtained control of the capital, and in May Innocent was forced to fly the city. But Innocent, who took refuge in France, was so fortunate as to receive the support of St Bernard. With this sponsorship he obtained general, though not universal, recognition in France, and was later approved by the Emperor Lothair and by most of the Church in Germany. Henry I of England was also reluctantly persuaded to accept him. By the summer of 1130 St Bernard could thus triumphantly declare that Innocent, 'having been expelled from the City . . . had been accepted by the World'.[85] In reply, Anacletus appealed to Rome, to Italy and (following the example of so many of his predecessors) to Roger and the Normans of the South.

Thus the ecclesiastical policy of Anacletus II and the political fortunes of Roger II became inextricably intertwined, and it was in these conditions that on 27 September 1130 Anacletus issued his famous bull conferring on Roger II the title of king. Its terms were admirably precise:

> We grant and give and sanction to you and to your heirs the crown of the kingdom of Sicily, and Calabria and Apulia, and of all the lands which we and our predecessors have granted to your predecessors the Dukes of

[84] See the *Invectiva* of Arnulf of Sées, later bishop of Lisieux (Watterich, *Vitae*, II, pp. 258–75).

[85] 'Pulsus Urbe ab Orbe suscipitur' (Bernard, Ep. 124, *Pat. Lat.*, 182, col. 268).

Apulia, namely Robert Guiscard and Robert [sic] his son. This kingdom is to be held by you in perpetuity and ruled by you always with all regal honours and all royal rights. We appoint Sicily as the head of your kingdom. Further we sanction and grant that you and your heirs shall be anointed and crowned as Kings by the hands of archbishops of your own kingdom and of your own choice and in the presence of such bishops as you may wish. And we give and sanction to you and your heirs the principality of Capua – and the 'honour' of Naples – and the support [auxilium] of the men of Benevento.[86]

In return Roger was to give to the pope homage and fealty and in addition to make an annual payment to Rome.

This notable bull only survives in a copy of the fourteenth century, but there is no reason to question its substantial authenticity, and it can be regarded as accurately heralding the policy and the achievements of the new reign. It saluted Roger with all the attributes of kingship. It enunciated the ecclesiastical prerogatives for which he was to strive. And with its references to Sicily, Apulia, Calabria, Naples, Capua and Benevento, it went far towards defining the boundaries of the later realm.

So favourable to Roger was the bull that it may be suspected that he was himself responsible for its issue and for its contents. In September 1130 Anacletus was sorely in need of Sicilian support, and Roger had evidently already decided that the time had come when he might claim the title of king. According to Alexander of Telese, his admiring biographer, he was repeatedly urged by his magnates to take this course, and most particularly by Henry, his mother's brother.[87] Sometime in 1130, therefore, a great court was held outside Salerno consisting of all Roger's greater vassals, both lay and ecclesiastical, and of prominent citizens from many of the chief towns.[88] It was probably at this assembly that it was determined that

Since Roger now reigned over so many of the provinces of Calabria and Apulia, and over so many of the regions which stretched almost as far as Rome, he ought to be vested not with the dignity of Duke but with the supreme majesty of a King. And they added that the capital of the kingdom and its head should be at Palermo the metropolis of Sicily.[89]

86 Text in Watterich, *Vitae*, II, pp. 193, 194. Cf. P. F. Kehr, *Italia Pontificia*, No. 137, p. 37.
87 Alex. Tel., II, c. 7.   88 Falco Benev., s.a. 1130.
89 Alex. Tel., II, c. 1.

And so, concludes Romuald of Salerno, writing at a slightly later date, 'after taking counsel with his barons and his people Roger caused himself to be anointed and crowned as King at Palermo'.[90]

Thus it was that on Christmas Day 1130 the first Norman king in Sicily came to his crowning. And Roger was evidently determined to make the occasion memorable. The magnificence of the entertainment, and the festivities which preceded and followed the coronation, made a profound impression on contemporaries. According to Alexander of Telese,[91] the royal palace was splendid with rich hangings, and the royal cortège passed to the great cathedral through crowded streets that were lavishly decorated, and even carpeted, with multicoloured fabrics. The coronation itself was conducted with impressive pomp and according to a ritual which has a considerable interest in the history of medieval royalty.[92] And after the ceremony there were banquets of sumptuous splendour at which the feudal magnates who had been summoned to acclaim Roger's crowning were waited on by attendants clad in silk. A vast concourse of people, we are told, came to watch the pageantry, and, if these descriptions approach to truth, they cannot have been disappointed. A new kingdom had been given to Christendom. But it had still to be seen whether Roger's realm could survive.

[90] Romuald, II, p. 7. [91] Alex. Tel., II, c. 3–6. [92] See below, pp. 83–7.

Chapter 3
KING ROGER OF SICILY,
1130–1154

I

The establishment in 1130 of the Norman realm in the South was an event of cardinal importance in European history, and Roger, the first Norman king of Sicily, must be regarded as one of the makers of medieval Europe. The lasting importance of his reign lies in the impact he made on his contemporaries, in the character of the government he created, and in the social and cultural conditions he caused to prevail throughout the wide dominions over which he extended his rule.[1] But all these far-reaching results of his career were dependent, at the outset, on his ability to surmount the hazards which accompanied his attainment of kingship. His advance to regality had offered a challenge not only to many important interests in Italy, but also to some of the strongest powers in Europe, and, for these reasons, at the beginning of his reign Roger had for long years to wage a continuous and perilous war for survival.

The wide issues that were here involved can be seen at once in the various parties which immediately became implicated in the conflict. First among these were the local magnates, and the problem which here confronted King Roger was further enhanced by the circumstances which had attended the original imposition of feudalism by the Normans in the South. In Sicily the Norman rulers, Robert Guiscard and Roger the Great Count, had been able to distribute fiefs very largely according to their pleasure. But on the mainland the Norman conquest had been in a sense a cooperative undertaking, and the various families who had shared in the subjugation of the land had often accepted only with reluctance the overlordship of the house of Tancred of Hauteville. Still less would they be ready to acquiesce without protest in the exaltation of a single king whose royal dignity, buttressed by the rites of the Church, would place a wide gulf between himself and even the greatest of his subjects. Feudal Apulia and feudal Capua might be expected immediately to revolt.

The new king could thus place only a limited reliance on his feudal

1 See below, chaps 5–8.

resources. He may perhaps, however, have hoped that he could derive some slight advantage from the primitive fortresses which he possessed on the mainland. It would seem that he and his predecessors had erected a certain number of these strongholds at strategic points such as Melfi, since some of the famous Italian castles later built by the emperor Frederick II are known to have been developed out of earlier fortifications.[2] But King Roger's castles were at first neither numerous nor particularly effective, and it is unlikely that they gave him much advantage. Far more important were his Saracen mercenaries. Saracen levies had been raised on a wide scale by his father, and these King Roger would enlarge and further employ. They were formidable warriors who inspired terror throughout the Christian provinces which they were wont to pillage. They were in fact the most effective troops that King Roger had at his disposal. Even so, his position at the outset of his reign remained lamentably weak, and his difficulties were further increased by the widely differing traditions which had for so long prevailed in the various provinces which had been brought under his single royal rule. In this respect, Lombard Capua might be contrasted with Byzantine Apulia and Calabria, and again with Moslem Sicily. The task here confronting the new king was thus not only to master a particularly intractable feudal baronage, but also to impose a unified royal government operating from Palermo on provinces which had cherished from a remote past their own separatist loyalties.

The crisis precipitated by the coronation of King Roger involved not only Italy but also Europe at large. In a sense the papal schism had assisted Roger, since he received recognition of his royalty from Rome sooner than might otherwise have been the case. But his association with Anacletus brought him into immediate conflict with Innocent II, and Innocent was soon to win the support of the Church both in France and Germany. King Louis VI of France and the emperor Lothair thus became implicated in their turn. To prove most menacing of all perhaps was the violent hostility of St Bernard, now the dominant figure in the Latin Church. For nine long years St Bernard was by his exhortations to sustain throughout the West a widespread and exceedingly powerful opposition not only against Anacletus, but also against the king whose usurped royalty had been blessed by the anti-pope and who could now be denounced both as an enemy of Christendom and as an ally of the Saracens.[3] Thus for nearly a decade after his coronation at Palermo

[2] G. Masson, *Frederick II*, pp. 190–201.
[3] H. Bloch, *Traditio*, VIII (1952), pp. 165 et sqq.

the Norman king was compelled to wage a continuous war against a vast and most formidable confederation made up of his own rebellious vassals and of the separatist principalities of Capua and Naples. It was also to be joined by the pope, by the two emperors of the West and the East, by the mercantile republics of Pisa and Genoa, and at times by the French king, and was consistently supported by the preaching of the most focal and influential ecclesiastic in Western Christendom. It is indeed a wonder that the new Norman kingdom survived.

The conflict began almost immediately after Roger's coronation.[4] The feudal revolt in Apulia was led by men such as Grimoald of Bari and Tancred of Conversano, while in the west Rainulf count of Alife, the king's brother-in-law, made common cause with Robert prince of Capua, Sergius duke of Naples and Geoffrey of Andria, near Bari. Many of the Apulian cities also joined in the revolt, notably Melfi, Venosa and Trani, and in July 1132, while Lothair and Innocent were still in northern Italy, Roger was defeated by the rebels in a pitched battle outside Capua. But the allies found it difficult to stay united, and the emperor's attentions were being diverted towards Germany. Roger could thus inflict heavy losses on his enemies separately by means of his dreaded Saracen mercenaries, and in this way the first crisis was passed. Grimoald was expelled from Bari, and those Apulian nobles who did not manage to escape suffered death, mutilation or imprisonment. The king's vengeance on the towns was still more terrible – Venosa, Trani, Troia, Melfi and Ascoli were all burnt, and the citizens subjected to savage and violent persecution. By the end of 1135, after this ruthless warfare, Roger found himself once again in possession of all the lands, with the exception of Naples, granted to him by Anacletus in 1130.[5]

Soon, however, the struggle was to be renewed on a far wider scale. Lothair returned to Italy with a large army, and through the efforts of St Bernard the cities of Pisa and Genoa were induced to join in the onslaught upon the Sicilian king. Even the Eastern emperor, mindful of past attacks by the Normans and jealous of Sicilian power in the Mediterranean, was at length brought to look favourably on the venture. Before the end of 1135 Venetian and Byzantine envoys arrived at Merseburg in Prussia to denounce the 'Count of Sicily' whose ships were preying upon those of Venice and Constantinople, and who, in addition, was contemplating the conquest of Africa, which 'is known to be a third part of the world'.[6] In the face of this

4 Falco Benev., s.a. 1132; Alex. Tel., II, cc. 29–32.
5 Jamison, *Apulia*, pp. 244–56.   6 Annals of Erfurt, s.a. 1135.

widespread and truly formidable coalition from all over Europe it seemed that the new Norman kingdom must surely be destroyed, and in fact by 1137 nearly all Roger's possessions in Italy had been overrun.[7] Robert had been restored as prince of Capua and Rainulf of Alife was invested by the pope with the duchy of Apulia.[8] In July 1137 Innocent and Lothair celebrated their successes at High Mass in the Norman church of St Nicholas in the midst of blood-stained Bari.[9]

But Roger's recovery, partly due to good luck but still more to his dextrous exploitation of the divisions among his enemies, was to be as complete as it was unforeseen. Pisa and Genoa remained in commercial rivalry, and neither Byzantium nor the papacy could be expected to view with enthusiasm the loudly voiced demands of Lothair for the restoration of the power of the Western empire in the Campagna and in Apulia. It is noteworthy, too, that Lothair showed an inclination to revive the issues that had been raised in the controversy over investitures, and the failure of Byzantium to support either the rebel barons in Apulia or the Western emperor in 1137 may have saved the Sicilian kingdom from destruction in that critical year. The Sicilian upstart must assuredly be destroyed but after this had been accomplished, whose claims would be recognized in the Italian lands which he had conquered? Opinions on this vital question would certainly differ in Rome, in Germany and at Constantinople.

The alliance against Roger was thus doomed to disintegrate. In the autumn of 1137, Pisa and Genoa feeling that they had little to gain from their cooperation beyond the approval of St Bernard, retired from the war, and shortly afterwards Lothair left for Germany.[10] He died there in December 1137, and was succeeded by Conrad III, a member of the rival house of Hohenstauffen. The old civil war between Welf and Hohenstauffen thus broke out afresh and it was zealously fomented by King Roger. During these years, indeed, Conrad's enemies in Germany were being financed by the king of Sicily whilst refugees from among Roger's feudal opponents in Apulia were receiving hospitality at the German court.[11] To this period too must be assigned the beginnings of a rapprochement between Sicily and the

---

[7] Chalandon, *Domination*, II, pp. 52–67.   [8] *Regesta Pontificum*, VIII, No. 150.
[9] *Annalista Saxo* (s.a. 1113) gives the fullest account of the solemn Mass of thanksgiving celebrated by Innocent II in the presence of the emperor.
[10] Chalandon, *Domination*, pp. 68–89; Jamison, *Apulia*, pp. 252–3.
[11] Geoffrey of Viterbo, c. XXXIII; Otto of Freising, *Chronicon*, VII, c. 23; John of Salisbury, *Hist. Pontificalis*, c. XXXII.

French monarchy. Finally, Roger was further assisted by two strokes of unexpected good fortune. Anacletus II died on 28 January 1138, so the king's cause was thus no longer linked to that of a discredited anti-pope, and three months later Rainulf count of Alife, Roger's main feudal opponent in Italy, was deposed.[12]

Among Roger's chief enemies in Italy there now remained only Pope Innocent II, and after the death of Anacletus the pope had no longer the same ecclesiastical excuse for continuing the war against Sicily, for though the papal schism was continued in the person of Victor II, Roger was not committed to the cause of the new anti-pope. Despite this, however, Innocent was determined to make one final effort to realize what had for so long been a major objective of papal policy in Italy – the prevention of the union of all the Norman dominions in the South under a single rule. With this in mind he resolved to support the independence of Capua as a separate state. He therefore moved southward against Roger, supported by Robert, titular prince of Capua, and by such of the rebel barons of Apulia who had survived the carnage of 1135. With singular incompetence, however, he allowed himself to be surrounded by the king's troops at Castel Galluccio near the banks of the Garigliano, and a large part of his force perished in a frenzied flight across the river. Robert of Capua escaped, but Innocent himself was captured and led a prisoner before Roger at Mignano.[13]

There it was on 25 July 1139 that Innocent, like his predecessor Honorius II, was brought at last to make an almost complete surrender to the Norman king of Sicily against whom he had fought so long. He lifted the excommunication on Roger and confirmed 'the illustrious and celebrated king in the possession of all the lands he had conquered with the exception of Benevento'.[14] Roger's triumph was complete. It is true that Innocent reserved his position on the vexed question of a metropolitan archbishop of Sicily, and it is true also that Roger, like his predecessors, paid tribute for his dominions and performed liege homage to the pope, but it was clearly to the advantage of the king that his realm should be regarded as a papal fief so that he could expect support from Rome against Germany. The new Norman kingdom in the South had thus been formally recognized. Innocent performed the final ceremony by the bestowal of three banners, one to the king and the others to the young Roger as ruler of Apulia and Alphonzo as

---

12 Falco Benev., s.a. 1138.
13 Falco Benev., s.a. 1139; *Chron. Fossa Nova*, s.a. 1138; Caspar, *op. cit.*, Reg. 124.
14 The papal bull is in *Pat. Lat.*, 179, col. 275. Cf. *Regesta Pontificum*, VIII, No. 159.

ruler of Capua.[15] The separate identity of both Capua and Apulia was thus acknowledged, but both had been brought under the single rule of Roger's Sicilian royalty, and very soon the inhabitants of Naples would make their own surrender.

It is customary, and legitimate, to regard the arrangements consequent on the treaty of Mignano as marking a turning point in the reign of King Roger. During 1140 he took a terrible vengeance on his remaining opponents. It is, in fact, from the events of these years that could best be illustrated the appalling brutality of Roger's Italian campaigns. In 1139 and 1140 Apulia and the Campagna were utterly devastated. 'Not even Nero, the cruellest of the pagan emperors,' it was said, 'had ever raged with so much fury as did this Christian king against his enemies.' The horrors which he perpetuated shocked even such distant commentators as Otto of Freising, and the Annalist of La Cava summed up the situation by saying that after the visitations of his Saracens, 'cowed Apulia stood silent wherever he appeared'.[16]

By such methods did Roger conquer his Italian realm, and after 1140 little more needed to be done to safeguard his kingdom. The chief remaining danger came from Germany. There is little doubt that the emperor Conrad felt himself betrayed at Mignano by his former ally Innocent II, and he was even to make an alliance with the emperor of the East against the 'Norman or Sicilian' tyrant who had robbed them both.[17] It was here that, despite ecclesiastical disputes, the feudal association of the Sicilian monarchy with the papacy was to stand Roger in good stead. The only wars that he was compelled to wage in Italy between 1140 and 1154 seem to have been small expeditions designed to maintain order or to safeguard his northern frontier.

II

By 1140 Roger's Italian kingdom had been established, and already its power was being extended overseas. The crucial part which Norman Sicily was to play in the political and economic life of the Mediterranean world during the twelfth century was being clearly indicated. So long as Sicily had remained a Moslem province, voyages to the East from Genoa, Pisa and

---

15 Falco Benev., s.a. 1139.

16 Falco Benev., s.a. 1134, 1138, 1139, 1140; *Falcandus*, ed. Siragusa, p. 5; *Ann. Cavenses*, s.a. 1140; Otto of Freising, *Chronicon*, VII, c. 23.

17 Wieruskowski, 'Roger II of Sicily', *Speculum*, XXXVIII (1965), pp. 61-4.

the other maritime republics of western Italy were too hazardous to be undertaken with any regularity. The Norman conquest, however, had opened the Straits of Messina to Christian shipping, and one of the most interesting documents of the period is the charter[18] which in September 1116 Roger, then still count, issued in favour of a certain Auger, a Genoese consul at Messina and his brother Ami. These men were apparently permanently charged with the interests of Genoa at Messina, and it is clear that the Sicilian city, now under Norman rule, had become a regular port of call for vessels proceeding from western Italy to the East. It was now also realized that a Norman fleet based on Sicily might in due course control the central Mediterranean. A new era of trade thus seemed to be opening between West and East, and one which would be strictly dependent upon Norman Sicily.

In these circumstances King Roger was fortunate in being able to rely upon, and to develop, the naval power which had been built up over the years by the Norman rulers of southern Italy and Sicily, and in particular by his father, the Great Count.[19] Many of the most spectacular of the Norman successes in the past, such as the capture of Bari in 1071, the conquest of Palermo in the next year, or the annexation of Malta and Gozo in 1090, had been the result of what might be aptly described as amphibious operations,[20] but the ships on which they had depended had for the most part not been built by the Normans themselves. They had been supplied by the conquered towns of the sea coast such as Taranto, Brindisi, Rossano and Reggio. For these cities, and others like them, had not only a great tradition of ship-building, but they had for long been associated with the maritime techniques of the Byzantine empire. As a result, not only the vessels but also crews of the navies used by the Normans at the beginning of the twelfth century were recruited from the lands they conquered, and particularly from the cities which had in the past been dominated by the Greeks.[21]

This was the policy which Roger the Great was steadfastly concerned to develop. Throughout his reign, therefore, no pains would be spared to sustain the royal fleets, and to increase their size and efficiency. The maritime organization inherited from the Eastern empire, and now reinforced by Moslem administration, was thus continued, and all the chief cities of King Roger's realm remained liable to make contributions, either of ships or of

[18] Cusa, *Diplomi Greci*, I, p. 359.   [19] Amari, *Musulmani*, III, pp. 340–3.
[20] Cf. D. P. Waley, 'Combined Operations in Sicily', *Papers Brit. School Rome* (1954).
[21] *Ibid.*

money, to the Norman navy. The capture of the great sea-faring city of Amalfi was here of particular importance. Elsewhere the provision of ships was often commuted into money payments so that great cities such as Naples and Bari were forced to secure special privileges in this respect.[22] Here too the immense financial resources of the king could be utilized to full effect. Ships could be chartered and crews hired, and at length the sea-power of Norman Sicily became such that it could challenge the maritime republics of Pisa and Genoa and even Venice and Byzantium itself. The rapidity of the growth of the Norman navy was shown when in 1113 Adelaide sailed to her marriage with King Baldwin of Jerusalem, the splendour of her naval escort exciting widespread admiration. In 1128, too, Roger the Great could afford to supply Raymond III count of Barcelona with fifty ships for use against the Moslems in Spain, and between 1146 and 1148 Norman sea-power was to deflect the whole course of the Second Crusade.[23]

III

The notable extension of Norman authority into North Africa during these years must thus be considered as at once an illustration and a result of the great increase of Norman power by sea and land which took place in the time of Roger the Great. It was also conditioned in part by the very complex political situation which developed in North Africa during his reign as count and which reached a climax of critical importance to Sicily in 1121–2, some eight years before he was recognized as king. Thus among the most important of Roger's neighbours across the sea were the Zirid princes who reigned at Al Mahdia, some forty miles north of Sfax. But these princes were constantly at war with the Fatimite dynasty of Egypt from whom they had originally won their independence and with the Berber rulers to the west who had established themselves in their fortified capital of Bougie. And across this welter of strife there had poured the invading flood of the Almoravids. These fierce puritan warriors who came originally from the Soudan had set up their first western capital at Marrakech. From there in due course they extended their authority over the whole province of the Maghreb from Oran to Tripoli, and eventually across the sea into Spain.[24]

These political rivalries among the Islamic states might in themselves tempt intervention by an invader from overseas, and Roger had strong

---

[22] Cahen, *Régime Feodale*, p. 73; *Cod. Dipl. Barese*, p. 80.
[23] Mas Latrie, *Traités de Paix*, pp. 13–72.   [24] *Ibid.*, pp. 24–5.

material reasons for concerning himself with North African affairs. There had always been commercial relations existing between Southern Europe and Moslem North Africa.[25] But from the beginning of the twelfth century these began to take on a form of special interest to Norman Sicily. The constant warfare which had ravaged North Africa for so long had caused terrible devastation through all the narrow territories between the desert and the sea,[26] and had produced recurrent famines of horrible intensity. In these circumstances, the Maghreb offered a ready market for Sicilian grain, and with their wonted versatility the Norman rulers of Sicily had been eager to exploit the situation. According to Moslem writers, Roger's father had drawn a large revenue from North Africa as a result of the traffic in grain,[27] and after his death during the first decade of the twelfth century the Normans of Sicily were maintaining commercial agents in many of the chief towns of the Maghreb.[28]

Roger the Great, both as count and as king, had thus perforce to face a special and a complicated challenge in the relations which he found existing between Sicily and North Africa. On the one hand there were obvious advantages in continuing a commercial cooperation which had proved profitable to both parties, but on the other hand there were developing tensions which could not be disregarded. The religious fervours stimulated by the First Crusade were slow to cool, and they might at any time be rekindled in North Africa. There was much piracy and slave-trading (perhaps under a religious excuse) by both Christians and Moslems, and open raiding was not infrequent.[29] None the less, during the regency of Adelaide it would seem that earlier traditions of friendship were maintained in the interests of commerce and in the succeeding years peaceful embassies passed between the two courts.[30]

The situation was, however, always delicate and in the time of Yahya, son of Tamin, who reigned at Al Mahdia from 1107 to 1116 and who was militantly hostile to the Christians everywhere, it began rapidly to deteriorate. Thus in 1113 a Moslem expedition from the Zirid province inflicted much devastation on the countryside around Naples and Salerno,[31] and under Yahya's son and successor Ali (1116–21) the tension grew. Ali was

[25] Lopes and Raymond, *Medieval Trade in the Mediterranean World*, pp. 29–35, 51, 54, *passim*.
[26] Amari, *Musulmani*, III, pp. 192, 193; Chalandon, *Domination*, I, p. 369.
[27] Ibn Athir, in Amari, *Bibl. Arabo-Sicula*, p. 115.   [28] Al Bayan, in *ibid.*, p. 153.
[29] Lopes and Raymond, *op. cit.*, pp. 29–35, 51, 54, *passim*.
[30] Chalandon, *Domination*, I, p. 370.   [31] *Ann. Cavenses*, s.a. 1113.

deeply involved in the rivalries which continued to ravage North Africa, and in particular he was perpetually at war with a certain Rafi ibn Makan, the ruler of Gabes. Rafi therefore placed himself under the protection of the ruler of Sicily, and Roger was quick to seize the opportunity for intervention. In 1118 a Norman fleet appeared off Gabes, and though it achieved little, its menace to the Zirid dynasty precipitated a crisis. For before his death in 1121 Ali had concluded an alliance with the Almoravids in Spain against the Normans of Sicily and the whole scope of the conflict in North Africa was thus widened.[32]

It was in these conditions that during 1121-22 a Moslem fleet from both Spain and North Africa came to ravage the coasts of Calabria and sacked Nicotera.[33] Roger's reaction was to organize a very large expedition against Al Mahdia, where Ali had been succeeded by his young son Hassan, who ruled under the guidance of his very able Grand Vizier, the eunuch Sandal, and who was not prepared to withstand the Sicilian threat. In July 1123 the Norman fleet left Marsala and, after a stormy passage, reached the island of Sorella some ten miles from the Zirid capital. From there was landed a large expeditionary force which took the stronghold of Al Dimas, and then advanced towards Al Mahdia itself. But at this crisis young Hassan and his Vizier acted with great energy and courage. They sallied out of Al Mahdia in considerable strength, took the Normans by surprise and completely routed them. The fleet could not send reserves in time to offer proper assistance, and it had to sail away leaving such Normans as survived to be killed or sold into slavery.[34] It was a disastrous reverse, and a few years later an Almoravid fleet was able again to raid Calabria with impunity, and then passing on to Sicily to ravage Patti and to fire Syracuse. Nearly a decade was to elapse before Norman power could once more be deployed on the southern shore of the Mediterranean.

None the less, young Hassan was never able fully to exploit his success against the Normans. In the midst of all the confused rivalries in North Africa he found it difficult even to protect his own sea-coast against the pirates who operated from the island of Gerba in the Gulf of Gabes. Then in 1134 he was suddenly called upon to face a direct attack from the Berber ruler of Bougie in the west.[35] In these circumstances he had to seek allies,

---

[32] Amari, *Musulmani*, III, p. 379; Chalandon, *Domination*, I, p. 273.

[33] Chalandon, *loc. cit.*

[34] For the expedition of 1123, see Amari, *Musulmani*, III, pp. 388-94.

[35] Ibn Athir; Ibn Dinar, in Amari, *Bibl. Arabo-Sicula*, pp. 117, 219.

and somewhat surprisingly he turned toward the Normans. Norman ships were already frequenting the Gulf of Gabes,[36] and in 1135 they occupied the island of Gerba itself. Hassan thereupon came to terms with them, and from that time forwards he was to be the reluctant, and sometimes the protesting, ally of King Roger, dependent both on Norman protection and on Sicilian grain. As a result, the Norman fleet was able to operate all along the North African coast, pillaging the sea provinces and bringing terror to the Moslem princes of the eastern Maghreb.[37] Roger had been given his great African opportunity, and he would not let it slip.

IV

Sporadic and purposeless raiding thus gave place to a constructive scheme of political conquest, and the man who under Roger II was responsible for bringing about this momentous change was himself one of the most interesting personalities of the age.[38] George 'of Antioch' was the son of Michael and Theodula, who were Syrian Christians presumably of Greek origin, and both he and his father had been connected in some way with the financial organization of Byzantine administration in Antioch. Early in life, George determined to exploit his own financial skill by taking service in the Treasury of Tamin, sultan of Al Mahdia.[39] Later, when relations between Sicily and Al Mahdia became closer, he transferred his career to the Norman court, and there he steadily rose to a position of preeminence.[40] And it was this man, familiar alike with Greek, Moslem and Sicilian administration, who was to be the chief architect of Roger's signal conquests in North Africa.

Through his organization and under his direction the Norman advance in Africa now became continuous and its success was demonstrated on 15 June 1146 when the Normans finally captured Tripoli.[41] Three years previously they had been beaten back from before its walls, but now this great Moslem city passed definitely into Norman hands. The effects were to be far reaching, and they were enhanced by the policy inaugurated and developed by George of Antioch, doubtless with the approval of his master. This was to respect the laws and customs of the Moslem inhabitants, and to entrust the adminis-

---

[36] Ibn Athir, *loc. cit.*   [37] Chalandon, *Domination*, II, p. 159.
[38] An excellent summary of his career is given in Ménager, *Emir*, pp. 44–54. Cf. Cohn, *Normannische . . . Sicilischen Flotte*, pp. 101 et sqq.
[39] Al Tigani, in Amari, *Bibl. Arabo-Sicula*, p. 161.
[40] *Ibid.*   [41] Chalandon, *Domination*, II, pp. 161–3.

tration of their cities to native *cadis*, who themselves became responsible for collecting taxes for the Sicilian king.[42] Tripoli became almost at once a most important centre for the commercial and political relations between the Norman king and his African subjects, and Roger thus won somewhat easily a reputation for clemency and moderation. He was, moreover, always able to count on a considerable measure of support from Moslem factions in Africa when making his own conquests. And these proceeded apace. It was early in 1148 that Al Mahdia itself was finally occupied and this success was rapidly followed by the capture of Zirid dependencies as far separated as Gabes, Susa and Sfax. By the end of 1148, Roger was master of the whole African coastline from the outskirts of Tunis to beyond Tripoli. It was an achievement which concerned not only Sicily and the Normans but the whole of Christian Europe.

George of Antioch died in 1151 or 1152, and the Norman king was to feel the need of his support in the ensuing years when a new upheaval in the Moslem world began to menace afresh the Norman conquests in Africa. This came with the rising from Morocco of the Berber Almohades. These fierce and zealous unitarians began at this time to threaten both the Almoravids in Spain and the Normans and Ziridites in Algeria and Libya. Many Moslem rulers in Africa now sought Roger's alliance, and the crisis was reached in 1152 when the Almohades, pushing eastward, occupied both Constantine and Bone. The Norman reply was to organize a large amphibious expedition in the next year under the command of a eunuch named Philip 'of Mahdia', who bore the title of emir, but who remains a most enigmatic figure. He may have been the son of a former Greek official at Roger's court, or (as his designation might indicate) he may have been a converted Moslem from North Africa who had advanced to power in the administrative service of the Sicilian king.[43] Certainly, the expedition he led overseas was a conspicuous success, and the campaign culminated when Bone itself was recaptured. The inhabitants were treated with the same consideration as had earlier been shown to those of Tripoli,[44] and in due course Philip the emir sailed back to Sicily with his honours and his booty. There, however, he became at once the victim of a plot which has never been explained. After a formal trial on charges which must remain unspecified, he was condemned to

---

[42] *Ibid.*
[43] Ménager, *Emir*, pp. 64–6.
[44] Ibn Athir, in Amari, *Bibl. Arabo-Sicula*, pp. 117, 219.

death, and in December 1153 he was dragged through the streets of Palermo at the heels of a vicious stallion and then publicly burnt.[45]

On the causes and the consequences of this atrocious crime, scholars have been unable to agree.[46] The fuller of the earlier accounts alleges[47] that Philip was condemned because he had remained a secret and practising Moslem. In view of Roger's known tolerance for Islamic practices both in Sicily and Africa, this explanation by itself would seem inadequate, and it is perhaps more probable that Philip was the victim of a struggle at the royal court where the feudal aristocracy were bent on ousting at last the foreign officials who had for years exercised such great power. It is also not impossible that Roger, in view of the criticism he had incurred for his apathy on religious questions, may have wished, under clerical pressure, to make some public expression of Christian zeal at the expense of another.[48] But unless the king can be acquitted of all knowledge of the affair – and this seems impossible[49] – the crime must take its place alongside the atrocities he had earlier committed during his Italian wars.

At all events, and whatever solution may be found for the mystery that darkens the final months of King Roger's reign, it remains true that the recapture of Bone in 1153 was the last major success achieved by the Normans in North Africa. The advance of the Moslem Almohades which had already begun under their great leader Abd el Moumen would hereafter proceed with inexorable force,[50] and after the death of Roger the Great the lands held by the Normans in North Africa began speedily to be lost, and soon there would be little left of the great African empire he had won and ruled.

V

King Roger the Great died on 26 February 1154, either from a heart attack or from overwork and excessive sexual indulgence.[51] Contemplating the man

---

[45] *Ibid.*, and cf. Romuald, s.a. 1153.

[46] Compare Caspar, *op. cit.*, pp. 432, 433, with Jamison, *Eugenius*, pp. 42–5, and with Lord Norwich, *Kingdom in the Sun*, pp. 158–60. An excellent summary is given in Ménager, *Emir*, pp. 64–6.   [47] Romuald, s.a. 1153.

[48] Ibn Athir remarks that there were some in Sicily who thought that the king was himself a Moslem. Roger may also have had in mind the criticisms that were made of his conduct during the Second Crusade.

[49] The argument of V. Epifanio in this sense (*Arch. Stor. Sicil.*, XXX, 1905) seems to me unconvincing.

[50] *Cambridge Medieval History*, V, pp. 190, 194, 200.

[51] 'Hugo Falcandus', cited by Lord Norwich, *op. cit.*, p. 156.

who made these conquests,[52] of his appearance there is scant evidence, but one early writer states succinctly that he was 'large of stature, and brawny, with the face of a lion and a voice like a growl'.[53] As to his character, it may bear comparison with that of his elder Norman contemporary, Henry I of England. The terrible cruelty of Henry I[54] compares with the particular savagery of Roger's campaigns in Apulia and Campagna. Of these, Otto of Freising says that

> He grievously afflicted the inhabitants and continues to oppress them. . . .
> When he captured Bari he not only persecuted the living with various
> tortures, but vented spite even on the dead. For he ordered the corpse of
> Duke Rainulf to be dug up and dragged through the streets.[55]

Most of the Italian and German annalists write in the same vein, and in describing his sacking of cities Falco of Benevento concludes: 'Never since the days of the Greeks and pagans had such destruction and arson been inflicted among Christians.'[56] The prolonged horrors attending the death of the Emir Philip also recall the castrations, the blindings and the mutilations which accompanied so many of the executions ordered by Henry I. It is not surprising that, like Henry, Roger inspired fear, and he too, according to Alexander of Telese, was wont on occasion to mask his ruthless purpose with a false geniality.[57]

Even so there were some of his contemporaries who, as was the case with Henry I, were ready to excuse his vices because of the good order he maintained. 'There are those,' remarks the disapproving Otto of Freising, 'who say that he does these things in the interests of justice rather than tyranny, and that he is, more than all other rulers, a lover of peace. They assert that it is to preserve peace that he holds rebels in check with such severity.'[58] Inevitably there were many to praise Roger at the time of his triumph. Indeed, when his support was needed for the Crusade, respected churchmen would join in these surprising tributes. Peter the Venerable, abbot of Cluny, for example, then extolled him as 'wiser than other princes', and as 'wielding

---

[52] A full citation from the authorities is given in Caspar, *op. cit.*, pp. 435–47, and in Wieruszowski, *op. cit.*, pp. 46–79.

[53] Romuald, *Mon. Germ. Hist.*, XIX, p. 427: 'Statura grandis, corpulentis, facie leonina, voce subrauca.'

[54] See above, p. 18.   [55] *Two Cities*, trans. Mierow, VII, c. 23.

[56] Falco Benev., s.a. 1138. Cf. *ibid.*, s.a. 1134, 1140.

[57] Romuald, *loc. cit.*; Alex. Tel., IV, c. 4. Cf. Will. Malms., p. 412, on Henry I.

[58] *Op. cit.*, VII, c. 23.

the sword of justice to crush those who transgressed the laws of God'. Even St Bernard was constrained to forget his earlier diatribes in order to salute one whose fame had 'spread all over the world'.[59]

Such eulogies, alas, always accompany success. It deserves note, however, that both Henry and Roger lacked the fashionable feudal virtues. Henry had no liking for war, and of Roger it was said that he pursued his ends by cunning rather than by force, and overcame his enemies more often by diplomacy than by war. He liked to leave it to others to win his battles in the field because for himself he 'preferred victory without bloodshed'.[60] In both cases a more modern technique of government seems to be foreshadowed. Roger was to be denounced for his avarice,[61] but it was to increase his power that he accumulated treasure. Like his older contemporary in the North, he excelled in the manipulation of men and raised up skilled administrators to carry his authority through his disparate dominions. Moreover, according to Alexander, he never ceased, like Henry I, to supervise personally the details of their work, particularly in connexion with the provision of revenue and the administration of justice.[62] His mental powers thus attracted somewhat grudging admiration. He was not, as it seems, ever called 'learned' like Henry I, but his intellectual curiosity, particularly in respect of antiquities, was noted, and for the rest he was 'wise', 'discriminating', 'subtle', and 'great in the formation of policy'.[63] Thus like Henry I he made a notable contribution to the evolution of secular government in Europe.

Both these rulers were in fact essentially secular in temperament, but Roger's indifference to religion was inevitably to be more openly displayed. He had acquired a realm which contained a large number of Greek Christians, and in Sicily he ruled over a large Moslem population. In these circumstances he exercised a wide tolerance which, while it helped to promote a brilliant cosmopolitan culture, could also be ascribed to a complete indifference to religious issues. His wars in Italy were won, with barbarous savagery, by his dreaded Saracen mercenaries, and he was thus described by a German annalist,

---

[59] *Epistolae* (*Pat. Lat.*, Vol. 189, esp. IV, No. 37, and VI, No. 16). See also the illuminating citation in Wieruszowski, *op. cit.*, pp. 73–5; St Bernard, Ep. 276, ed. Scott James, pp. 348, 349.

[60] 'Hugo Falcandus', ed. Siracusa, p. 5; Romuald, s.a. 1154; cf. Will. Malms., p. 412, on Henry I; Alex. Tel., IV, c. 4.

[61] Otto of Freising, *op. cit.*, VII, c. 23; Alex. Tel., IV, c. 3; cf. Henry of Huntingdon (Bk VIII) on Henry I.

[62] Alex. Tel., IV, c. 3.   [63] Romuald, s.a. 1154; cf. Wieruszowski, *op. cit.*, p. 75.

who was not alone in his opinion, as *semi-paganus*.[64] Again, in North Africa Roger was eager to win the alliance of Moslem rulers when it suited his purpose, and Archbishop Romuald of Salerno tacitly admitted the absence of any religious motives in these wars, which he says were waged solely because of personal ambition,[65] as was Roger's decisive intervention in the Second Crusade.

The significant similarity between the early descriptions of Roger the Great and those which had formerly been given to Henry I of England is very noteworthy, and certainly both in his character and in his career King Roger might bear comparison with any of his Norman contemporaries or predecessors. His rise from obscurity to his plenitude of power is in fact one of the most remarkable episodes in the whole history of medieval Europe. He had begun his career as a count at a perilously early age, but in 1140 he could style himself without fear or contradiction as king of Sicily by the grace of God, and, as such, king also of the duchy of Apulia and the principality of Capua, of the duchy of Naples and the county of Calabria.[66] He had thus brought together under a single rule five very ancient provinces of widely differing racial stocks, and of contrasting political traditions; and during the next decade he would buttress the unity of the composite realm he had created by a unified administration operating efficiently from Palermo. Nor was this all. Roger had also won for himself an overseas empire. Towards the end of his life he was master of the whole sea-coast from Tripoli to Bone. He had established a series of garrisons in North Africa from which his authority might be exercised and all this shore could be regularly patrolled by the Norman fleets. Many Arab tribes in the interior turned to him for protection, and for a short period, with the exception of Tunis and Kairouan, all the chief cities of the Maghreb of Tripolitania and of Numidia paid him tribute. Not without reason was King Roger accustomed towards the end of his reign to style himself *Rex Africae*,[67] for the additional title called final attention to the political transformation he had brought about. Nor is it surprising that a contemporary poet at Rouen should have saluted him as one of the heroes of the Norman race:

> You Roger have glorified your Norman ancestry for you reign as a conqueror in wisdom and splendour. You are the most illustrious of Kings.

[64] *Annalista Saxo*, s.a. 1154.　　　　　　　　　[65] Romuald, s.a. 1137–44.
[66] Charter cited by Kehr, *Urkunden*, p. 248.
[67] Kehr, *Urkunden*, p. 246 n. 3. Cf. Wieruszowski, in Setton and Baldwin, *Crusades*, II, p. 27.

Italy, Sicily and Africa have submitted to you. Greece, Syria and Persia fear you. The Ethiopians and the Germans, the blacks and the whites, are alike eager for your protection.[68]

The exuberance is excessive. But it is none the less true that it was in the special nature and in the consequences of his conquests, rather than in the details of his wars, that the chief interest of Roger's achievements will be found. By adding to his Sicilian dominion all the Italian mainland south of the Garigliano, Roger had created a powerful new European state, and in it would be developed new principles and practices of government. By his conquests in Africa he had completed his control of the narrows of the Mediterranean in such a manner as might have been expected to modify the southern frontiers of Christendom. His royal authority stretched from Syracuse almost to Benevento, and it was felt even in Tripoli. His Saracen mercenaries controlled Apulia and Calabria. His fleets dominated the sea from Malta to Bougie, from Barka to Sardinia. The conquests of Roger the Great would make him the wealthiest and not the least powerful monarch in Western Europe, and no change in the relations between the Latin West and the Eastern empire could henceforth take place without reference to the realm he ruled.

[68] Quoted by Herval in *Studi Ruggeriani*, I, pp. 103–4.

Chapter 4
THE BALANCE OF EUROPEAN POWER

I

The consolidation of the Norman realms during the earlier half of the twelfth century contributed to the modifications in the European balance of power which were effected at that time. Thus the development of the two great kingdoms under Norman rule helped to diminish between 1106 and 1152 the preponderance of the Germanic empire in Western Europe. It also virtually affected the history of France during a period when the prestige of the Capetian dynasty was being enhanced. For the monarchy at Paris found itself faced during these years not only by a great confederation of French fiefs under the rule of the Norman kings of England, but also by rival feudal coalitions such as those based upon Blois and upon Anjou. It was in these circumstances that the French monarchy entered into new political relations with the papacy which would in due course affect the whole of the West. Meanwhile, in the South, the balance of power in the Mediterranean had been radically altered by the expanding strength of the Norman kingdom of Sicily. And during these same decades, and partly for these reasons, the political might of Latin Christendom was notably increased by comparison with that of the Eastern empire.

II

The effects of these changes on the European future needs no emphasis, but they are easier to record than to explain. Many different explanations have, for instance, been given of the decline of German imperial power during these years.[1] The older view that the German monarchy had been hampered from the time of its foundation by special and insurmountable difficulties is now being replaced by the opinion that as late as the second half of the eleventh century the imperial monarchy was 'vigorously grasping at new opportunities' and was 'already on the path which fifty years later the Norman rulers were to tread in England, and which the Capetians were not to reach before the second half of the twelfth century'.[2] Perhaps there is an element

[1] On Germany in this period, see *Cambridge Medieval History*, Vol. V, chaps III and X; also Barraclough, *Medieval Germany*, 2 vols (1928).   [2] Barraclough, *op. cit.*, I, p. 73.

of exaggeration in both these approaches, and at all events it now seems generally agreed that the civil wars in the latter part of the reign of the emperor Henry IV, and under Henry V (1106–25), marked the end of a period of German history. And the consequences were to prove enduring, since we are now told that

> the decisive point in German history lies at the close of the eleventh and in the opening years of the twelfth century, and it is impossible to understand the physiognomy of modern Germany without appreciating the abiding results of that critical period.[3]

Evidently there are wide general reasons for noting a modification of German influence in Europe during the six decades which preceded the advent of Frederick Barbarossa in 1152.

Any contribution which the Normans may have made towards bringing this about needs, however, to be very cautiously assessed. For whatever may have been the strength of the imperial power in the middle of the eleventh century, the German monarchy had always to face problems which were peculiar to itself.[4] Chief among these were the claims to virtual independence put forward and often realized by the four great duchies of Saxony, Franconia, Swabia and Bavaria,[5] and within all these duchies there remained between 1106 and 1152 a long-established and powerful landed aristocracy which had not as yet been brought into any strict feudal dependence on the Crown.[6] As the twelfth century advanced, moreover, the duchies themselves passed under the domination of princely families possessed of vast territorial wealth, and fortified by the support they could command from their dependants. Yet another element of disunion was thus intruded into German politics at this time, and the way was opened for the struggle between the great houses of Welf and Hohenstauffen which were to dispute the imperial authority between themselves.[7]

The civil wars which were thus promoted, and the aristocratic turbulence which they engendered, were largely responsible for the spread of social anarchy in Germany during the earlier half of the twelfth century. The

[3] Barraclough, *Origins of Modern Germany* (1946), and cf. his *Medieval Germany*, I, p. 26.
[4] Cf. Douglas, 'Development of Medieval Europe', in Eyre, *European Civilization*, III, pp. 158–62.
[5] Cf. G. Barraclough, *Medieval Germany*, Vol. II (1961), pp. 23–47.
[6] M. Bloch, *Feudal Society*, pp. 177–9.
[7] *Cambridge Medieval History*, Vol. V, chaps III and X.

rivalry between the duchies, and the Welf–Hohenstauffen feud which it produced, had in short proved fatal to the establishment in Germany of a strong centralized and hereditary monarchy such as was being developed at this time in England, France and Sicily. Thus during these decades the successive rulers of Germany – Henry V (1106–25), Lothair II (1126–37) and Conrad III (1138–52) – all struggled against difficulties which they were unable to overcome.

These developments might be considered as sufficient in themselves to explain the decline in the European influence of the German monarchy during the earlier half of the twelfth century, but it would none the less be rash to exclude Norman policy from among the factors which promoted this change. The advance of Norman power in Italy and more particularly the inauguration in 1130 of the new Norman royalty in the South offered a special challenge to the imperial monarchy in Germany. For Roger had thereby acquired territories and rights which had formerly been vested not only in Byzantium but more immediately in the Western empire. St Bernard was quick to seize on this point, and to stress the unity of the ensuing struggle. Of course the saint's special concern was with the schism between Innocent and Anacletus, but King Roger was the ally of Anacletus, and he could also at the same time be denounced as an *invasor imperii* – a usurper of imperial rights. Thus while it was the duty of all Christians to support the rightful pope against Anacletus and the 'Tyrant of Sicily', a special duty rested on the shoulders of a Christian emperor whose rights had been particularly invaded. As St Bernard wrote to Lothair,

> It is not my business to incite to battle, but I declare without hesitation that it is the concern of any friend of the Church to save her from the mad fury of schismatics. Equally it is the special duty of Caesar to uphold his crown against the machinations of the Sicilian usurper. Just as it is an injury to Christ that a Jew should seize for himself the See of Peter, so also is it against the honour of Caesar that anyone should make himself King of Sicily.[8]

The matter was not, however, devoid of complexity. It will be recalled that the Norman conquests in the South had been made during the period when the conflict between the empire and the papacy was reaching its climax, and successive popes had turned to the Normans for support, or taken refuge with them when they were driven out of Rome by the imperial troops.[9] The papacy

[8] Bernard to Lothair, in *Letters*, ed. Scott James, No. 142.   [9] See above, Chap. 2.

could in fact be seen as consistently favouring the advance of the Normans in Italy, and as a result there had been created that special feudal relationship between the Normans and the Holy See whereby the rulers of all the Norman principalities in the South held the dominion they had won as liege vassals of the popes.[10] Here, however, a distinction might be made between those territories such as Capua which could be regarded as being in the pope's gift, and provinces like Apulia and Calabria which the pope could only grant in defiance of other powers such as the empires of the East and West. The papal feudal overlordship over all the Norman lands in the South, including Sicily, was thus bound to entail serious repercussions north of the Alps.

It was also in due course to present the papacy with a grave problem. At the height of the Investitures contest it was doubtless an advantage to Rome to be able to use Norman strength against the empire. But later it was realized that the Norman advance might prove an even greater menace to the papacy. It thus became a cardinal principle of papal policy to prevent a union between the Norman principalities in the South, and the progress of Roger the Great could thus be seen both in Rome and in Germany as a challenge and a threat. It was partly for this reason that the papacy came to modify its attitude towards German affairs, and in due course became an ally of an emperor ruling in Germany. Lothair II's rise to the imperial dignity in 1125 was largely due to an alliance between Honorius II and a powerful group of German magnates supporting the Welf cause,[11] the result being that two years later the pope and the emperor, with the same motives, conducted together their savage campaign in Italy in order to prevent the count of Sicily from succeeding to the duchy of Apulia.[12] Their defeat was thus a new reverse of the empire in Western Europe.

This was further enhanced in 1130 by Roger's achievement of royalty, and the manner in which this was done further complicated the German situation. For Roger now had support from Rome, but it came from a pope who was hardly recognized north of the Alps. The alliance between Innocent II, the legitimate pope, and the emperor was thus further strengthened, and it was in close cooperation that in 1137 they waged their terrible war in Italy against the tyrant of Sicily.[13] Once again, therefore, Roger's triumph damaged the empire even more than the papacy. When on 4 December 1137 Lothair died in the Tyrol on his way back from Italy, he was a defeated prince. And

[10] See below, chaps 6 and 7.
[11] W. Holtzmann, 'Regno di Ruggero', *Studi Ruggeriani*, pp. 40–2.
[12] *Ibid.*   [13] See above, pp. 40 et sqq.

he left the Norman king in full possession of all the territories south of Rome which had once belonged to the empire.

It is not surprising, therefore, that Conrad III should have found himself helpless in face of the increasing power of the king of Sicily. Roger went to some pains to subsidize in Germany the Welf opponents of this Hohen-stauffen emperor,[14] and the victorious peace he made with Innocent II in 1139 at Mignano robbed the German ruler of his best ally in the West. Thus Conrad, as emperor, never felt able even to cross the Alps, and the efforts he made to join forces with Byzantium against Sicily were likewise to prove unavailing. Nothing, moreover, came of the strange embassy which in 1143 John Comnenus II sent to Germany in order to foster an alliance between the emperors of the East and West against 'the arrogance of Roger of Sicily'.[15] Meanwhile, conditions in Germany lapsed into further disorder, and Conrad's later participation in the Second Crusade was to prove an in-glorious fiasco, which King Roger was quick to exploit.[16]

III

The general consequences to Europe of these developments were in fact soon to be displayed. An immediate beneficiary from the diminution of German power was the French monarchy which was represented during this period by Louis VI, who reigned from 1108 to 1137, and then by his son and suc-cessor Louis VII.[17] Not only did these kings now have less to fear from armed attack from the East, but they could dispute with greater confidence the special religious sanction which had long been claimed by the imperial monarchy in Germany. In this they were powerfully assisted by the closer relations which grew up during this period between the French royal house and the papacy. Urban II was a Frenchman, and after his time it became the practice that if any pope should find his residence in Italy insecure, he should take refuge in France. Correspondingly, the papacy came to foster the theo-cratic claims of the French kings. When, for instance, the young King Louis VII was crowned in 1131, he was anointed with the Holy Oil which was said to have descended from Heaven for the baptism of Clovis, and the

---

[14] Otto of Freising, *Chronicle*, VI, c. 27; Geoffrey of Viterbo, c. XXXVIII.
[15] Otto of Freising, *Gesta Friderici*, I, c. 23; Caspar, *op. cit.*, p. 361.
[16] See below, chap. 11.
[17] Luchaire, *Louis VI*; Pacaut, *Louis VII*.

unction was performed in the hallowed city of Rheims by Innocent II himself.[18] Elsewhere, too, the special position asserted by the House of Capet was to be recognized. The First Crusade sponsored by Urban II was predominantly a venture from the Latin West in which the Germanic empire played a subordinate part, and in the Second Crusade Louis VII posed as the natural leader of the Western warriors of God.[19]

The enhanced prestige of the French monarchy was matched during these years by a very limited and gradual increase in its material power. At the beginning of his reign Louis VI, whose commands were often resisted even in his own demesne, was able to make his direct authority felt, though in varying degrees through an area comprising some twelve modern départements. He was also sporadically recognized, though less securely, as suzerain over many of the great French fiefs. Indeed in 1124, when he launched his 'crusade' against the emperor Henry V for the relief of Rheims, contingents came to his banner not only from the churches of Chalons, Laon, Soissons and Étampes, but also from the great fiefs of Blois, Champagne, Nevers and Vermandois.[20] This was of course an exceptional occasion. But French royal power was none the less being frequently appealed to at this time. In 1127 Louis VI intervened vigorously in the affairs of Flanders, and both in Britanny and Burgundy the royal protection was sought by local churches and lesser feudatories against their immediate overlords. Thus was the overriding authority of Capetian royalty beginning to be recognized over much of France. But the achievement was very restricted, and it must not be viewed in isolation. Just as the decline in German influence during these years had in part been promoted by the Norman kingdom in the South, so also were the results of the westward shift in the balance of power consequent on that decline to be profoundly modified by the action of the kingdom which the Normans had founded in the North.

The matter was not, however, to be concluded without long and complicated conflict.[21] Between 1106 and 1135 Henry I of England, who regarded all his dominions as forming a single and indivisible realm, controlled a great confederation of French fiefs, and possessed resources as great as those of the French monarchy. It is not surprising, therefore, that Louis VI should have waged perpetual war against his Norman rival. Moreover, the fluctuations of

---

[18] Ullmann, *Papacy*, p. 177.   [19] Cf. Runciman, *Crusades*, II, pp. 247–78.

[20] L. Halphen, in *Cambridge Medieval History*, V, pp. 593–6.

[21] The details are fully set out in the *Cambridge Medieval History*, Vol. V, chap. XVIII; in A. L. Poole, *From Domesday Book to Magna Carta*; and in David, *Robert Curthose*.

that struggle permitted the formation of other feudal coalitions, the most important of which was centred on Anjou.[22] The essential condition of Angevin expansion had been the acquisition by its counts of most of Touraine, for their seizure of the great city of Tours gave them control of the route between Paris and Poitiers and thus blocked the westward expansion of the French monarchy. Thus fortified, Anjou could challenge the Norman dominance further to the north. Norman claims both in Britanny and in the Vexin were thus resisted at this time, and in 1126 Maine, which had long been an object of contention, was formally joined to Anjou.[23]

In these circumstances both Henry I and Louis VI were actively to contend for Angevin support. One of the daughters of Fulk V count of Anjou had been married to the Norman prince, William, who perished in 1120 in the wreck of the *White Ship*. In 1123 her younger sister Sibyl was married to Henry's enemy William Clito, the son of Robert Curthose, at the instance of the French king. But Henry I succeeded in getting this marriage annulled by Pope Calixtus II on the alleged ground of consanguinity. Finally, in 1127 the Norman king achieved a truly remarkable diplomatic triumph with the union of his daughter Matilda, the widow of the emperor Henry V, to Count Geoffrey of Anjou.[24] The implications of this marriage were indeed to be far reaching, for it detached Anjou from the French king and at the same time made possible the future union of Normandy, Maine, Anjou and Touraine under a successor of the Norman kings of England.

Meanwhile, however, yet another great feudal confederation had been formed, for it was precisely at this period that the house of Blois rose to the peak of its power.[25] Theobald IV, grandson of William the Conqueror, who succeeded to the combined *comtés* of Blois and Chartres in 1102, and who was to survive until 1152, was chiefly responsible for this steady increase in strength, and in 1125 he also acquired[26] the *comté* of Champagne which had been held by his uncle Hugh. During these same years the power of the family was being vastly enhanced by the wide lands gained both in France and in England by Theobald's younger brother, Stephen, who was now count of Boulogne and the favourite nephew, and eventual successor, of King Henry I.[27]

---

[22] On the rise of Anjou, see Powicke, *Loss of Normandy*; Haskins, *Norman Institutions*, pp. 123–56; Chartrou, *L'Anjou, 1109–1151*; Boussard, *Comté d'Anjou*; and O. Guillot, *Le comté d'Anjou au XIe siècle*, 2 vols (1972).

[23] Latouche, *Comté du Maine*, pp. 31–56; cf. Luchaire, *op. cit.*, Nos 156, 157.

[24] Luchaire, *op. cit.*, p. cx.   [25] *Ibid.*, p. lxxxvi; Davis, *Stephen*, p. 28.

[26] Davis, *op. cit.*, p. 4.   [27] See above, pp. 26, 27.

A third great complex of power had thus been created. In 1135, at the time of King Henry's death, the house of Blois exercised a strong and sometimes controlling interest from the borders of Lancashire and Yorkshire through much of eastern England and across the Channel by way of Boulogne onwards towards Chartres, Meax and Troyes and southwards over the whole of Champagne. The seizure by one of its members in 1135 of the Anglo-Norman realm, whose unity had been so carefully sustained, was thus a matter of wide general concern. Indeed, the war waged by King Stephen over the English succession against Matilda, Count Geoffrey and their son Henry, must have seemed to most contemporaries a continuation of the long-standing rivalry between Anjou and Blois. But now England and Normandy with all their dependencies were thrown in as an additional prize. The reign of Stephen is often dismissed as merely an unfortunate episode in English history. In reality it reflected a crisis in the power politics of Western Europe.

The ensuing conflict between King Stephen and Matilda with her Angevin associates was thus watched with interest and considerable apprehension throughout the West. A significant stage in the struggle was reached when Geoffrey count of Anjou was accepted in Rouen as duke of Normandy, and after 1144 Louis VII was forced to recognize the position of the Angevin count in the Norman duchy, until in 1150 Geoffrey handed over his Norman rights to his son Henry, the future king of England.[28] Of equal importance to Europe were the arrangements by which in 1153 Henry was recognized as Stephen's heir in England.[29] Certainly some concessions had here to be made to the house of Blois. For William, the son of King Stephen, was confirmed in all his vast possessions as count of Boulogne, count of Mortain, and through his marriage with Isabel of Warenne, earl of Surrey.[30] Such was the price which Henry of Anjou had to pay for his acceptance as the successor of King Stephen of Blois in England. But the bargain was to be to his spectacular advantage, for by it he would become the most powerful ruler in Western Europe.

The way had in fact been prepared for the climax which came in 1154 when, on the death of Stephen, Henry achieved royalty as king of England, and was saluted as 'Holy and Anointed of the Lord'. All the resources of England were now at his disposal. As duke of Normandy, count of Anjou, count of Maine and count of Touraine, he was master of most of the north and west of France and much of its centre. Moreover, in 1152 he had married

---

[28] Haskins, *Norman Institutions*, pp. 150, 151; Round, *Cal. Documents*, No. 726.
[29] Warren, *Henry II*, pp. 51, 52.   [30] Round, *Peerage and Family History*, pp. 171, 172.

Eleanor, the heiress of Aquitaine, who had been repudiated by Louis VII,[31] so the king of England was also dominant in the French south-west. So far as the political structure of Western Europe was concerned, the transformation effected during the earlier half of the twelfth century was now completed. The balance of power had moved westward from Germany. But west of the Rhine the dominant power in 1154 was not the French king, but the king of England, who as count of Anjou had acquired and enlarged the empire which the Normans had created.

IV

The alteration in the balance of power which had thus been brought about within Western Europe was also to be felt on all the frontiers of Latin Christendom. In Britain, for example, the consolidation of the Anglo-Norman realm could of course result in no extension of Christian belief. But it did involve the penetration into other lands of ideas relating to the ecclesiastical order which had been established in the Latin West. If, however, the Norman advance circumscribed the Celtic elements in British culture, care must be taken not to exaggerate the consequences of this. It would for instance be unwise to place the deployment of Norman influence in Ireland much before 1166 when Dermot, the exiled king of Leinster, sought and obtained the support of Henry II of England through the intervention of Robert FitzHarding of Bristol.[32] But in Wales the situation was very different. Norman progress into Wales from the three great palatine earldoms of Chester, Shrewsbury and Hereford had for long been remorselessly prosecuted even though the Norman advance had been less assured in the north than in the south. In 1100 the penetration of Cardigan and Carmarthen was only beginning but before the death of Henry I in 1135 South Wales could be considered as almost a Norman province dominated by Norman lords and controlled from Norman castles.[33] It is true that the Normans would be eager to use existing Welsh institutions, and it is true also that a successful reaction against Norman influence would soon begin under the leadership of Owen of Gwynned,[34] but the results of Norman action here were sufficiently impressive, and they would colour much of the later history of Wales.

---

[31] Warren, *op. cit.*, pp. 42–7.   [32] Orpen, *Ireland under the Normans*, I, chap. III.
[33] Lloyd, *History of Wales*, II, pp. 374, 375; Armitage, *Early Norman Castles*, pp. 273–80.
[34] J. G. Edwards, 'The Normans and the Welsh March', Brit. Acad. *Proceedings*, XLII(1956).

In Scotland, moreover, the development was equally noteworthy.[35] Partly as a consequence of the dependence on Henry I of the royal sons of St Margaret – Edgar, Alexander II and David I – the political and social structure of Scotland was modified during their reigns. The loss by Scotland in 1092 of the southern portion of Celtic Strathclyde centred on Carlisle had been matched with the acquisition by Scotland of Anglian Lothian north of the Tweed. The strange diagonal frontier which now divides England from Scotland was in fact in the process of formation, and the results were soon apparent. Before the twelfth century the essential Scotland had been a kingdom, largely Celtic in culture, and situated to the immediate north of the isthmus of Forth and Clyde. But during the early decades of the twelfth century there was a constant extension in Scotland of Anglian and Norman influence radiating from Lothian and Fife, and while no ruler of Scotland would ever be able to ignore the Highlands with impunity, the political centre of Scotland now ceased to lie in Perthshire. It became a realm ruled by kings from Dunfermline or Edinburgh.

And these kings were not only dependent on the Norman king of England: they were themselves enthusiastic admirers of Norman institutions. Thus after 1124, David I, who had previously been earl of Huntingdon, modelled his administration on that of Henry I. He conducted a survey of his lands in Galloway which was based upon the principles of the Domesday Inquest. He surrounded himself with Norman magnates, and French became the language of his court. Even his chancery imitated Norman practice; and in one charter at least he could actually address his subjects in Scotland as *Francis et Anglis*.[36] There never was a Norman conquest of Scotland. None the less, it would seem that the Normans helped to bring Scotland more closely into touch with the governmental practices of Western Europe. And Britain as a whole was carried by the Normans more intimately into the political orbit of Latin Christendom.

V

Very different and much more subtle problems are posed in respect of any influence which the Normans may have had in determining the frontiers of that Latin Christendom which marched with Islam in the South. How far, if at all, the wars waged by Roger the Great in North Africa[37] contributed

---

35 See Ritchie, *Normans in Scotland*.
36 Lawrie, *Early Scottish Charters*, No. LIV.   37 See above, pp. 56–60.

to any permanent enlargement of Christendom remains to be considered, for this was the age of the crusades, and in the crusades the Normans were to play an individual and decisive role.[38] The Norman conquests in Africa might therefore reasonably have been expected to extend the Christian frontiers, and for a time at least they seemed destined to do so. Since these conquests were made shortly after the Normans had wrested Sicily from Islam, and were won over Moslem principalities and powers, it must have seemed for a while as if the Normans might regain for Christendom what had been one of the fairest provinces of the Roman Empire, and other consequences of this advance could be glimpsed when the Normans captured the Hippo of St Augustine. Most of these hopes were to prove illusory, however, but there were wider implications of the wars waged by the Normans on the southern frontier of Latin Christendom.

At the opening of the twelfth century there still remained after centuries of Moslem rule a considerable Christian population in North Africa. Travellers in the Maghreb could find there monuments of Roman and presumably Christian antiquity, and it was specifically reported that at Tlemcin a church and an altar were regularly used by Christians.[39] Indeed a Christian hierarchy of many bishops subjected to the metropolitan see of Carthage had been fully recognized by the papacy.[40] These Christian communities were doubtless scattered and probably subject to disabilities, but they survived, and practised their own religious observances. They were thus a force to be reckoned with in North African politics, and they might have been expected to welcome a Christian invader from overseas.

There were thus many factors which might have transformed the Norman invasion of North Africa into a religious war over a new frontier between Christendom and Islam. Indeed, the leaders on both sides were often very ready to exploit this idea for their purposes. Roger the Great and his father had used such propaganda, and similar action had on occasion been taken by their Moslem opponents. The Zirid rulers had been particularly active in this respect and when Hassan succeeded at Al Mahdia in 1121 he was able to pose effectively as the champion of his faith. His crushing victory over the Normans in 1123 was proclaimed as a signal triumph for Islam, and widely saluted as such in prose and verse throughout the Moslem world.[41] God – it appeared – sent the enemy a storm which brought them to disaster so that

---

[38] See below, chaps 10 and 11.   [39] Mas Latrie, *Traites de Paix*, pp. 3–5.   [40] *Ibid.*, p. 5.
[41] Al Tigani, Ibn Athir, Ibn Hamdis, in Amari, *Bibl. Arabo-Sicula*, pp. 116, 157, 158, 250, 254.

'the cold waves slew them without need of the blue lanceheads or the white blades of the sabres'. As for Hassan himself, he was a hero to Islam.

Son of Ali, lion in the Holy Garden of the Faith, to whom the lances are a living hedge. Woe to the blue eyes of the Franks. They shall receive no kiss from thy lips.[42]

It is the authentic voice of religious propaganda appropriate to a conflict relating to the boundary between Christendom and Islam. And it was to be continued. The curses of the God of Islam are called down upon Roger's head by Ibn Athir. According to Ibn al Dinar, Roger was the enemy of God, whilst Ibn Haldan speaks of his campaigns in Africa as part of a general war between Christians and Moslems.[43] Similar declarations in the opposite sense could be cited from Christian writers such as Robert of Torigny and Peter the Venerable.[44]

Despite such developments, however, Norman military action in North Africa never promoted a war of religion. It is perhaps significant that according to the continuator of the chronicle of Sigebert of Gembloux the exiled archbishops of Al Mahdia took refuge for many years at Palermo and were only restored to their see after the capture of the city by the Normans in 1148. But as observers familiar with opinions current at the Sicilian court were quick to notice, Roger in his African campaigns was not moved by any religious zeal but rather by material considerations – the desire for wealth, the lust for conquest, and the promotion of commercial advantage. And the same secular interests predominated among the Moslems. North Africa was in political chaos. The Zirid rulers of Al Mahdia, who had earlier emancipated themselves from the caliphs of Egypt, were now faced not only by the Berbers at Bougie but also by the dynasty of Berni-Khoracin at Tunis. And all these rulers had themselves great difficulty in maintaining their own supremacy within their separate dominions. In these conditions, the Moslem princes were eager to obtain the alliance of the Normans against each other, and the political disunion of North Africa was to prove a cardinal factor in the success of Roger the Great on the southern shore of the Mediterranean.[45]

Religious motives thus played only a minor part in the warfare which took

42 Ibn Hamdis, cited by Curtis, *Roger the Great*, p. 116.
43 Amari, *Bibl. Arabo-Sicula*, pp. 118, 202, 203, 218, 219.
44 Constable, *op. cit.*, p. 236.
45 *Mon. Germ. Hist. S.S.* VI, p. 454. Cf. J. Mésnage, *Le Christianisme en Afrique*, pp. 219, 220.

place on the southern frontiers of Christendom during the earlier half of the twelfth century. It was notable, for instance, that just as the Norman rulers of Sicily made copious use of Saracen mercenaries in their campaigns, so also did Christian mercenaries assist the Moslem rulers both in the wars which they waged against each other, and in those conducted against the Christians.[46] As for King Roger, he would make little distinction between his Christian and Moslem subjects, and this fact was complacently noted even by Islamic writers. As Ibn al Dinar wrote at a later date:

> This enemy of God restored the cities of Sailah and Al Mahfie, furnished capital for the merchants. He did good to the poor, confided the administration of justice to *cadis* acceptable to the people, and ordered the government well.[47]

A similar indifference to questions of faith could be found among the competing Moslem rulers. The religious enthusiasm generated by the Almoravid conquests had evaporated before 1100, and it was long before it was rekindled. When this did take place, however, the Norman successes, which were essentially secular in character, were speedily brought to an end.

The Moslem counter-attack against the Normans in North Africa was conditioned by the rise between 1120 and 1150 of the new Islamic sect of the Almohades.[48] These fanatical unitarian warriors derived from southern Morocco. They received their religious inspiration from the preaching of the mystic and in due course they produced their own great military leader in Abd-el-Moumen. Under him their success was to be spectacular. By 1134 Abd-el-Moumen was established at Sale, and fiercely engaged against the Almoravids whom he regarded as his particular enemies because of their anthropomorphic beliefs. Before 1147 he had captured from them the fortified strongholds of Fez, Tlemcin, Algiers and Oran. He then pushed his conquests eastward towards Tunis and northwards into Spain, where his troops occupied Xeres, Cadiz, Cordova and Seville. And in Africa his conquests had been equally rapid. He had, in short, made himself lord of a great empire that was militantly united for the defence of Islam. Almost the whole of the Maghreb was in his power, and by 1155 only such strongholds as Al Mahdia, Tripoli and Bone remained in Norman hands.[49] And these were soon to fall.

[46] Mas Latrie, *op. cit.*, pp. 32-3, citing Ibn Athir and Ibn Khaldun.
[47] Quoted by Curtis, *op. cit.*, p. 254.
[48] Mas Latrie, *op. cit.*, pp. 32-46.   [49] *Ibid.*, p. 41.

The Norman conquests on the southern shore of the Mediterranean in the time of Roger the Great thus proved at last to have caused but a temporary interruption of Moslem domination. From lack of power, and still more from lack of purpose, the Normans had failed to establish a frontier of Christendom in northern Africa. And soon the muezzin would once again ring undisturbed from Bone to Algiers, from Tripoli to Marrakech.

VI

No survey of Latin Christendom itself in 1154 can, however, fail to recognize the extensive influence the Normans had exercised on its political structure during the previous fifty years. For within Western Europe the changes they had helped to bring about were profound. A wide-stretched empire founded by the Normans was in 1154 ruled by a count of Anjou who had succeeded to the Norman inheritance as king of England, and this dominion included not only Britain but the greater part of France. In the South, too, a strong Norman kingdom had been established to comprise nearly all of southern Italy and the whole of Sicily. Meanwhile the relations between the imperial monarchy of Germany, the Capetian dynasty of France and the papacy had been basically modified. Undoubtedly there were many changes still to come. Under Frederick Barbarossa, for example, the imperial monarchy would begin at once to recover much of the power it had recently lost, and while the medieval future would lie predominantly in the hands of France, the Capetian dynasty would need to overcome many obstacles before it could aspire to its later distinction. But the fundamental conditions underlying the developing structure of medieval Europe had clearly been established; and in it the papacy would in due course be accepted as the 'focal point' in the political order of the West. Even the position later attained by Innocent III at the apogee of papal political power had been formulated in all its essentials by St Bernard before his death in 1153.[50]

The corporate strength of Latin Christendom had thus been enhanced, and at the same time the growth of the Norman realms had substantially increased the relative power of Western Europe by comparison with that of the Eastern empire. The emperors Alexis I (1081–1117) and John Comnenus (1118–43) had to some extent been successful in combating the decline which was inexorably threatening Byzantium, but even so the situation of the Eastern empire at this time was not happy. The control by the emperors of

50 Ullmann, *Papal Government*, pp. 426–37.

the Balkan peninsula had become precarious, and the Slav rulers both of Serbia and Dalmatia had achieved virtual independence. The kingdom of Hungary, which was waxing in strength, was hostile, and the northern frontier across the Danube was continually menaced by barbarian raiders such as the Petchenegs. It was thus against an empire that was already weakened that the great Turkish advance was made which was a preliminary to the Crusades.[51]

But the Eastern empire had also suffered directly from the Normans. The earlier Norman conquests in Italy had been made at the expense of Byzantium, and for their own political reasons the Normans in the past had always supported the papacy in its claims over the see of Constantinople. Indeed, there had in the past been occasions when Norman leaders had with papal approval carried their offensive across the Adriatic to occupy parts of the coasts of Dalmatia, and even to threaten Constantinople itself.[52] In the meantime the rich provinces of Apulia and Calabria had passed through Norman action completely out of Byzantine control, and the climax was reached when in 1130 there was founded the unified Norman kingdom of Roger the Great. For this most powerful realm, ever waxing in strength, comprised all the territories in Italy which had once been ruled from Constantinople together with the whole of Moslem Sicily, and in the future it continuously and successfully challenged the authority of Byzantium both by sea and land.[54] It was indeed a notable achievement, but it must be considered as part of the wider development, for from their own great kingdoms in the North and South, and through the spreading influence which they exercised, the Normans between 1100 and 1154 had been able to modify and to fortify the political structure of Latin Christendom in such a way as to ensure in the future the enduring preponderance of Western over Eastern Europe. The balance of European power had been radically and permanently changed.

[51] Cf. *Cam. Med. Hist.*, IV, chaps XI and XII; Runciman, *Crusades*, I, pp. 70–5.
[52] Cf. Douglas, *The Norman Achievement*, pp. 150–62.

PART TWO

THE NORMAN IMPACT UPON EUROPE

Chapter 5
ROYALTY AND FEUDAL SOCIETY

I

During the earlier half of the twelfth century when the Normans helped to transform the balance of European power, they also entered constructively into the European political and social system. Its modification was, moreover, by no means so automatic as is sometimes assumed. At the beginning of the century the Normans were still regarded – and with some justice – as intruders into the European social order, and European men had not yet fully acquiesced in the conditions which had been created by their conquests.[1] By 1150, however, this had been changed. The Normans could then no longer be viewed as aliens within the civilization of Latin Europe. Indeed, they had themselves adopted as their own some of the basic institutions of Europe, and these they were both to strengthen and to develop, an achievement to prove of enduring consequence to the European future. But it was not inevitable. And no feature of it was more influential, or of greater significance, than the manner in which the Normans, first in England and then in Sicily, attained and glorified royalty with all that this implied in the twelfth-century world.

In 1100, almost immediately after the sudden death of William Rufus, his younger brother Henry was chosen king by 'those counsellors who were near at hand'. He then went to London, and on the next Sunday (5 August)

before the altar at Westminster he vowed to God and to the people to put down the injustices that were done in his brother's time, and to maintain

[1] Cf. K. Leyser, R. Hist. Soc. *Trans.* 5, Vol. IV, p. 65.

the best laws that had stood in any King's day before him. And after that, Maurice, Bishop of London, consecrated him King.[2]

This sequence of events is itself of interest since it exactly reflected the procedure that had long been practised in Latin Europe for the succession and establishment of kings – one which was later crystallized in a coronation ritual that would be almost universally adopted.[3] The consecration of a king in one of the most solemn rites of the Church – his crowning and particularly his anointing – was not performed until he had been formally accepted and acclaimed (the *collaudatio*), and until he had promised to discharge all the high duties of kingship.[4] Henry I, the most secular minded of men, evidently thought it profitable to lose no time in buttressing his disputable claim on the English throne by obtaining in haste the religious sanctions which had been accorded in Western Europe to royalty since the days of Charlemagne.

Thus were displayed the abiding consequences to the Normans in Europe of the royal coronation of William duke of Normandy which had taken place in Westminster Abbey on Christmas Day 1066.[5] It is of course true that the Conqueror on that famous occasion had been mainly concerned to appear as the legitimate successor to King Edward the Confessor. He was *Rex Anglorum*, and that assumption would colour the government of his English realm. But the ceremony had also wider and more personal connotations. He was now a king as well as a duke, with all the additional prestige which this implied. Certainly he had been consecrated according to a rite which had hallowed previous kings in England. But the ceremony also followed tradition common to the whole of Europe. And both his solemn promise of good government and his acclamation had been made in the presence of both Norman and English magnates. This too was to prove of future consequence. Both William Rufus and Henry I would be saluted as kings by Normans and by English,[6] and the coronation of Stephen as king was specifically stated to apply both to Normandy and England.[7] Clearly the implications of the establishment of Norman royalty in England stretched across the Channel.

[2] A.S. Chron., 'E', s.a. 1100.
[3] On this see generally Schramm, *English Coronation* (1937).
[4] Richardson and Sayles, *Governance*, p. 138.
[5] Douglas, *William the Conqueror*, chap. 10.
[6] Schramm, *op. cit.*, pp. 45, 46; Freeman, *William Rufus*, I, pp. 19–23; II, pp. 346, 347.
[7] *Gesta Stephani*, p. 8.

It may also be possible to detect certain changes introduced by the Normans from Europe into English coronation practice. The famous questions put by the bishops in French and English to the congregation in the Abbey in 1066 and the shout of acclamation they provoked were certainly due in part to the special circumstances. But they none the less bear all the marks of a *collaudatio* such as had already been widely adopted in Europe, though less notably in England, and which would under the Normans in due course become part of the English coronation rite.[8] Again, if a very early commentator is to be believed, William in 1066 had been sacramentally anointed with Holy Oil in a manner not hitherto employed at royal coronations in England. After the *Kyrie Eleison* and the Litany of the Saints had been sung,

> The archbishop bade the people pray and forthwith began the rite itself. He said the collect, and raised the King from the dust. Then with the chrism poured forth, he himself anointed the King's head and consecrated him King in the royal manner.[9]

Thus had the duke of Normandy been set apart as king from other men, and we are already in the atmosphere of veneration for divinely appointed monarchy. The practical importance of this to the ruler was to be demonstrated by the speed with which in 1087 William Rufus caused himself to be consecrated by Lanfranc, and still more in the hasty coronation of Henry I. Between 1100 and 1125 Western Christendom had been brought to recognize that the acquisition and exploitation of semi-sacred royalty would form an essential part of the developing Norman impact upon Europe.

II

It is in the light of these considerations that must be considered the exaltation in 1130 of Roger count of Calabria and Sicily and duke of Apulia as king at Palermo. But here there was no question of a Norman acquisition of an ancient kingdom. It was the creation of a new realm to be ruled by a newly consecrated Norman king. Perhaps for this reason a certain mystery still hangs over the acquisition of royalty by the first Norman king in the South, and almost everything connected with the momentous events in southern Italy and Sicily during 1130 has been a matter of controversy. The early narratives are unusually precise,[10] but they are also on many points mutually contradictory,

[8] Will. Poit., ed. Foreville (1952), p. 220; Schramm, *op. cit.*, pp. 151–5.
[9] *Carmen*, ed. Morton and Muntz, p. 52.   [10] Above, pp. 31 et sqq.

and modern scholars have been almost as divided as were contemporaries about the implications of what then took place.[11] It is probable for instance that the 'petition' to Roger to become king made by the magnates led by Count Henry took place at Palermo, and not at the great assembly that was undoubtedly held near Salerno some time in 1130. But the exact sequence of events as recorded by Alexander of Telese has not been established beyond all conjecture, and it is likewise uncertain whether the initiative for the papal bull of investiture came from the pope or from Roger. Should the great court held outside Salerno be placed before the bull, or did it take place after its issue, and as a result of its promulgation?

The relative importance of the parts played in these events by Roger himself, by his feudal vassals, and by Anacletus, is therefore left vague, and in view of the relations which were later to develop between the papacy and the king of Sicily, who was at once a powerful Christian prince, a feudal monarch and a nominal papal vassal, this was clearly a vital question. Nor is it answered in the copious descriptions of what finally took place at Palermo at Christmas-time in 1130. Roger certainly summoned to his capital a great feudal court to acclaim his crowning, but what were its precise functions, and how many of Roger's greater vassals attended from the Italian mainland, is doubtful. Some obscurity likewise hangs over the coronation itself.[12] According to one early account, Anacletus sent his nephew, Cardinal Conti, to perform the consecration, but it was Robert prince of Capua who, as chief vassal, placed the crown on the head of the new king.[13] Also, while Peter the Deacon (who is himself notoriously unreliable) alludes to the bull of Anacletus, and while Falco of Benevento speaks of the pope's legate at the coronation, neither Alexander of Telese nor Romuald archbishop of Salerno even mention Anacletus or the papacy in connexion with the establishment of the Norman kingdom in 1130.

In considering the origin of these contrasting arguments and comparing them with those used by the apologists for the establishment of that other Norman kingdom in the North sixty-four years earlier, the detailed parallelism between the writings of William of Poitiers on William the Conqueror

11 See, for instance, Caspar, *op. cit.*, pp. 85–7; E. Pontieri, *Tra in Normanni*, p. 205; Fuiano, 'La Fondazione del Regum Siciliae', *Papers Brit. School of Rome*, XXIV (1956); Ménager, 'L'Institution monarchique', in *Cahiers*, Vol. II (Poitiers, 1958), pp. 303–31, 445–68; Wieruszowski, *op. cit.*, pp. 53–60.
12 Caspar, *op. cit.*, Reg. 66 (69).
13 Falco Benev., s.a. 1130.

and those of Alexander of Telese on Roger the Great are particularly illuminating.[14] Both William of Poitiers and Alexander of Telese have, as authors, been respected and distrusted for the same reasons. They were both contemporary with the events they described, and wrote about them with knowledge and in considerable detail. On the other hand, they were both perfervid and boastful partisans seeking to exalt the stature of their heroes, and to disparage their opponents. They cannot, however, be ignored.[15] That Alexander knew the book of William of Poitiers is possible but extremely unlikely, and in any case the propaganda element in the work of both these writers may be fully compared, inasmuch as it indicates how the Normans themselves both in the North and in the South wished their attainment of royalty to be regarded.

Such a comparison leads, in fact, to some remarkable results. Like William the Conqueror before him, Roger in 1130 apparently needed to be 'persuaded by his followers before he consented to become a King'. And if in each case this may reflect a formal election in the traditional manner, it is none the less noteworthy that the chief spokesman in 1130 as in 1066 at the critical discussion was not a Norman but an ally.[16] For Haimo *vicomte* of Thouars, who was so eloquent in this sense at Berkhamsted, came from Poitou, while Count Henry, who spoke for Roger, came from northern Italy. Like William also, Roger is said to have become a king by right of conquest. This is implicit in the whole narrative of William of Poitiers, and the claim was specifically made by Alexander on behalf of Roger. Moreover, in both cases the achievement had been specifically assisted by God, inasmuch as William in England was stated to have waged a war for religion, while Roger could boast that his father had won back Sicily from Islam. It is scarcely surprising, therefore, that both these rulers should be finally shown by their apologists as justifying the divine assistance they had received by giving peace and order to the distracted lands they ruled.[17]

More curious however is it that both these writers managed also to assert a legal and hereditary justification for the succession of the two new Norman kings. Edward the Confessor, who was without issue, is said to have designated Duke William of Normandy as his heir, and in 1126 Duke William of Apulia, knowing that he would die childless, is reported to have nominated

---

[14] The comparison which follows has been stated by Douglas in *Mélanges . . . Perroy*, p. 106.
[15] Stenton, *Anglo-Saxon England* (1945), pp. 586, 687; Chalandon, *Domination*, I, pp. x, xi.
[16] Will. Poit., p. 219; Alex. Tel., II, c. 1.
[17] Will. Poit., pp. 230–31; Alex. Tel., I, p. 85.

Roger as his successor.[18] Nor is this all. Roger, we are told, acquired Sicily 'by paternal inheritance' and

> he took possession of Apulia, Calabria and the other lands not only by virtue of conquest by war but also by right of succession in virtue of his near relationship to the Dukes who had preceded him.[19]

As for William, the victor at Hastings:

> If it be asked what was his hereditary title let it be answered that a close kinship existed between King Edward and the son of Duke Robert whose aunt Emma was the sister of Duke Richard I, and the mother of King Edward himself.[20]

Even more remarkable, however, is the manner in which in both cases the new royalty was made to appear as the restoration of earlier conditions. William, in accepting royalty, it is said, yielded to the prayers of the men he had beaten in battle because they urged that the English are wont to have a king for their lord, and throughout his reign the Conqueror consistently claimed that he was the legitimate successor to the Old English monarchy after a usurpation. The same strange character of a restoration was ascribed, albeit with greater difficulty, to the events of 1130. 'Palermo,' it is said, 'had long ago been the seat of Kings but owing to the inscrutable will of God' it had been deprived of them for a very long time.[21] That is why Roger, having been duly crowned, made Palermo his capital so that a kingdom might be restored not only to Sicily but to the other lands he had been called upon to rule.[22]

This notion of a restoration was in fact to be exploited by Roger II throughout his reign. It appears for instance in the famous bull which the Sicilian king extracted from Pope Innocent II in 1139. Roger had not created a new legal authority, but had revived a kingdom which 'according to ancient writers', had existed of old time.[23] Roger himself in the next year restated the same idea in a charter in which he referred to 'the kingdom

---

[18] Chalandon, *Domination*, I, pp. 322–4.
[19] Alex. Tel., II, c. 2.
[20] Will. Poit., p. 222.
[21] Alex. Tel., II, c. 1.
[22] *Loc. cit.*
[23] P. F. Kehr, *Italia Pontificia*, No. 159; *Pat. Lat.*, 179, col. 279; Sicilia quod utique prout in antiquis refertur historiis regnum fuisse.

which had for so long been in abeyance, and which, by the mercy of the Redeemer, had in our own days been restored to its pristine royal status'.[24] It has even been suggested that such arguments may have been based on some precise knowledge of ancient Greek history on the part of the Norman writers in the South, and certainly the opponents of Roger II were to claim that Sicily had always been a breeding ground of tyrants.[25] In like fashion William of Poitiers had compared Duke William's crossing of the English Channel in 1066 to the passage of Xerxes over the Hellespont, and related the Conqueror's restoration of political unity in England to what had been achieved in this country by Julius Caesar.[26] Such knowledge of ancient history as was possessed by Norman writers either in the North or in the South could, however, easily be overemphasized. None the less, the assertion by Alexander of Telese of a *restitutio regni Siciliae* might have derived from the manner in which the empire had been restored to the West.[27] Nor perhaps is it wholly without significance that at the other end of Europe a monk could salute the memory of William the Conqueror in a long passage taken almost word for word from a ninth-century panegyric of Charlemagne.[28]

Such similarities command attention. It is a far cry from Poitiers to Telese, from Salerno to Berkhamsted, from Westminster to Palermo, and certainly no single or simple explanation can be given to both the coronations which took place in such widely differing circumstances. But of the related and enduring consequences of the Norman events of 1066 and 1130 there was no doubt in the minds of contemporaries. In both England and Sicily the Normans had taken to themselves one of the most hallowed political institutions of Christendom. The monarchies which they established derived from the time-honoured Christian conception of European royalty.

III

The Normans not only accepted the religious sanctions of royalty: they enhanced them. In the whole large literature devoted in the Middle Ages to political theology there is no stronger assertion of the sanctity of kingship

---

[24] Caspar, *op. cit.*, p. 231 n. 1.

[25] Wieruszowski, *op. cit.*, pp. 53–60.

[26] Will. Poit., pp. 163, 250–4.

[27] Cf. Fuiano, *op. cit.*, pp. 74, 75.

[28] Printed in Guillaume de Jumièges, *Gesta Normannorum Ducum*, p. 145.

than that which is to be found in certain tractates issued about 1100 by an anonymous Norman writer either from York or from Rouen.[29] In these treatises the sacred dignity of the royal office was exalted to quite extraordinary heights. The king has been transformed by his anointing; he is henceforth to be regarded as much as priest as king; for 'being the Lord's Anointed he cannot be called a layman'. He has in fact been made a *Christus Domini*; he has become a *sanctus*; and there may even be found in his office a reflection of the authority of God Himself.[30] Such were sentiments and beliefs that were widely prevalent when in 1100 Henry I, who had possibly murdered his brother, seized the English kingship; and he was quick to take advantage of them. It is true that ecclesiastical writers in support of the Hildebrandine reforms had already begun to make clearer distinctions between the priestly office and that held by any layman – even the king. Thus at royal coronations unction would soon perhaps lose some of its solemnity.[31] It is not, however, certain whether the coronation *Ordo* commonly associated with St Anselm was used at the consecration of Henry I, as it certainly was for that of Henry II.[32] And in any case Henry I assuredly had no cause to complain of the veneration which was accorded to his royalty.

Thus three times a year – at Easter, at Whitsuntide and at Christmas – following the custom of his father, he would display himself crowned, robed and exalted before all the most powerful men in England, 'archbishops and bishops, abbots and earls, thegns and knights'.[33] And at these 'crown-wearings', held successively at Winchester, Westminster and Gloucester, on the greatest Feasts of the Church, there would be chanted in front of him the royal *Laudes* which had been sung at the time of his coronation. These *Laudes*, with their refrain 'Christ conquers; Christ Reigns; Christ rules', were a litany of a special type designed to invoke Christ, the victor, the ruler and the commander, and to acclaim in Him with Him and through Him, His royal vicar on earth.[34] Such were the attributions accorded to Norman royalty in England in the first quarter of the twelfth century. And if its

[29] Ed. Böhmer, in *Mon. Germ. Hist. Lib. de Lite*, III, pp. 642–78.

[30] G. H. Williams, *The Norman Anonymous of circa 1100* (1951); E. H. Kantorowicz, *King's Two Bodies* (1957), pp. 43–61.

[31] Schramm, *op. cit.*, p. 27.

[32] *Ibid.*, pp. 27, 74–8, 106–8.

[33] Cf. A.S. Chron., 'E', s.a. 1087.

[34] 'Christus vincit; Christus regnat; Christus imperat.' The fascinating history of the *Laudes* and their variations is told in E. H. Kantorowicz, *Laudes Regiae* (1946).

prestige owed much to earlier developments, its sanctions were none the less extremely impressive. As the Norman Anonymous declared:

> The power of the King is the power of God. This power is God's by nature, and the King's by grace. Hence the King is God and Christ, but by grace; and whatever he does he does not simply as a man, but as one who has become God and Christ by grace.[35]

The rhetoric may well appear fantastic, but it was not entirely out of touch with the realities of twelfth-century public opinion. It is probable for instance that Henry I was credited with performing miraculous cures by virtue of his kingship, and he seems to have been the first ruler of England who regularly 'touched' for scrofula specifically because of his royalty.[36] Something of the glory of this regality would undoubtedly depart during the civil war which followed Henry I's death, but the earlier traditions were not allowed to die. And when Henry II had been installed as king of the English he was hailed by Peter of Blois with the words 'He is Holy, and the Anointed of the Lord'.[37]

Such was the royalty which had been adopted and exalted by the Normans in the North. And it was into a regality similarly conceived that in 1130 Roger, grandson of Tancred of Hauteville, entered in the Norman South. There are of course some distinctions, for the Norman kingdom of Sicily was inevitably susceptible to ideas derived from the Eastern empire which had so long governed Apulia, and the development of Norman royalty in the South was to be given a special turn by the fact that the first of the Norman kings of Sicily was subjected by liege homage to successive popes. But these conditions were to prove mainly important in connexion with Norman administration, and in respect of the relations which this induced between the temporal and spiritual powers.[38] The dominant characteristics of the royalty seized by Roger the Great were certainly acquired independently of any special relations with either Rome or Byzantium.[39] They were the product of a European tradition eagerly adopted and carefully fostered. As

[35] *Mon. Germ. Hist. Lib. de Lite*, III, 664; Kantorowicz, *King's Two Bodies*, p. 48.

[36] M. Bloch, *Royal Touch*, pp. 46, 47. It is possible, though not certain, that William the Conqueror used the 'royal touch' (Douglas, *William the Conqueror*, pp. 254, 255). The miraculous cures assigned to Edward the Confessor were attributed to his personal sanctity, and not to his royalty.

[37] *Mon. Germ. Hist. Lib. de Lite*, III, p. 687; Kantorowicz, *King's Two Bodies*, pp. 48, 49.

[38] See below, chaps 6 and 7.

[39] Fuiano, *op. cit.*, esp. pp. 76–7.

with Henry I, so also did Roger the Great acquire a Christ-centred liturgical kingship.

The similarity in this respect between Norman royalty in the north and south of Europe is the more remarkable in that whereas in the south they added a new kingdom to Christendom, in the north they ruled over a realm that had long existed. Yet the comparison could be closely pressed and copiously illustrated. Alike in the chronicles which record his acts, and in the charters which he issued, Roger the Great is made to appear as the royal deputy of Christ. Alexander of Telese depicted him as wielding a sharp sword by the command of God for the punishment of the wicked,[40] and the same notion is expressed even more forcibly in the charters. From the beginning of his reign he issued charters as 'Roger by the grace of God King of Sicily and Italy'.[41] He is moreover 'the champion of the Christians and their shield'.[42] In Greek he is described as a 'most holy King crowned of God'.[43] The reiteration is continuous. In 1144 in a grant for Abbot Blasius of S. Nicolo le Fico he styles himself 'Roger pious servant of the Divine Christ, strong King and protector of the Christians',[44] and in the next year he makes a gift to Cefalú in the name of God 'who has given us honour and adorned our name with the royal title'.[45] There were other and extraneous inspirations for these assertions,[46] but there can be no doubt that the first Norman king of Sicily claimed to an enhanced degree the religious sanctions traditionally accorded to royalty in Western Christendom.

Here as in England, however, the same qualifications have to be made. In 1100, in his coronation charter, Henry I proclaimed to all his subjects:

> Know that by the mercy of God, and by the common consent of the barons of the whole kingdom of England, I have been crowned King of this realm.[47]

Alongside the divine sanction of his regality there is thus here expressed the feudal support which had made its acceptance possible. Roger of Sicily has

[40] Cf. Jamison, *Apulia*, p. 265.
[41] Kehr, *Urkunden*, Nos 7 and 8.   [42] *Ibid.*, No. 5.
[43] Cusa, *Diplomi Greci*, pp. 19 and 389; Kehr, *Urkunden*, p. 247; Ménager, *Cahiers*, II, p. 307 n. 34.
[44] Collura, *Studi Ruggeriani*, No. V, p. 614. In like fashion Innocent II can term him 'christianae religionis diligens propugnator' (Jaffé-Lowenfeld, No. 8043).
[45] Pirro, *Sicilia Sacra*, p. 800; Ménager, *Cahiers*, II, p. 307 n. 34.
[46] See below, chap. 7.
[47] Douglas, *English Historical Documents*, II, No. 19.

also been seen as receiving the essential election and acclaim of his greater vassals whose acts in this respect might be equated with the formal election and *collaudatio* of the coronation rite.[48] The power of the Norman monarchies and their character would in fact depend very directly on this combination. The Normans claimed for their newly established king the semi-sacred authority ascribed to medieval royalty. But they also accepted a social order based upon the principles of European feudalism which they imported into the lands they conquered. A situation of considerable interest to the future was thus created, for 'the clearest legacy of feudalism to modern societies is the emphasis placed upon the notion of political contract'.[49] And it was precisely this notion which in due course counterbalanced the older tradition of the sanctity of kingship which had been so steadfastly sustained in the Norman realms between 1100 and 1154.

IV

There are in fact many reasons why the part played by the Normans in the history of European feudalism may be regarded as possessing a special interest. 'The establishment of the Duke of Normandy in England,' remarked Marc Bloch, 'was one of a series of examples of the migration of legal institutions – the transmission to a conquered country of French feudal practices.'[50] And 'this phenomenon', he added, 'occurred three times in the course of the same century' – in England, in Italy and in Syria. But it was not until after 1100 that the full consequences of this would be disclosed, for the Normans not only brought feudal practices with them, they made those practices contribute to the maintenance of public order in a manner hitherto unknown in any country in Europe. The feudal influence of the Normans on Europe was in fact to be profound. It affected not only the Norman realms, but also the older European states.

It was largely for this reason that the earlier half of the twelfth century was to prove a period of fundamental importance in the development of feudal society in Europe. Of course many of the basic feudal institutions had already been established. The practice of claiming the protection of a lord in return for service had for instance been a feature of the social structure of the Carolingian empire at the time of its decline, and in 1100 men had long been

---

[48] Cf. Douglas, *William the Conqueror*, chap. x.
[49] M. Bloch, *Mélanges*, I (1963), p. 188.
[50] M. Bloch, *Feudal Society*, p. 187.

familiar with the fief as a service tenement whose hereditary possession was dependent upon the performance of specified duties. Also, by the beginning of the twelfth century the men of Western Europe had come to recognize the supremacy of a class of mounted warriors specially trained and equipped who were bound together with each other, and to their lords, by ties of allegiance that had assumed the distinctive form of vassalage.[51]

But at the time when the great Norman kingdoms were established it still remained uncertain whether the fragmentation of political authority implicit in many of the earlier feudal arrangements could be checked, or whether those feudal inspirations which had taken so firm a hold on the minds and habits of European men could be made to serve as the foundation of larger and more effective systems of secular government. Between 1100 and 1160 an affirmative answer to both these vital questions had been given over large areas of Western Europe. Less emphasis came gradually to be paid to the intense personal relationship between man and man than was originally inherent in the feudal tie, and more attention was paid to its public implications. It was the fief and its obligations which was now stressed, and an effort was made to inculcate the notion that the fief was not a possession conferring private rights, but rather a delegation of public powers. In many quarters there was even visualized a regular feudal hierarchy culminating in a prince who would be the ultimate source of all feudal authority including those of the subordinate vassals.[52]

The hazardous advance towards the establishment of feudal order out of feudal separatism was effected to very different degrees in the various countries of Christendom. East of the Rhine, in the empire which had recently been the strongest political power in the West, feudal progress was slower and less thorough than elsewhere. The central authority vested in the emperor had been weakened by the investitures conflict, and older systems of land tenure continued to survive alongside newly introduced feudal arrangements. Characteristic of the empire at this time was the prevalence and extent of allodial estates whose owners were subject to no lord, and in Germany the laws regulating fiefs and vassalage were for long treated as a separate system applicable only to particular estates and persons. Here a comparison might be made with France, where before 1150 the allod had almost disappeared, and where feudal law had been inextricably woven into the whole legal fabric. The history of France in the earlier half of the twelfth

[51] *Ibid.*, pp. 145 et sqq.
[52] Cahen, *Régime féodale de l'Italie normande* (1940), pp. 137, 138.

century is essentially the history of the great fiefs, and of their relations with a monarchy which had only a very imperfect control over their actions.[53]

But the most striking contrast is that to be found between the Norman realms and the rest of Western Europe. The basic institutions of feudalism had been given their first form in the western portion of Charlemagne's empire, and it was from there that they spread to other lands. But there is a profound truth in the observation by Marc Bloch that where feudalism was imported it was much more systematically organized than where its development had been purely spontaneous.[54] For this reason the three great Norman conquests of England, Sicily and Antioch were to mark a cardinal stage in the history of feudal institutions, and by the sixth decade of the twelfth century the two great Norman kingdoms in the North and South were the most completely organized feudal states in Western Christendom. There and there alone could be seen in its social completion a whole feudal pyramid with its apex in the king.[55] Neither Henry I nor Henry II at the beginning of his reign would have tolerated as did the king of France a tenant-in-chief such as the count of Toulouse, who was nominally a vassal, but who in fact rendered no service to the king and resented any royal interference in his affairs. And no king of France, or emperor in Germany before 1150, exercised the same power over his vassals as did King Roger II of Sicily.

V

These conditions deserve close scrutiny in any assessment of the Norman contribution to the feudal structure of Europe. The basic evidence for feudal society is to be found in the feudal charter, and such charters are numerous in illustrating conditions in the twelfth-century Norman realms. Moreover it is symptomatic of the royal authority established in the Norman kingdoms that the feudal arrangements both of Norman England and of part of Norman Italy were codified and described in two surviving royal registers of feudal tenants and their services. The *Catalogus Baronum*,[56] which relates to wide areas of southern Italy, and particularly to Apulia, was drawn up during

[53] M. Bloch, *Feudal Society*, pp. 176–90.
[54] *Ibid.*, p. 188.
[55] Cf. Ganshof, *Feudalism*, p. 60.
[56] This is printed in Del Re, *Cronisti e Scrittori* (1865), pp. 571–615. A critical edition by the late Miss Evelyn Jamison is in process of publication. See also C. H. Haskins, in *Eng. Hist. Rev.*, XXVI (1911), pp. 655–69.

the last quarter of the twelfth century, and it embodies material of various dates. But its most fundamental sections refer to the reign of King Roger the Great, that is, to the period before 1154. Similarly, the famous *Cartae*[57] of feudal services drawn up for Henry II of England in 1166, and for Normandy in 1172, supply a mass of material relating to conditions in the reign of Henry I (1100–35), and demonstrate that the arrangements characteristic of feudal England were all operative in his time.

The *Cartae* and the *Catalogus* have inevitably been widely cited in connexion with the vexed question whether feudalism was first introduced by the Normans into England, Italy and Sicily. It was, for instance, long believed that English feudal institutions were evolved gradually out of the Anglo-Saxon past, and even as late as 1940 a distinguished French scholar concluded that in pre-conquest England there 'existed everywhere a semi-feudal regime'.[58] Earlier, however, that view had been effectively challenged in the magisterial work of J. H. Round and F. M. Stenton,[59] and it is now generally (though not universally) held that the feudalism characteristic of Norman England was brought to England by the Normans. The long debate about the origins of feudalism in England has not yet ended,[60] but in the meantime it may be safe to conclude that

> the more clearly the Anglo-Norman aristocracy of barons and knights is seen in the light of records written from its own standpoint – the more misleading it seems to apply the adjective feudal to any aspect of English society before the Norman Conquest.[61]

It would in fact be 'turning a useful term into a mere abstraction' to do so. Evidently the feudal structure of twelfth-century England should be regarded as a Norman creation.

A similar conclusion can be drawn in respect of southern Italy and Sicily.[62] As in England, in Italy there has been at times a tendency among historians

[57] Printed in *Red Book of the Exchequer*, I, pp. 186–444. Exhaustively discussed by J. H. Round in *Feudal England*, pp. 225–316.

[58] Cahen, *Régime*, pp. 34, 136.

[59] Round, *Feudal England*, pp. 225–316; F. M. Stenton, *First Century of English Feudalism* (1931).

[60] See, for example, M. Hollings, in *Eng. Hist. Rev.*, LXIII (1948), pp. 453–87; C. W. Hollister, in *American Hist. Rev.*, LXVI (1961), pp. 641–64; and *Anglo-Saxon Military Institutions* (1962).

[61] Stenton, *English Feudalism*, p. v.

[62] Cahen, *op. cit.*, *passim*.

to minimize the consequences of the Norman conquest, and to attribute the origin of all later medieval institutions in Italy to a period before the coming of the Normans. In the case of feudal organization and practices such a theory might, however, be hard to sustain. Certainly, before the advent of the Normans feudal ideas had been carried to Italy from France in the wake of Charlemagne. But they had never taken firm root in the peninsula, and, south of Rome, their influence was very tenuous. It is true that dependent tenures had been created in the Lombard principalities of Capua and Salerno, but they had never been coordinated into a regular feudal regime. In Apulia and Calabria, moreover, under Byzantine rule such tenures were rare, whilst in Moslem Sicily they were virtually non-existent.[63] In the South, therefore, the Normans had introduced feudal principles and practices into regions which were largely unfamiliar with them, and they applied those principles to many different provinces which had hitherto submitted to distinct traditions of extreme diversity. It is hardly surprising therefore that feudal progress under the Normans was slower, and more precarious, in the South than in the North. None the less, the feudal structure of southern Italy and Sicily in the twelfth century must be regarded as a Norman innovation.

The main distinction between the Norman states in the North and South derives from the very different political foundations upon which the Normans had to erect their own political edifice. In England they found a kingdom subject to a single monarchical rule, and acknowledging, albeit with some divergencies, a single system of law. The local customs, and even the administrative practices of the various provinces, could not be ignored, and there was an appreciable divergence in this respect between the Danelaw and the rest of England. But there was nothing in the differences that separated Mercia from Wessex, or Northumbria from East Anglia, to compare with the political, legal and ethical divergencies that divided Lombard Capua from Byzantine Apulia, and both from Moslem Sicily. The reaction of these several provinces to Norman feudal innovations was bound to be distinct, and their opposition to them was inevitably to be different.

Such variations were moreover enhanced by the manner in which the Norman conquests had been conducted. In England a single monarchy had been displaced and the Normans had thus been able to impose their feudal arrangements over the entire realm. The feudal unity that had thus been achieved in England by the time of Henry I is indeed wholly remarkable. The greater tenants of the king held their estates widely scattered over the

63 *Ibid.*, pp. 21–41.

kingdom, but the military duties they owed to the king were clearly specified in the *Cartae* of knight-service. The number of knights they must bring to the royal service is in each case formally set out, and it depended not on the amount of the baron's lands but on individual bargains with the king which could be regularly and legally enforced over all the land.[64] A similar situation had been created in Sicily where the conquest had been rapidly completed over the whole island by two of the sons of Tancred of Hauteville. As a result, Roger the Great Count had been able, before his death in 1101, to distribute fiefs throughout Sicily according to his pleasure and largely on his own terms.[65] But if in this respect the feudal situation in Sicily could be compared with that in England, conditions in southern Italy were different. There the conquest over distinct provinces had been made by leaders of individual contingents. The result was a multiplication of small fiefs unregulated at first by any strong central control, and the establishment of a feudal aristocracy that for long was more conscious of its privileges than its duties.[66]

These distinctions could be widely illustrated. Reference might for instance be made to the earls and counts established at this time in the Norman lands. Considering the size of his realm, comparatively few earldoms are to be found in England in the time of Henry I. Some of the earldoms established by his father had in fact been abolished, and only one of these remained after 1100 in the possession of the family to which it had originally been granted.[67] All the earldoms in England between 1100 and 1135 were moreover held by men who were closely connected with the king, and who were kept rigidly under his control. The forfeiture of the Montgomery earldom in 1102 demonstrated how effective such control might be, and not until the nineteen unhappy years that followed the death of Henry I did earldoms multiply in England and become a source of disturbance. Not the least disastrous consequence to England of the civil war between Stephen of Blois and Matilda from Anjou was their lavish grants of rival earldoms in order to attract support from the magnates to whom they were given.[68] Men such as Geoffrey de Mandeville, earl of Essex, and William de Mohun, earl of Dorset, were creatures of new and anarchic conditions. During the reign

[64] Round, *Feudal England*, p. 261; Cahen, *op. cit., passim*.

[65] Cf. Douglas, *Norman Achievement*, pp. 175–7.

[66] Cahen, *op. cit.*, p. 138.

[67] Southern, 'Place of Henry I in English History', Brit. Acad. *Proceedings*, XLVIII (1962), p. 133.   [68] Davis, *Stephen*, pp. 129–44.

of Henry I the earldoms, speaking generally, were a support rather than a menace to the unity of the realm.

A comparable situation was to be found in contemporary Sicily, where only two local *comtés* seem to have been established. One of these – that of Syracuse – was created by Count Roger I for his nephew Tancred, and lapsed after his death,[69] whilst the other – that of Paterno – was granted by the Great Count to one of his sisters as a dowry and passed eventually into the family of the Aleramici,[70] who were strong supporters of the Norman regime. Not less than thirty-six feudal *comtés* existed at this time in Norman Italy,[71] and while some of these were ephemeral, many of them were of high importance. The history of the Norman dominions in the South could not be written without frequent references to the comital families of Loritello and Molise near the Abruzzi, of the 'Principate' in the neighbourhood of Naples, or of Conversano and Montescaglioso in the region of Bari.[72] Several of the Norman *comtés* in Italy passed into the possession of men closely connected by marriage or relationship with the house of Hauteville.[73] But all of these comital families would during the early decades of the twelfth century claim, and sometimes exercise, a virtual independence.

Nevertheless, it is the feudal similarity existing at this time among the Norman dominions, rather than the differences between them, which must command attention. After all, the Norman feudal settlement had everywhere been effected by closely associated or inter-related groups of families, many of whom came to hold land both in the North and in the South. If the history of such families as those of Grandmesnil Barneville, Craon, Laigle, Avenel, Sourdeval, Blosseville and Courbepine[74] should ever be written in detail, much new light would be thrown on the Norman influence upon European feudalism. It is noteworthy that most of the basic institutions of feudalism are to be found in England, Italy, Sicily and also Antioch almost immediately after the Norman domination had been established.

In each case they had evidently been imported by the Normans. Thus the fief and liege-homage, and the practice of subinfeudation, appear almost at once in the Norman realms of the North and South,[75] where in each case

[69] Ménager, *Messina*, p. 59.
[70] Cahen, *op. cit.*, pp. 59–61; Douglas, *Norman Achievement*, p. 178.
[71] Chalandon, *Domination*, II, pp. 567–8.
[72] Cahen, *op. cit.*, pp. 58–62 and *passim*.   [73] *Loc. cit.*
[74] Jamison, *Sicilian Norman Kingdom*, pp. 4–5; Douglas, *Norman Achievement*, chap. VI.
[75] Alex. Tel., II, c. 67; Cahen, *op. cit.*, pp. 42, 43; Stenton, *op. cit.*, *passim*.

there was swiftly established a military aristocracy conscious of its special position in society.[76] Even the detailed regulations of feudal military service are often stated in almost identical terms. The knight is a mounted warrior specially trained and equipped; his expenses must be met in part at least by his lord; and the normal duration of his service will be of forty days.[77] Castle-guard was known in Italy as in England, and in the South scutage – the commutation of knight-service into money payments – was even more important than in the North.[78] And all this was a result of Norman innovation. But what gave Norman feudalism its special character in Europe was not only the establishment of feudal institutions, but the coordination of those institutions by the Norman monarchs to serve as a basis of the strength of the Norman kingdoms.

VI

The dominant position attained by the Norman kings in the feudal states they ruled has been abundantly illustrated in the case of England,[79] where feudal organization in the early twelfth century was brought to a higher pitch of efficiency than in any other contemporary country in the West. This result was in fact achieved early in the twelfth century under the rule of Henry I, and particularly after 1106 when that king triumphed over his elder brother at Tinchebrai. It is true that owing to his weak title Henry had been compelled to make some concessions to his greater barons in the charter that he issued at the time of his coronation in 1100.[80] But from that same document it can be concluded that the king already relied on the feudal support he could command, and that very much of the royal revenue was derived from the dues he could exact as feudal overlord. Henry I was in fact to take full advantage of this situation, and the reign is marked by his unscrupulous exploitation of what were known as the 'feudal insidents' – fees payable to the lord on such occasions as when his vassal married or inherited his estate.[81]

In this the king was certainly helped by the fact that his father had avoided

[76] Cahen, *op. cit.*, pp. 51–62; Stenton, *loc. cit.*   [77] Cf. Ughelli, *Italia Scara*, V, p. 700.
[78] Stenton, *op. cit.*, chap. VI; Cahen, *op. cit.*, pp. 73–5.
[79] Round, *Feudal England*, p. 261; Stenton, *loc. cit.*; Douglas, *William the Conqueror*, chap. II.
[80] Liebermann, *Gesetze der Angelsachsen*, I, p. 521; Douglas, *English Historical Documents*, II, No. 19. See further Strayer, *Twelfth Century Europe*, pp. 80, 81.
[81] Southern, *op. cit.*, p. 151.

the creation of compact fiefs for his greater barons in England, whose estates were in consequence widely scattered over the country. Henry I was thus able to benefit by quasi-legal means from the tenurial complexity which had been caused.[82] And at the same time the military service to which he was entitled, or the money payment for which it might be commuted, were clearly specified. The feudal rights of the king in England between 1106 and 1135 were set out with quite exceptional precision, and this reflected the realities of royal power. The strength of the feudal order prevailing in England under Henry I can indeed be judged by the fact that it survived the troubles that followed his death. Thus in 1154 the feudal structure set up by the Normans in England was inherited by Henry II, and the new king from Anjou was to develop it afresh to serve once more as a buttress to the monarchy.

The situation in England in 1100 had in fact been particularly favourable to Norman feudal policy. The new Norman king could rely on the feudal tenures which had been created by his father throughout a kingdom which had long been politically united. Conditions in the Norman South were in this respect very different, however. There, a united dominion was only slowly and with difficulty to be established. In 1101 Roger the Great Count had left to his young sons a legal supremacy over Sicily and Calabria, but during the next three decades it would need perpetual warfare before the dominance of the ruler of Sicily could be extended over all the Norman territories on the mainland. And only after this had been accomplished could feudal institutions in the Norman South be coordinated into such a regime as had already been set up by Henry I in England. A cardinal stage in the growing impact of Norman feudalism on Europe was thus reached in 1129. In that year Roger the Great – who was not yet king – had already received the homage of the princes of Capua, and begun to extend his claims northwards as far as Ancona and southwards towards Naples and Gaeta. Then in August he was acknowledged as duke of Apulia by the pope whom he had beaten in battle, and finally in September he convoked at Melfi a great assembly of all the magnates (*optimates*) of Apulia, and proclaimed the principles which would henceforth determine his overlordship over all the Norman feudal realm in the South.[83]

The court at Melfi in 1129 bears the same relation to the history of feudalism in Italy as does the assembly at Salisbury some twenty-nine years

[82] *Loc. cit.*
[83] Jamison, *Apulia*, pp. 237-9.

earlier to that in England.[84] Its proceedings are described by Alexander of Telese and by the interpolator of the chronicle of Romuald of Salerno,[85] and while these two writers naturally emphasize different aspects of what then took place, the general impression they leave is clear. 'All the counts of Apulia in Calabria' were compelled to take an oath of fealty to Roger the Great and to his two sons Roger and Tancred. At the same time the magnates were forced to swear obedience to a solemn edict issued by Roger which proclaimed a general peace in the interests of all his subjects and, in particular, prohibited for ever the practice of private war among members of the knightly class. Roger's paramount position in the feudal state was thus asserted in the most spectacular manner, and the significance of these declarations was soon to be further enhanced. For Roger's accession to royalty in the next year was due in large part to a feudal 'promotion'.[86] It was by the advice and acclamation of his barons and people that he was brought to be king at Palermo, and it was the magnates of his realm that decided that he who already exercised such power over so many lands should be raised from the high rank of duke to the culminating honour of king.[87]

In one sense the proclamation of a general peace by Roger the Great at Melfi in 1129 was not original. It could be derived from notions ealier developed both in Normandy and England,[88] whereby the efforts formerly made to promote public order by means of such institutions as the 'Truce of God' might be enforced by temporal rulers. And indeed it is probable that the Great Count had proclaimed a general peace in Sicily at some period between 1091 and 1094.[89] But nothing comparable to this had been attempted by the Normans on the Italian mainland. The importance of Roger's action in 1129, and of its repetition after he became king, lay therefore in the fact that the peace of the Norman king had now been extended over all the Norman lands in the South, and was indeed to prove an important agent in their political unification. Its enforcement would, moreover, largely depend on the fact that its original proclamation was made just at a time when the Norman king of Palermo was achieving his dominating position within the feudal structure of his entire realm.

[84] A.S. Chron., 'E', s.a. 1085 (equals 1086).

[85] Alex. Tel., I, c. 21; Romuald, p. 9.

[86] Ménager, *Institution monarchique*, pp. 445 et sqq.   [87] See above, p. 46.

[88] Pollock and Maitland, *Hist. Eng. Law*, I, p. 42; Douglas, *William the Conqueror*, pp. 83 et sqq.

[89] See his diploma for the church of Patti in Pirro, *Sicilia Sacra*, p. 770.

The advance of the king within the feudal order in the Norman South could be watched in many directions. It is apparent, for instance, in the oaths of liege-homage offered to the king by even his greatest barons and it is further remarkable how often this was coupled with a reservation of fealty by their own subtenants in favour of the king. Thus in 1134 when Alphonzo, Roger's son, was installed as prince of Capua, he not only swore liege-homage to his royal father at Palermo, but all his tenants at the same time took an oath that they would be faithful to the king 'against all men and women'.[90] And in the next year similar action was taken by the duke of Gaeta.[91] Almost equally important was the king's position with regard to the lesser feudatories in his realm. In England it had proved an advantage to Henry I that there were no compact baronies in the country so that the royal will could be exercised more directly upon near vassals. In Italy a similar benefit to the monarchy was the existence of a multitude of small fiefs. In Apulia this was a result of the circumstances of the original conquest. In Sicily, too, the Great Count after 1093 had subdivided many of the large fiefs which had earlier been created by Robert Guiscard.[92]

As a consequence there existed in 1130 a very large number of small feudatories holding directly – and 'in chief' – from the king.[93] A comparison between the *Cartae* and the *Catalogus Baronum* is illuminating, for in the former less than a quarter of the lay fiefs held in chief owed service of as few as ten knights, whilst many had been assigned a service of between thirty and a hundred,[94] while in the latter it is rare to find any tenant owing a service of as many as five knights, a service of ten knights or more being quite exceptional.[95] It seems surprising that King Roger does not appear to have exacted homage from the rear vassals in his realm, as was perhaps done on occasion by the king in England,[96] but his immediate feudal authority evidently extended directly over a very large number of the holders of small fiefs.

[90] Alex. Tel., III, c. 31.
[91] *Codex Caiet.*, II, No. 234.
[92] Douglas, *Norman Achievement*, p. 178.
[93] Cahen, *op. cit.*, pp. 71–2.
[94] Round, *Feudal England*, pp. 253–6.
[95] Haskins, *Eng. Hist. Rev.*, XXVI, p. 661.
[96] In 1086, for example, the king called to Salisbury 'all the people occupying land over all England no matter whose vassal they were and they all submitted to him and became his vassals and swore oaths of allegiance to him that they would be loyal to him against all other men'. A.S. Chron., 'E', s.a. 1085 (equals 1086).

Thus neither in England, Sicily, nor Italy was there ever any question of the Norman monarchy seeking to combat feudalism. On the contrary, both Henry I and Roger the Great sought in their several ways to strengthen the feudal structure of the realms they ruled, to give that structure further coherence, and to utilize the feudal institutions within their kingdoms to increase the royal power. Their success in this respect was wholly remarkable even though there were differences in the manner in which it was brought about. The dominance of the Norman king within the feudal order was attained later in the South than in England, and perhaps was never there so complete as in the North. But the Sicilian realm did not have to face the social disturbances which befell England between 1135 and 1153; and the final result was the same. The Normans had created what were between 1154 and 1160 the best ordered feudal realms in Christendom. It was indeed through a combination of feudal overlordship, carefully established, with royal authority, strongly asserted, that the Norman rulers were enabled during the earlier half of the twelfth century to give a new turn to the development of secular government in Western Europe.

Chapter 6
SECULAR GOVERNMENT

I

No aspect of the influence exercised by the Normans on Europe between 1100 and 1154 is more noteworthy than the special contribution they made at that time to the development of secular administration in the West. This was partly due to kings who at first relied both on the traditional sanctions accorded to royalty in the past, and also on long-established feudal principles which they brought with them into the countries they conquered. But these kings were also able to erect on these foundations a wholly new edifice of power. They adapted, and sometimes distorted, feudal organization to their own advantage, and at the same time they established new institutions of government operated by men of their own choosing. Nor were they reluctant, when need arose, to rely on traditions that had been operative before their coming in the lands they ruled. The manner in which all this was accomplished was, however, very complex. But its results were to prove so influential in the growth of the Western European states that the beginning of the process during the earlier half of the twelfth century merits careful note. And in any such analysis the reigns of Henry I of England and Roger the Great of Sicily invite particular attention and comparison, for they witnessed the opening stages of developments which naturally took different forms in the Norman North and the Norman South but which none the less possessed many common features.

Both Henry I and King Roger owed their achievement of royal status in large measure to the support of the feudal magnates in their realms. Henry, for instance, was thus enabled to gain the English throne despite the prior claims of his elder brother Duke Robert, and it was the Norman magnates in Italy and Sicily who decided that Roger, who had come to rule over so many provinces, ought in consequence to be given the title of king rather than that of duke.[1] Each of these princes would thus be expected to rule *ut dominus et rex* – both as feudal lord and as king – and this was made abundantly clear in the documents which recorded their advance to royal power. The great charter which in 1100 Henry I issued immediately after his

[1] Alex. Tel., II, c. 1.

coronation[2] was specifically addressed to 'all his barons and faithfull vassals both French and English', and it was almost exclusively concerned with the payment of feudal dues, the performance of feudal services, and the regulation of the feudal relations between the king and his tenants-in-chief. Promises were there given that such malpractices in these matters as had taken place during the previous reign should be discontinued; and though these promises were in the event not to be kept, the assurance reflected the feudal basis of the new king's power.

Similarly, charters issued in the years immediately preceding Roger's coronation at Palermo display the young ruler surrounded by Norman prelates and barons. Here were the archbishops of Palermo and Reggio, the abbots of S. Eufemia and Lipari, and among the lay magnates men such as Robert Avenel, Ralph of Beauvais, Robert Borel, Rannulf of Troina and Robert of Bassonville.[3] These, with others like them, were in constant attendance upon Roger at this time and were doubtless active in promoting his royalty in 1130, and when, five years later, Roger's son, Alphonzo, became prince of Capua it was 'by favour of all the magnates and knights'.[4]

In respect of the constitutional developments which he sponsored, Henry I achieved something more lasting even than the Conqueror.[5] Correspondingly, the special characteristics which were later to be found in the Norman kingdom of Sicily probably owed more to Roger the Great than to any other single man. In view of the great changes which were to be effected during the reigns of these kings, the feudal structure of the realms they ruled, and the feudal resources which contributed to their power, merit considerable emphasis. England between 1106 and 1135 was a feudal state and, despite all the unique features it later exhibited, the kingdom founded by Roger the Great was at its inception an integral part of feudal Europe.[6]

The chief organ of government in both the Norman realms at this time is to be found in the omnicompetent feudal court of the king, the *curia regis* to which the king's vassals came as in feudal duty bound, and which was also attended by the prelates of the realm, and by members of the king's household. Alongside the greatest barons of the realm appear the chancellor, who was the keeper of the king's seal, and holders of household offices

[2] Liebermann, *Gesetz*, I, p. 521, trans. in Douglas, *English Historical Documents*, II, No. 19.
[3] Ménager, *Emir*, Nos 4, 12; Caspar, *op. cit.*, Reg. 12.
[4] Alex. Tel., III, c. 31.
[5] Southern, 'Place of Henry I', Brit. Acad. *Proceedings*, XLVIII (1962), pp. 127-62.
[6] Ménager, *Institution monarchique*, pp. 466, 467.

designated by humble titles such as butlers, chamberlains or stewards – offices which were in fact held by some of the most important men of the land. This royal and feudal court discharged under the king's direction all the functions of government, and from it, during the reigns of Henry I and King Roger, specialized departments of administration were to be derived.

A survey of these royal and feudal courts illustrates at once the essential similarities and also the wide differences in the constitutional structure of the Norman kingdoms. In 1107 a charter of Henry I for Binham Priory[7] was attested in the royal court by two archbishops, eight bishops, six abbots, two counts, the chancellor, a chaplain, and no less than seventeen barons. In 1121 a grant for St Peter's Abbey, Shrewsbury,[8] was similarly witnessed, and the composition of the magnificent court held by Henry at Woodstock in 1128 has already been noted.[9] But all these charters could be set alongside those which were being issued during the same years by Roger as count before even he became king. In 1117 Roger, 'holding his court with his barons', made grants in favour of Hugh abbot of Holy Trinity, Venosa, in the presence of Robert Avenel, Rannulf of Troina, Bon the protonotary, Basil the chamberlain, John the emir, and Racher the butler.[10] In 1125 a dispute was settled by Roger in favour of Maurice, bishop of Catania in the presence of the bishops of Messina and Troina, together with the 'archons' Robert Avenel and Matthew de Creun, the emirs John and Christodoulos, Paen the chamberlain and Philip the logothete.[11]

Evidently both in England and in the South the Norman rulers were governing through a court consisting of their prelates and barons, but they were buttressing this court with officials of their own choosing who might be expected to give a fresh expression of their power. Some of these officials, however, bore very different titles in the Norman South, for there was nothing in the charters of Henry I to correspond with the emirs, the archons, or the logothetes of the Southern documents. Indeed, some of these designations evidently perplexed the Normans in England, as may be seen from an anecdote recorded by John of Salisbury. In 1150 he says,

> a certain count named Hugh, born in Apulia but of Norman origin, had long been striving to secure a separation from his wife who was sprung from

[7] *Regesta Regum*, No. 828.
[8] *Ibid.*, No. 1245.
[9] See Davis, *Regesta*, II, No. 1389.
[10] Ménager, *Emir*, No. 12.
[11] *Ibid.*, No. 18.

the noble stock of Lombards and Romans. . . . Finally he appeared in person before the Lord Pope bringing with him catapans of the Sicilian King and other officials and nobles from Apulia and Calabria in order to obtain a dissolution of the marriage.[12]

These catapans, the author adds, 'are powerful officials who exercise the authority of princes in the cities and castles of that region'. In fact, of course, the catapans had been charged with local administration in southern Italy under the Eastern empire, and the Normans had here taken over an office from Byzantium. The Greek origin of Roger's *strategoi* is likewise self-evident. As for the logothetes, they may have been judges or chancery officials, or auditors of accounts,[13] but they too clearly bore a title derived from the Eastern empire. Equally obvious was the Arabic source of the designation of those kaids who were local officials under the Norman king,[14] and still more notable was the title of emir which was borne by so many of those who were most prominent in contributing to spectacular achievements of Roger the Great.

II

Of all the titles given to officials in the Norman kingdom of Sicily, that of emir has properly attracted most attention from historians.[15] This was due partly to the fact that in its Latinized form, *Admirabilis* – Admiral – the title came to be used throughout Europe as denoting specifically a high naval command. But in fact it is extremely unlikely that at least before 1177 the emirate in the Norman South was ever specifically or exclusively connected with naval organization.[16] The fame of the Sicilian emirate at that time depended more simply on the fact that some of the most important men in his realm were thus described during the period when King Roger was wielding his greatest power. At this time, however, the title of emir was given fairly commonly to persons of standing who were connected with the royal court, and the style may thus be regarded as a court distinction conferring special prestige but not in itself indicating specific duties. The

---

12 *Historia Pontificalis*, ed. Chibnall, p. 80. This is Hugh II, count of Molise.
13 Jamison, *Eugenius*, p. 40.
14 Cusa, *Diplomi Greci*, pp. 129, 155, 157, 265, 478; Ménager, *Emir*, pp. 2, 83.
15 Recent studies are embodied in Jamison, *Eugenius*, and Ménager, *Emir*.
16 Ménager, *Emir*, p. 86.

emirate was thus held by John the Archon, who shortly after 1130 commanded the king's troops in front of Amalfi,[17] by Nicholas, who was at one time strategotos of Lentini,[18] and by Theodore, who in 1133 gave judgement in the company of the chancellor Warin in a dispute involving the inhabitants of Patti.[19] Such men must be placed alongside the magnates who, bearing the title of emir, so notably enlarged the power of Roger the Great and conditioned much of the Norman impact upon Europe in his time.

The great emirs of King Roger were men of Greek origin rejoicing in an Arabic title; and they stand in the forefront of the history of their age. The first emir, Eugenius, had risen to power under the Great Count, and was the founder of an important family of administrators.[20] The more imposing Christodoulos, who controlled so much of the government of Sicily during the regency of the Countess Adelaide,[21] thus preserved the continuity of Norman administration in the island, and made possible the later achievement of Roger the Great. But most notable was George of Antioch, who was saluted in 1137 as Emir of the Emirs and Archon of the Archons,[22] and was the chief agent in the Norman conquest of North Africa. At home too he came to occupy much the same position as was enjoyed by the Grand Vizier at an oriental court, and he was active in developing the royal administration, particularly on its financial side. His death in 1151 or 1152 was to signalize the end of a period in Roger's reign.

These men were in fact to prove themselves the architects of the Norman kingdom of Sicily. Indeed, so dominant did the power of the emirs become that there was, perhaps inevitably, a reaction against it. The terrible fate of the emir Philip of Mahdia in the last year of Roger's reign was probably caused by feudal and ecclesiastical opposition to the authority vested in his office. It is significant also that Maio of Bari, who after 1154 became chief emir, was a Latin, not a Greek. Even so, the tension which had been created was not relieved. Maio was murdered in 1155, and after his time the authority of the 'Emir of Emirs' waned. And it was never fully restored. But it is not without significance that the greatness of the Norman kingdom in the South, and its secular structure, was in large measure created under a

---

[17] Alex. Tel., II, c. 8.

[18] Ménager, *Emir*, p. 62.

[19] Scacci, *Patti e l'amministrazione del commune* (1907); Ménager, *Emir*, p. 63.

[20] Jamison, *Eugenius*, pp. 35–56.

[21] See above, chap. 2.

[22] Ménager, *Emir*, Nos 28–9.

grandson of Tancred of Hauteville by a series of very powerful constructive statesmen who were Greek by race and proud to possess an Arab title.

III

A comparison between the Norman realms must serve to call immediate attention not only to the achievement of the Norman kings of this period but also to what were the basic causes of their success. They established a centralized government concentrated on a feudal royal court, and operated by trained officials, and adapted their administration everywhere to the special needs of the contrasting provinces they ruled. They created a constitutional regime of abiding strength by the careful building of new institutions on old foundations.

The debt of the Norman monarchy in England to the Anglo-Saxon past has been abundantly illustrated in recent years, and perhaps even exaggerated, but it was certainly very large. The greatest asset which the Anglo-Norman kings possessed was undoubtedly to be found in the fact that the West-Saxon monarchy had submitted all England to its rule, and created the rudiments of an administration which might be made to operate over all the kingdom. It was not for nothing that William the Conqueror had claimed to be the legitimate successor to Edward the Confessor after Harold's usurpation, or that in 1086 most of the landowners in England before the coming of the Normans were recorded in Domesday Book. During the reign of Henry I, therefore, the king with his expert advisers could exploit with masterly skill many of the institutions which they found at work in England. The earlier royal secretariate was to be transformed into the Anglo-Norman chancery, and the taxational system of the Anglo-Saxon kings combined with the fiscal expedients of feudalism, and brought under the control of an organized Exchequer. More particularly, the Norman monarchy sustained the local courts of shire and hundred, and enlarged the power of the shire reeves of sheriffs, who had been the chief link between the king and the communities which made up his realm.

The institutions of local government had perhaps been the strongest elements in the Anglo-Saxon state, and, if only for this reason, the wording of Henry I's famous writ[23] issued between 1108 and 1111 concerning the holding of the courts of shire and hundred merits careful attention. These

[23] Liebermann, *Gesetz*, I, p. 524, trans. in Douglas, *English Historical Documents*, II, No. 43.

courts, the king commands, 'Shall meet in the same places and at the same times as they were wont to do in the time of King Edward.' And the Norman king continues: 'I do not wish that my sheriff [*vicecomes*] should make them assemble in different fashion because of his own needs and interests.' Finally it is ordained that 'if in the future there should arise a dispute concerning the allotment of land . . . let this be tried in my own court if it be between my immediate tenants. But if the dispute be between the vassals of two different lords, let the plea be held in the shire court.' The implications of this emphatic phraseology are clear. The new royal and feudal justice of the *curia regis* over the king's tenants-in-chief is safeguarded. But other disputes respecting land will be tried by the sheriff. And the sheriff (here styled *vicecomes* or viscount) will now be a Norman magnate exercising with increased powers the authority of an Anglo-Saxon official, and dispensing justice in an Anglo-Saxon court according to the legal traditions of the shire.

Such arrangements not only indicate the methods of the Norman administration in England, they also illustrate by comparison the much more complicated problems facing the Norman government in the South, and the means by which these too were successfully solved. For Roger the Great did not inherit a well-established monarchy. He created a new kingdom which brought under a single rule provinces of differing traditions and even of different religions. He was, in fact, not only 'King of Italy and Sicily',[24] but more specifically 'King of Sicily, of the Duchy of Apulia and of the Principality of Capua'.[25] In his time, therefore, the centralized monarchy which he founded never attempted to impose a uniform legal system on the various parts of his kingdom. Certainly feudal law was applied to the Norman magnates,[26] and certainly also the royal administration became ever more pervasive and efficient. None the less, Greek legal traditions continued to be respected in the provinces which had been subject to Byzantium. In northern Apulia and the principality of Capua, Lombard law could be applied, and throughout Sicily Moslem legal customs for long remained in operation.[27]

So striking was Roger's success and so important was the influence which he would exercise on Europe that this aspect of his policy deserves some illustration. English scholars are familiar with the spectacle of a Norman sheriff

[24] Kehr, *Urkunden*, Nos 7 and 8.
[25] *Ibid.*, No. 12.   [26] Ménager, *Institution monarchique*, *passim*.
[27] Ménager, in *Normanni e la loro espansione*, pp. 439–97.

holding a trial according to the Saxon customs in the Saxon court. But a similar procedure was at the same time being adopted in vastly more difficult conditions in the Norman South. In 1114, for example, George *vicomte* of Juto (in the province of Palermo) ratified on Roger's orders the divisions within the township of Mirto in the presence of Roger 'de Pappaville', monk of St Bartholomew of Patti, and of 'many other Christians and Saracens'.[28] Some years earlier, when Roger Borsa was in litigation with the archbishop of Salerno, he based his case on the customs of the Lombards,[29] and later, at Sulmona, Hugh son of Gerbert, who was of French descent (*de genere francorum*), declared that henceforth he would submit to the Lombard laws of the land.[30]

This recognition of local customs and provincial laws formed an integral part of the policy of Roger the Great even after he had established the unity of his kingdom, and the results were notable. In 1153, for instance, towards the end of his reign, he issued an important charter[31] to sanction the gifts which had been made by Peter abbot of S. Maria Latins at Jerusalem to certain Sicilian churches, by specifically confirming the boundaries of the estates as these had been established by his justiciars on the testimony of 'senior dwellers in the vicinity both Christian and Saracen'.[32] The analogy to the sworn inquest of neighbours which was part of the legal administration of Anglo-Norman England is at once apparent. But the results in the South were perhaps even more spectacular. In 1168, less than twenty years after the death of Roger the Great, John bishop of Catania declared that all the communities under his rule – Latins, Greeks, Jews and Saracens – could be judged according to their own laws.[33]

Such was the success achieved by the Normans in their attempt to reconcile the racial and cultural differences existing in their kingdom in the South. But something more would be needed if the political unity of that kingdom was to be sustained. Anticipating a procedure later to be adopted by Henry II of England, King Roger sought to solve this problem by establishing his sons as titular rulers over the several provinces in his realm.[34] In the years immediately following his own coronation those sons were, it is true, too young to assume such responsibilities. At first, therefore, the king governed Apulia

28 Collura, No. 14. 29 Ménager, in *Normanni e la loro espansione*, p. 446.
30 *Ibid.* 31 Kehr, *Urkunden*, No. 14.
32 'In presentia veteranorum Christianorum et Saracenorum' and again 'in presentia vicinorum christianorum at Saracenorum'. 33 Ménager, in *Normanni*, p. 448.
34 On what here follows see Jamison, *Apulia*, pp. 370–82.

person of Roger bishop of Salisbury something very like the later justiciar-ship emerged,[42] and like later justiciars he acted fairly consistently as the president, or at least as the dominating member, of the king's court.

He was therefore intimately concerned with what was perhaps the most important constitutional development of the reign of Henry I – the evolution, out of the *curia*, of the Exchequer as financial organization. By the beginning of the twelfth century the primitive arrangements whereby in England the royal finances had been concentrated in the king's *camera* or chamber was proving inadequate. Early in the new reign therefore certain changes occurred. In the first place, alongside the *camera*, which looked after the king's house-hold expenses and followed him on his travels, there was established a separate institution known as the *Treasury*, which was apparently situated at West-minster under the control of a Treasurer. Soon, however, the Treasury was itself superseded by another body known as the Exchequer.[43] Both the name and the practices of this new institution deserve note, for the word 'exchequer' indicated a revolution in the method of auditing the accounts. It signified

> the introduction of a precise system of calculation worked out by counters on a chequered board and recorded on rolls. Thereafter the Treasury was limited to the payment or the storage of money; the business of account passed to the Exchequer.[44]

There is convincing evidence that this new body was in existence within a very few years after the reunion of Normandy and England in 1106,[45] and the earliest surviving example of the characteristic Exchequer records – the Pipe Rolls – is for the year 1131. Most certainly, the Exchequer was a creation of the reign of Henry I.

However, the Anglo-Norman Exchequer always remained part of the royal *curia*. The king evidently 'holds his court in his Exchequer and the pleas which came before the court of the Exchequer related not only to financial matters but to all the business of Government'.[46] It was, moreover, in the court of the Exchequer that in the king's absence Roger bishop of Salisbury exercised his great judicial powers.

The chief problem facing Anglo-Norman England at this time was to make the royal justice pervade the whole of the land. Thus by the beginning of the reign of Henry I it had already become the practice to appoint in each shire or

---

[42] *Ibid.*, p. 30.   [43] Chrimes, *op. cit.*, pp. 29–32.
[44] R. L. Poole, *Exchequer*, pp. 40, 41.
[45] Richardson and Sayles, *op. cit.*, pp. 165, 166.   [46] *Ibid.*, 228.

group of shires a local judge who would conduct those pleas of the Crown which had been removed from the jurisdiction of the sheriff.[47] At this time too a new development of great importance to the future was beginning to take place. Judges from the central court of the king would go 'on eyre' – on circuit – through wide areas of the kingdom to hear specially important pleas, and these 'itinerant justices' speedily became in England an integral part of Norman and Angevin government. This institution in its origins owed much to the bishop of Salisbury, and he himself frequently went 'on eyre' throughout the land, as did other justices appointed by the king such as Geoffrey Ridel, Robert Bloet bishop of Lincoln, Ralph Basset, Alfred of Lincoln and perhaps Geoffrey de Clinton, William d'Aubigny, Walter Espec and Eustace FitzJohn.[48]

V

The most cursory survey of the financial and judicial history of England at this time thus demonstrates the rapid development of royal administration in the Anglo-Norman realm during the reign of Henry I. It remains to be seen, however, whether in very different conditions a similar process could be detected in the kingdom of Roger the Great.[49] Certainly here too reference must be made to the royal and feudal *curia* and to the growing importance within it of officials chosen by the king. In this sense it might be tempting to seek a parallel between the influence exercised by the Greek emirs at Roger's court and that of the bishop of Salisbury in England, but it would be rash to push this comparison too far. Certainly, though, as the reign of King Roger advanced, the introduction into the court of new royal officials such as constables and chamberlains is very noteworthy, and since they were directly appointed by him these contributed to the king's power.[50]

As in England, so also in the South the scope of the royal jurisdiction was steadily increased. The most important pleas, especially if they related to Sicily or Calabria, were often heard by the full *curia*, but sometimes certain of its members – feudal magnates or royal officials – sat apart to give judgement in particular cases. And even more than in England use was made of justiciars appointed to dispense the royal justice in the several parts of

[47] D. M. Stenton, *English Justice*, pp. 80–3.   [48] *Loc. cit.*
[49] On this question, see in particular the magisterial article of C. H. Haskins, 'England and Sicily in the twelfth century', *Eng. Hist. Rev.*, Vol. XXVI (1916).
[50] Jamison, *Apulia*, p. 267.

Roger's disparate realm. Although 'the title justiciar does not appear in the South until 1136, many years after it was in current use in England and Normandy',[51] the duties later associated with the office were consistently discharged throughout Roger's reign. In 1136, for example, royal judgements were given by the king's judges at Trani, and also at Taranto, while during the next decade records of such pleas have survived from Salerno and Capua, from Barletta, Pascara and Aquino, and for many regions of Sicily. The names of a number of these local justices have been recorded – Lampus of Fasanella and Florius de Camerata at Salerno, William de Tivalla at Bari, and Henry de Ollia, who appears in the north at Viesti on the sea-coast near Monte Gargano. Sometimes too these local justices would sit alongside local magnates such as Hugh count of Molise or William archdeacon of Salerno.[52] It is possible also, though not certain, that in Sicily and Calabria, as in England, royal officials such as William of Pozzuoli and Avenel of Petralia acted from time to time as itinerant justices, but elsewhere, and particularly in Capua and Apulia, this is less likely.[53]

Such details illustrate the manner in which the royal justice spread throughout the Norman South in the time of the first Norman king of Sicily. A comparison with the North in respect of financial organization raises, however, much more difficult problems. There seems no doubt that at the outset the royal finance was concentrated as in England in the royal *camera*.[54] But the Normans found in existence in Sicily an elaborate financial bureau of Saracenic origin known as the *diwan* or *duana*, and according to their wont the Normans immediately made full use of it.[55] The matter was further complicated by the fact that during the reign of Roger the Great the whole fiscal organization passed under control of the Greek emirs who served the king. It was they who coordinated the work of the *camera* and the *diwan*. In the former they were served by Greek officials, whilst the *diwan* remained an Arab bureau manned by men who have been aptly described as 'sheiks of the *diwan*'.[56] And both the *camera* and the *diwan* were made to form part of the all embracing *curia* of the king, even as in England the Exchequer remained a specialized part of the omnicompetent royal court.

The differences between the fiscal organizations developed in the two

[51] Haskins, *op. cit.*, p. 643.   [52] *Ibid.*, pp. 642–6.
[53] *Loc. cit.* But see Jamison, *Apulia*, pp. 269, 270, 302–11.
[54] Jamison, *Eugenius*, pp. 34, 35.
[55] Jamison, *Eugenius*, pp. 33–42; Haskins, *op. cit.*, pp. 652–3.
[56] Jamison, *Eugenius*, p. 40.

Norman kingdoms are self-evident, the more especially as during the reign of Roger the Great the responsibility for royal finance came to be vested almost exclusively in the hands of Greek and Saracen officials working under the orders not of Latins but of Greek 'emirs'. In these circumstances it is unlikely that there was here any conscious imitation between the Anglo-Norman realm and the Sicilian kingdom. Already, however, before 1154 officials such as Thomas Brown and Robert of Selby were moving between the two courts, and doubtless they brought with them suggestions as to accounting and taxational practice.[57] Any essential similarity in the developing institutions of the two Norman kingdoms must, however, be sought elsewhere. And it will be found in the outstanding success which these institutions achieved. The creation of the Exchequer during the reign of Henry I, and its operations, made that king richer than any of his neighbours in the North. And Roger the Great became indisputably the wealthiest monarch in the whole of Western Europe. The revenue he derived from Palermo alone was said to be greater than that which could be exacted from the whole of any other kingdom in the West.

VI

The whole machinery of government was made to work with ever greater efficiency under the direction of the Norman kings. Theirs in both cases was the operative will. For obvious reasons the issue of royal orders by the chanceries in the Norman realms showed considerable divergencies, but in both instances use was made of practices that had been operative before the Normans came. The famous Anglo-Norman writs whose Latin language invested command with all the terseness of efficiency had their prototypes in texts, couched in the vernacular, which had been issued in Anglo-Saxon England,[58] and in the South the Normans imitated Byzantine usage in their Greek acts, and frequently modelled their Latin texts upon papal usage.[59]

None the less, a certain correspondence in chancery practice has been detected between the Norman kingdoms which might be contrasted with the rest of Western Europe. The writs (*mandata*) of Roger the Great and his officials never achieved the masterly brevity of the writs of Henry I, but the Sicilian kingdom was, with the Anglo-Norman, the only government in the twelfth century to make constant use of such writs which 'constitute the

[57] On Thomas Brown, see Haskins, *op. cit.*, pp. 439–43.
[58] Cf. *Regesta Regum*, Vol. I, Introduction.   [59] Haskins, *op. cit.*, p. 443.

surest index of the efficiency of a medieval administrative system'.[60] In both the Norman realms it was in fact the Norman king who was the most active agent not only in creating administrative institutions but also in determining the use to which they should be put. And it was precisely in this connexion that would be most conspicuously displayed the Norman success in blending older traditions with new methods of government.

Henry I, for instance, never ceased to claim that he was a king appointed by God, and he was an expert in exploiting the feudal organization which he had inherited from his father. But the essential secularity of his policy has recently been emphasized afresh in a notable essay,[61] which also demonstrates the extent to which his rule anticipated many developments of a remote future which might be as distant as the eighteenth century. In the time of Henry I, for example, but not before, royal patronage began to be systematically practised as a means of government. And then for the first time this became what it always remained in England – a potent factor of social change.[62] Henry I raised men up to do his service and the history of England in the twelfth century could not be written without plentiful reference to the careers of such as Geoffrey de Clinton, Ralph Basset, Humfrey de Bohun, Eustace and Pain FitzJohn, William d'Aubigny and their like.

Even so, the full implications of this extensive use of royal patronage deserve the further emphasis they have now received. For these men needed to be rewarded, and the king recompensed them not only by grants of offices and exemption from taxes, but more particularly at the expenses of the older feudal families. Henry I was ruthless and adroit in exploiting the dues he could exact from his greater vassals, and in particular those payments he could extract by way of the wardship of heirs and the disposal of heiresses. As a result, the fortunes of nearly all his trusted officials would be founded on marriages to the heiresses of great estates. And these same officials unscrupulously used their wealth and power not only as royal agents to enrich their master, but also to advance their own careers.

They worked and paid for what they got, but they got what they paid for, generally in the form of other men's widows, daughters, heirs and lands.[63]

At the same time they were in a position to take advantage of every difficulty experienced by the older aristocracy in the shape of debts which could not be

[60] *Ibid.*, p. 444.   [61] Southern, 'Place of Henry I'.
[62] *Ibid.*, pp. 129, 130, 145, 146.
[63] *Ibid.*

paid or suits that could not be prosecuted. They also acquired from the king privileges and remissions of tax, and the perquisites of office.

Their success in these respects depended directly on the more sophisticated system of administration which was created during Henry I's reign. It was largely as members of the king's household, as purveyors of royal justices, as collectors of fines due to the king, that they waxed rich, and as manipulators of the royal finance at the Treasury, in the Exchequer and throughout the shires of England. Here it was that they found their opportunities, and these they seized. Government under Henry I was no longer a sacred duty but a matter of business. For his officials it provided the assurance of a career, and the means by which new families might be founded. Once again, all this anticipated many modern developments in English history which have challenged the attention of scholars:

> Whether the gentry were rising or falling in the century before 1640, they had certainly played a more important part in England since the twelfth century than anywhere else in Europe, and much of the credit for this – if it is a credit – must be given to Henry I.[64]

Ideals and principles, loudly voiced and sometimes realized in a theocratic society, such as medieval Europe aspired to be, found little place in the rule of England by this son of William the Conqueror. The motives which now impelled men to take part in the royal administration might be more aptly compared with those that are said to have prevailed in eighteenth-century England. It was the desire to better their families and their friends and to emerge richer than they began which inspired most of those who made so efficient the secular government of England by Henry I.

VII

Henry I and his advisers never propounded any theory of kingship; they were content to devise practical solutions to particular problems. A somewhat different atmosphere, however, came to pervade the Norman kingdom in the South after 1130. The new and influential principles which underlay the revolutionary conception of the royal power of Roger the Great were clearly displayed in the *assizes* which are alleged to have been promulgated at a council held by that king at Ariano in 1140.[65] More particularly were they

[64] Southern, 'Place of Herny I', p. 130.
[65] Falco Benev., s.a. 1140.

enunciated in the prologue which is made to introduce these legislative enactments. It is true that the value of this testimony is now made more difficult to assess in that a learned attempt has recently been made to refer both the assizes themselves and the prologue to a period subsequent to the reign of King Roger.[66] And both the feudal basis of Roger's power and his recognition of the diverse legal traditions in his realm have already been noted. On the other hand, most modern scholars accept the assizes and the prologue as representing conditions in King Roger's reign,[67] and as enactments made at an assembly at Ariano in 1140.[68] In any case, considerable complementary evidence could be cited to illustrate the new and revolutionary conception of royalty which became current in the Norman South during his reign.

A different emphasis was for instance now given to the older notion of the priest-king. It is as a law giver that the king now offers his work to God. For 'by this oblation the royal office assumes for itself a certain privilege of priesthood; wherefore some wise men, and learned in the law, called the law-interpretors the Priests of Justice'.[69] The reference is to the Digest, and 'the point of reference of this new ideal of priest-king was no longer the Anointed of the Lord but the Legislator as depicted in the law books of Justinian'.[70] Indeed, Roger himself makes precisely this claim: 'It is the duty and care of the king to declare laws, to govern the people, to promote good conduct and to punish malefactors.'[71] Small wonder that Romuald of Salerno could assert that King Roger promulgated his own laws in his kingdom, and by that means assured its peace.[72] It was as supreme legislator that Roger sought the sanction of his royalty, and the justification of his sovereignty.[73]

Power in his kingdom was thus concentrated in the person of the king, and the function of the king was to proclaim and enforce the law. His authority

---

66 Ménager, *Institution monarchique*, pp. 467–8; and *Cahiers*, II, pp. 303–31, 465–8.

67 E.g. M. V. Anastos, in *Twelfth Century Europe*, ed. Clagett, p. 167. And see the discussion reported in *Normanni*, pp. 599–615, especially the remarks of A. Marongiu.

68 E.g. Caspar, *op. cit.*, pp. 275–87; Jamison, *Apulia*, p. 255; Fuiano, *op. cit.*; and Kantorowicz, *King's Two Bodies*, p. 118, *passim*.

69 Prologue to Assizes.

70 Kantorowicz, *Laudes Regiae*, p. 100; cf. *King's Two Bodies*, pp. 117–23.

71 Prologue to Assizes.

72 Romuald, p. 226; Ménager, *Legislation sud-italienne*, p. 465.

73 See generally, A. Marongiu, 'Concezione della sovranta di Ruggero II', in *Studi Ruggeriani*, I, pp. 213–54.

was, moreover, made effective by a closely controlled hierarchy of officials established both at the centre of government and throughout the provinces. The Norman kingdom in the South thus emerged as a closely structured secular organization under a ruler who would share his judicial and political powers with no other party within or outside his kingdom. Here was a realm that in many ways anticipated the modern state, for its very existence offered a challenge to the whole conception of government which prevailed in Latin Christendom. Certainly, the kingdom of Roger the Great was unique in Europe. The only realm which in respect of the secularity of its administration could in any way be compared with it was that which had been ruled by Henry I and which would soon be governed by Henry II. Evidently the Norman rulers everywhere, and particularly in the South, had initiated in Europe a new development in secular government.

Chapter 7
SPIRITUAL AND TEMPORAL LOYALTIES

I

The rapid development of secular government in the Norman realms raised questions of vital consequence to the whole of Western Christendom. The Church became more deeply involved in its relationships with secular rulers, and Christians at large were confronted with new problems in reconciling the demands of their spiritual and temporal loyalties. Moreover, during these decades Western Christendom, albeit for these reasons often disturbed, had been materially strengthened against its rivals by the firm establishment of the powerful Norman kingdoms. Thus the papacy in its assumed leadership of Latin Christendom would not only be fortified by increased resources but would at the same time be confronted by a challenge to its political authority from the rulers of the new realms.

An element of paradox therefore might be detected in the Norman ecclesiastical impact on Europe at this time. It is tempting and just to visualize Henry I of England and Roger the Great of Sicily as outstanding opponents of ecclesiastical pretensions, but the growth of the Norman kingdoms took place at a time when Latin Christendom was experiencing a great revival to which the Normans had made their own contributions. The reforming papacy at an earlier date had owed much to the support of the Normans of the South, and the Norman invasion of England in 1066 had been blessed by a pope. William the Conqueror had fought at Hastings under a papal flag, even as at a later date Roger the Great and his sons would receive banners from the pope to indicate their legitimate tenure of papal fiefs.[1] The Norman rulers in the North and in the South were to pose as the friends of the Church, and this was of some significance when the Church was producing the first fruits of a great renaissance. Despite its violence, this was a profoundly religious age, and there can have been few among the ordinary folk of Western Christendom who could wholly escape from the circumambient atmosphere of a lively faith which by means of force, mansuetude or love commanded their unquestioning allegiance. The epoch that saw the flowering of such movements as those associated with Cluny and Camaldoli, of Chartreuse,

[1] Falco Benev., s.a. 1139; Romuald, s.a. 1139; Jaffé-Lowenfeld, I, p. 850; Caspar, *op. cit.*, Reg. 123b, p. 536.

Citeaux, Paremontré and Savigny must be acclaimed as a great period in the religious history of Europe. And in the fostering of religious orders and in the production of Christian saints the Norman kingdoms could claim their full share.

The Norman boasts of sympathy with the reformed Church were not in fact entirely misplaced. The Anglo-Norman realm was, for example, graced by two outstanding archbishops of Canterbury, Lanfranc and Anselm, who came to England from Italy by way of the Norman abbey of Le Bec Hellouin. The Normanization of the prelacy in England which followed the Conquest was not only astonishingly drastic, it was also judiciously effected. Some deplorable appointments were certainly made, but the new rulers of England were here guided in the main by the advice of great reformers in the Church such as Hugh abbot of Cluny or John abbot of Fécamp. Most of the Norman bishops who acquired English sees were conscientious and hard-working men, and often great builders whose work has endured to this day. Some of them, such as Gundulf bishop of Rochester, Robert bishop of Hereford and Osmund bishop of Salisbury (who was later canonized), left behind them a reputation for personal sanctity. In the same way, despite some lamentable exceptions, most of the new Norman abbots reputably discharged their duties, and brought to England 'a new discipline, and a new, or at least a revitalized, observance'.[2]

The consequences of these developments persisted throughout the earlier decades of the twelfth century. Thomas I archbishop of York, who survived until 1100, was the brother of Samson bishop of Worcester, who died in 1112, whilst Thomas II, archbishop of York from 1114 to 1140, was a son of Samson. Again, Abbot Paul of St Albans was a nephew of Archbishop Lanfranc, whilst Abbot Anselm of Bury St Edmunds (1121–48) was a nephew of St Anselm of Canterbury.[3] The first Norman king of the English has been justly described as a ruler who 'was resolved of set purpose to raise the whole level of ecclesiastical discipline in his dominions',[4] and the result of this would be apparent in the more difficult conditions which characterized the reign of Henry I from 1100 to 1135. Nor were these earlier traditions to be wholly lost even during the troublous years which followed the great king's death. During the civil war between Stephen and Matilda of Anjou the power of the monarchy over the Church in England suffered a sharp decline. But the ecclesiastical influence on English politics never waned.[5]

[2] Knowles, *Monastic Order*, p. 121.
[3] See Le Patourel, 'Norman Colonization', in *Normanni*, p. 422; Knowles, *Eng. Hist. Rev.*, XLV (1930), pp. 273–81.
[4] Knowles, *Monastic Order*, p. 99.   [5] Cronne, *Reign of King Stephen, passim*, esp. chap. 4.

In the South, too, the policy of the Norman rulers cannot entirely be described as anticlerical in tone. Europe was not allowed to forget that Sicily had been regained for Christendom by Norman arms, or that the Sicilian Church had been reconstituted by Norman action. The prelacy in the island and in the Norman provinces on the mainland does not seem to have been as distinguished as that in contemporary England, but at a slightly later date at least two prelates from the provinces, Romuald archbishop of Salerno and Alexander abbot of Telese, wrote admirable chronicles, whilst William bishop of Syracuse, who was himself probably a Norman, enjoyed a high reputation and was a friend of Adelard of Bath.[6] A long list of Roger the Great's benefactions to the Church could also be easily compiled. As count, for instance, he made grants to the abbeys of S. Filippo of Gerace and St Michael of Monte Scaglioso, and after he became king the monasteries of Grottaferrata, St Nicholas of Casale and S. Maria della Grotta at Marsala were among those which benefited from his largesse.[7]

Nor was the secular Church neglected. The cathedral of Trani was finished in 1139, and that of Melfi, which had been wholly built by the king, was completed in 1153.[8] Similar activity is also recorded as having taken place at Bitonto, Lecce, Barletta, Troia, and above all at Bari, where the great Norman church of St Nicholas was finished in 1139.[9] Further gifts during this reign were also made to the bishoprics of Taranto, Monopoli and Patti.[10] Roger the Great was the most secular minded monarch of his age, and he could be fairly denounced by ecclesiastical spokesmen as a menace to the existing structure of Christendom. But towards the end of his tumultuous reign he could pose with some success as the friend of both Cluny and Citeaux.[11] And some of the most intransigent exponents of the new political aspirations of the Church were constrained (perhaps for interested reasons) to praise him. As Peter the Venerable, the famous abbot of Cluny, declared:

> Before your time, Sicily, Apulia and Calabria were the refuge of the Saracens. But now through you they have become an abode of peace. They have been made into a magnificent kingdom ruled by a second Solomon.[12]

It is, however, as the resolute opponents of papal political claims that the Norman rulers of this age, and particularly Henry I and Roger the Great,

---

6 Haskins, *Medieval Science*, pp. 20–42; Douglas, *Norman Achievement*, p. 209.
7 Collura, Nos 20, 26, 30, 32, 36, 40, etc.   8 Curtis, *Roger of Sicily*, p. 395.
9 *Loc. cit.*   10 Collura, Nos 46, 47, 48, 56, 58, etc.
11 White, *Latin Monasticism*, pp. 163–5.   12 *Pat. Lat.*, 139.

will probably be most vividly remembered. Partly this was due to the firm character of these rulers, but it must also be considered in connexion with the general reaction which the new papal policy had provoked in all the king-doms of the West. For the papacy, with its theory of the ultimate supremacy and the unique sanctity of the papal monarchy, and with its insistence on the 'freedom of the Church from any temporal control', had offered a chal-lenge to all secular rulers of Western Christendom, not only the Norman Kings, but also the emperors, the Capetian dynasty and the princes of Christian Spain.[13]

II

None the less, Norman ecclesiastical policy at this time was not merely part of a conflict that was common to the whole of the Latin West. It possessed its own particular and individual characteristics, for in both the Norman realms the papacy could put forward demands for a special allegiance derived from past history. It was, for example, asserted that in the time of St Augus-tine of Canterbury the Church in England owed its establishment directly to Rome, and it was stressed that the Norman dynasty had been set up with papal support. The Norman rulers of England were therefore the vassals of the papacy, and the Norman kings owed fealty to the popes. Indeed it was concluded that this had been fully recognized by special payments from England to Rome of the tax known as 'Peter's Pence'.[14] The repudiation of these demands by William the Conqueror in his famous letter to Alexander II is well known:

> I have not consented to pay fealty, nor will I do so, because I never promised it, nor do I find that my predecessors ever did it to your pre-decessors.[15]

But the demand continued to be made with great consistency. In 1101, immediately after the accession of Henry I, it was renewed by Paschal II through the mouth of Anselm.[16] The question continued to colour much of the relationship between the Anglo-Norman monarchy and Rome and after

[13] Cf. Ullmann, *Papal Government*, esp. chaps IX and XIII.
[14] See Z. N. Brooke, *English Church and the Papacy*, p. 143.
[15] Lanfranc, *Opera*, p. 12; Douglas, *English Historical Documents*, II, No. 101.
[16] Z. N. Brooke, *op. cit.*, p. 151.

1135, when that monarchy entered on a period of weakness, it began to assume a greater significance.

The original conquests of the Normans in Italy and Sicily had been made with papal approval, and the earlier Norman rulers had performed homage to Rome in respect of the lands they had won.[17] These conditions had likewise persisted. Thus Duke William of Apulia had performed liege-homage for his duchy successively to Paschal II in 1114, to Gelasius II four years later, to Calixtus II in 1120, and to Honorius II in 1123.[18] Then when Roger the Great acquired Apulia after Duke William's death he was held to have inherited not only the duchy but the vassalage to the pope, which he duly performed to Honorius II in 1129.[19] Nor was this all. Anacletus II, the anti-pope, in his bull of 1130 successfully demanded liege-homage from Roger in return for recognition of the latter's Sicilian royalty,[20] and still more remarkably did Roger at the moment of his triumph over Innocent II at Mignano in 1139 proffer liege-homage to the defeated pontiff.[21] The significance of this relationship was later to be blurred by the social and political developments in Roger's Sicilian kingdom, but it was never to be forgotten at Rome, and after Roger's death in 1154 Pope Hadrian IV felt able to recognize Roger's son William as lord of the Sicilian dominions, but not to confer on him the dignity of king.[22]

In short, the popes of this age, and more particularly Paschal II, Honorius II and Innocent II, always demanded from the Norman realms both in the North and in the South something more than the normal obedience which they claimed from the Church as a whole. From the Church in the Norman lands they claimed the submission of a daughter, and they also demanded from the Norman kingdoms a recognition of political subordination.[23] Meanwhile the Norman kings, who from time to time protested, and sometimes displayed, a zeal for the reform of the Church, were ruthlessly successful in strengthening the power of the secular authority against all ecclesiastical encroachments. It is the combination of these factors which imparts a special interest and a general significance to the Norman impact on the Western

---

17 Holtzmann, in *Studi Ruggeriani*, I, pp. 39–40.
18 Chalandon, *Domination*, I, pp. 319–25.
19 *Regesta Pontificum*, VIII, No. 132, p. 36.
20 *Regesta Pontificum*, VIII, No. 127.
21 *Pat. Lat.*, 179, col. 478; *Regesta Pontificum*, VIII, No. 159, p. 42.
22 *Regesta Pontificum*, VIII, No. 177, p. 46.
23 For England in this respect, see Z. N. Brooke, *op. cit.*, pp. 177–9.

Church between 1100 and 1154, and more particularly to the changing relations between the Norman kings and the papacy during these years.

III

The first Norman king of England had shown himself not only a resolute defender of his temporal rights but also a supporter of the reforming movement in the Church. Indeed, the success of his uncompromising ecclesiastical policy was due not only to his own political strength, but also to his genuine concern for the welfare of the Church in his dominions. He could always in an emergency count on the support not only of Lanfranc, the great archbishop of Canterbury, but also of all the prominent ecclesiastics in his realm. During the fourteen years which followed his death in 1087, however, these conditions were substantially changed. William Rufus, violent and brutal, lacked none of his father's determination to resist the political claims of the papacy, but unlike his father he used his power to exploit the Church for his own gain. He was addicted in particular to the traffic in ecclesiastical appointments and to the appropriation of the property of the Church. William Rufus showed himself, in fact, precisely the type of secular ruler which the Hildebrandine papacy was justly most concerned to withstand, and the ecclesiastical esteem won by his father for the Norman monarchy in the Church was thus forfeited.[24]

There now grew up in England for the first time since the Norman Conquest a parity within the Church which might be prepared to support the pope against the king in a dispute between them.[25] Small in number, and at first of little power, this group received a great accession of strength with the appointment of St Anselm in 1093 as archbishop of Canterbury, for Anselm was not only a steadfast supporter of papal policy but also himself one of the most respected figures in the Western Church. In 1098 he made his views known on many of the points at issue during a session of a council held at Bari,[26] and he was soon to receive in the North ever increasing support from the monastic revival which was taking place in England. The Cistercian influence was now particularly strong in England. Indeed, from 1110 to 1133 the great abbey of Citeaux was under the rule of an Englishman, Stephen Harding, whose monastic constitution the Charter of Love (*Carta Caritatis*)

[24] *Ibid.*, chap. X.
[25] *Ibid.*, pp. 159–61.
[26] Hefele-Leclerc, VI (i), pp. 461–3.

as later confirmed by Calixtus II was accepted as a model for much of Western Europe.[27] Similarly, the greatest son of Citeaux, St Bernard of Clairvaux, came during the earlier half of the twelfth century to extend his influence over the whole of Latin Christendom, and not least to England.[28]

King Henry I at his accession thus faced a difficult ecclesiastical situation. There is no doubt that he wished to amend many of the abuses which had grown up during the reign of his brother, but he was naturally concerned lest his own monarchic authority should be sapped by political concessions to the Church, a problem related to the continuing dispute respecting the investiture of prelates which, although of general concern to the whole of the West, reached a climax in England during the early years of the reign of Henry I. The king claimed that he could not be indifferent to the appointment of men who were among the greatest of his feudal tenants. The papacy retorted that secular rulers, and notably William Rufus, had intruded many unworthy persons such as Rannulf Flambard bishop of Durham into high ecclesiastical office. The famous compromise was reached in 1107.[29] It recognized more clearly than ever before a distinction between the spiritual and temporal connotations of ecclesiastical office. The king gave up his claim to invest prelates with the rod and staff denoting their hierarchical authority in the Church, but he retained, with papal consent, the right to exact homage from all prelates in respect of their temporal possessions. This proved advantageous to the king, since he cleverly interpreted the arrangement as signifying that no prelate should be consecrated before he had rendered homage.

The appointment of bishops, however, was to remain a crucial issue between Henry I and successive popes. Here Henry I was able to retain much of his father's power, though he might always be resisted, as he was in the institution of the bishopric of Ely in 1109.[30] Nor can he be entirely acquitted of the malpractices which had disfigured the rule of Rufus. Thus, after Anselm's death in 1109, the king allowed the see of Canterbury to remain vacant for five years in order that he might collect the revenues for his own use. But in general the control he exercised over ecclesiastical appointments was not only effective but also generally creditable. On one matter, however, he was to suffer a considerable reverse. Like Roger the Great in Sicily at a later date, Henry was anxious that the whole Church in his English realm should be

27 Douglas, *English Historical Documents*, II, No. 115.
28 Cf. Ullmann, *Papal Government*, pp. 426–37.
29 Eadmer, *Hist. Novorum*. p. 186.
30 Bentham, *Antiquities of Ely*, pp. 219–26; Jordan, in *Moyen Age*, XXIV, p. 267.

united as a single province. He therefore wished to maintain the former temporary subordination of York to Canterbury, which had earlier been supported by documents forged during the primacy of Lanfranc. But papal judgement was eventually given in favour of the independence of the separate province of York, and Henry felt it wise not to resist.[31]

In all these disputes the crucial issue concerned the position which the papacy occupied in Christendom. No Norman king of England would have wished to create a national or independent Church, for all the Anglo-Norman kings would have recognized the supremacy within the Church of the pope who was acclaimed as the Vicar of Christ and the successor of St Peter. The policy of these kings was in fact confined to limiting the pope's authority (which was fully recognized) to strictly ecclesiastical affairs, and to resisting its extension towards a control of temporal matters. But in view of current theories of ecclesiastical functions such distinctions were very hard to draw. For that reason the delegation of papal authority to legates which might be sent to the various kingdoms of Europe became for the Norman governors of England – as indeed for the Norman rulers in the South – a matter of extreme difficulty and tension.

Among the 'customs' said to have been established by William the Conqueror was the stipulation that no papal legate or papal letter should enter England without the king's consent, and that no ecclesiastical council should be held within his realm without his permission. These rules, however, became increasingly difficult to enforce.[32] Controversy took place, for instance, between Henry I and St Anselm very early in the reign of the new king, and when in 1116 Anselm returned from the South with the legatine commission he was refused permission to enter England. Three years afterwards the matter was the subject of discussion between the king and Pope Calixtus II at Gisors, and in 1121 a papal legate named Peter Piereleone was admitted to England. Four years later he was followed by John of Crema, who actually held a legatine council in English. The royal protests were, however, vigorous, and in 1126 a compromise was reached whereby Honorius II appointed as his legate William archbishop of Canterbury. This arrangement, though not binding on the future, was acceptable to both parties. The pope acquired a permanent personal representative in England, whilst the king was saved from the perpetual threat of visiting legates.[33]

[31] Z. N. Brooke, *op. cit.*, pp. 170–3.
[32] Douglas, *English Historical Documents*, II, p. 68.
[33] Z. N. Brooke, *op. cit.*, 164–71.

1. The church of
S. Giovanni
degli Eremiti,
Palermo

2. (Above) *Interior of the Cappella Palatina, Palazzo Reale, Palermo*

3. (Right) *'The birth of Jesus Christ' — mosaic in the Cappella Palatina*

4. *Interior of the church of the Martorana, Palermo, founded by George of Antioch. The architecture is partly Norman and partly Arab*

5a. (Above) *'The Lamb of God', St Mary's Byton, Herefordshire*

5b. (Left) *The Prior's Doorway, Ely Cathedral*

5c. (Below) *Durham Cathedral from the north-west*

6a. *The emir George of Antioch at the foot of the Virgin – mosaic in the church of the Martorana*

6b. *The coronation of Roger the Great by Jesus Christ – mosaic in the church of the Martorana*

7a. (Above and below) *Seal of Stephen*

7b. (Right) *Seal of Matilda*

8a. *Seal of Henry I*

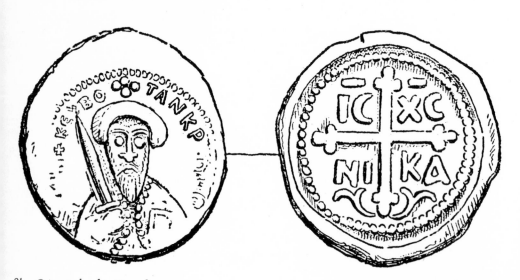

8b. *Coin attributed to Tancred*

On the whole, Henry I managed, in circumstances of increasing difficulty, to sustain the barriers which had been erected by his father against papal encroachment on English temporal affairs. But in the changed conditions of the twelfth century there was always something precarious in his ecclesiastical policy, and its success depended directly on the king's political strength. Thus it was that after his death in 1135 the disturbed reign of Stephen witnessed the final disruption of the special relationship which has been characteristic of the connexion between the Anglo-Norman monarchy and the reforming papacy. A new period in English ecclesiastical history was about to begin.

IV

The king was no longer able to exercise any effective control over the Church, and at the same time his own position became ever more dependent on ecclesiastical support. This was fully recognized in the charter he issued at the time of his coronation, and it was probably the papacy which was the chief agent in securing his succession. Innocent II, for instance, approved his claims in 1136, and this decision was confirmed at Rome after debate in 1139.[34] In this situation the power exercised by the papacy in England began steadily to increase. After the death of William archbishop of Canterbury in 1136, for instance, Cardinal Alberic was immediately sent from Rome to England as papal legate, and the king was compelled to acquiesce in the consecration by the legate of Theobald, William's successor at Canterbury. Even the fact that the most powerful man in the English Church was now the king's brother, Henry bishop of Winchester, did little to ease the situation, for Henry received the legatine commission and was in general obedient to the papal commands. In 1143 he signalized his independence by holding a legatine council, but in the same year he forfeited his papal office with the accession of Celestine II. The ecclesiastical weakness of the king was not, however, remedied, for in 1145 Lucius II sent a new legate, Cardinal Ymar, from Rome. Not until 1150 did Eugenius III in different circumstances restore the earlier situation by making Theobald archbishop of Canterbury his permanent legate in England.[35]

During the same years the king also lost his control over the appointment of bishops and abbots in England. Henry of Winchester as legate had made himself the effective agent in such appointments between 1135 and 1143.

[34] John of Salisbury, *Historia Pontificalis*, ed. Poole, pp. 107 et seq.
[35] Z. N. Brooke, *op. cit.*, pp. 180–3.

And in the following years, though 'free elections' were nominally guaranteed, it was in fact the pope or his agents who usually made the decisions. As a result, appeals to Rome which had been exceptional in the time of Henry I became ever more frequent, and the right of any prelate to make such an appeal was becoming generally recognized. In all these developments the influence of St Bernard, who took a keen interest in English affairs, was evidently pervasive. He was always opposed to Henry of Winchester, whom he distrusted as a secular prelate, but after Henry ceased to be legate, the saint was able to implant in England many of the more extreme papal claims. The process reached its climax after 1145 when St Bernard's pupil, Eugenius III, became pope, and papal influence on temporal as well as ecclesiastical affairs in England came to be dominant. The policy of the Church and of Rome was, for example, to be of decisive importance in securing the promise of the English succession to Henry of Anjou.[36] In short, the relationship between the spiritual and temporal powers which had been characteristic of Anglo-Norman England was destroyed between 1135 and 1154, and it would only be restored at a later date and with great difficulty. It is thus not with the reign of Stephen but with the conditions prevailing in the time of Henry I that the impact of the Normans of the South on ecclesiastical affairs needs to be compared.

V

The circumstances surrounding the achievement of royalty by Roger the Great in 1130 may be vividly contrasted with those that had attended the accession of Henry I in 1100. Certainly, Henry could by some be regarded as a usurper who had illegally seized the inheritance of his elder brother, Robert, and it was not until after 1106 that his power in fact became secure. On the other hand, the monarchy he had acquired had been blessed by the pope when it was established by his father, and many considered that it had made a substantial contribution to the reform of the Church. By contrast, the establishment of the Norman monarchy in Sicily in 1130 could be legitimately viewed as a revolutionary act. It was seen as a challenge to the empires both of the West and of the East, and as especially damaging to the papacy and to the unity of the Church.[37] The earlier alliance between the papacy and the Normans of the South had been definitely abandoned in 1124 by

[36] R. H. C. Davis, *Stephen*, pp. 121-3.
[37] See above, chap. 3.

Honorius II, who was determined to prevent the political union of Apulia, Calabria and Sicily under a single Norman ruler.[38] Considerable ecclesiastical consequences were to follow from this policy, since Honorius committed both the temporal and the spiritual prestige of the papacy to the venture. Besides collecting allies from among all Roger's opponents in south Italy, he also excommunicated the Sicilian count, and even preached a crusade against him promising indulgence to all those who took part in the holy war.[39] In the event this policy, with all its ecclesiastical connotations, proved a disastrous failure and in 1128 Honorius had been compelled to lift the excommunication, and to recognize Roger as ruler not only of Sicily but of all the Norman lands in Italy, including the principality of Capua.[40]

As Roger's greater subjects had been quick to realize, these conquests might justify the assumption of the title of king by the ruler of so wide a dominion. There was thus from the start an inherent opposition between the papacy and the Sicilian realm, whose establishment was regarded by many at Rome as an outrage. It was certainly not lawful, remarked one observer, since 'it is common knowledge that Sicily belongs to the patrimony of St Peter, and both Apulia and Capua were papal fiefs'. The king, however, claimed he had a right to do this, because after the Church of God had lost Sicily to the invading Saracens, his valour and that of his ancestors had restored it to the Faith.[41] It was a clear-cut confrontation.

Moreover, Roger had not only achieved royalty by means of a victory over the papacy. His triumph was also to be sanctioned from Rome by a pope who was soon to be denounced as an illegitimate occupant of the Holy See. From the standpoint of the ecclesiastical history of Europe, therefore, the early struggles of the Norman kingdom of Sicily can be viewed as an essential factor in promoting a prolonged schism in the Western Church. Thus during the first critical and perilous years of his reign the Norman king appeared before Europe as both the protégé and the foremost champion of Anacletus II against the legitimate pontiff Innocent II. The schism of Anacletus was in fact to affect the whole of Latin Christendom, and as a result the new Norman king was made the object of the most violent denunciation by prominent ecclesiastics from all over the Western Church. He was a tyrant. He was an ally of Saracens. He had intruded a Jew into the seat of St Peter. He was a

[38] H. Bloch, in *Traditio*, VIII (1952), p. 174.
[39] Falco Benev., s.a. 1127; *Regesta Pontificum*, VIII, No. 127, p. 34.
[40] See Chalandon, *Domination*, I, pp. 394–5.
[41] John of Salisbury, *Historia Pontificalis*, p. 69.

usurper of imperial rights. Most notable of all he was an oppressor of the Church whose integrity he aimed to destroy.[42] This was the constant theme in particular in the preaching of St Bernard. Roger had attacked the unity of Christian peoples which was embodied in the person of the Vicar of Christ.[43]

It was in such conditions that were built up the famous coalitions against the Norman king of Sicily. The king of France was here followed by the emperor and the king of England, and the incessant denunciations of St Bernard emphasized the crusading nature of the struggle. As a result southern Italy was plunged for nine years into a welter of war which implicated the rulers of France and Germany together with the cities of Genoa and Pisa, but in which the chief opponents were always the pope and the Norman king.[44] The conclusion of the conflict, and its character, were thus fittingly signalized when in 1139, a year after the death of Anacletus, Innocent II was brought before the king at Mignano as a defeated captive, and forced to ratify Roger's claim to be king of Sicily and, as such, legitimate ruler over all the Norman lands in Italy. Roger's royalty had thus been once again recognized by Rome, but this time by a legitimate pope who had been defeated in battle.

The long warfare which had been waged against successive popes with their allies, the defeat of Honorius II in 1128 and the humiliation of Innocent II in 1139, together with the invective which had been inspired by the schism, inevitably coloured all the relations between the spiritual and temporal authorities in the Sicilian realm, and in particular the relations between its ruler and successive popes. Here was a legacy of strife which had no parallel in the Norman kingdom of Henry I of England. Indeed, the ecclesiastical policy of Roger the Great was for these reasons in some sense set apart from that of any of his contemporaries. None the less, it is remarkable how many of the problems arising between Rome and Roger the Great concerned issues that had been of particular importance to Anglo-Norman England.

VI

The matter of papal legates is of special interest. The famous bull of Urban II[45] which is alleged to have conferred on the father of Roger the Great the

---

[42] H. Wieruszowski, in *Speculum*, XXXVIII (1963), pp. 54–62. Reference may be made in particular to the letters of St Bernard.

[43] Letters of St Bernard, *Pat. Lat.*, 182, Nos 127, 139, *passim*.

[44] See above, chap. 4.

[45] Malaterra, *Historia Sicula*, IV, c. 29; *Regesta Pontificum*, VIII, No. 81, p. 25.

power of a papal legate has been much criticized by scholars both in respect of its purport and its authenticity, and it has for generations been a subject of controversy.[46] Certainly, in the past, its significance has in some quarters been exaggerated, and any disruptions of the so-called 'Sicilian monarchy' which is said to have been thus created should be received with caution. In any case, so far as Roger the Great was concerned the grant to his father must be considered in the light of a letter[47] sent by Paschal II to Roger himself while still a count in 1117, wherein the privilege claimed by the ruler of Sicily seems to have been restricted to his right to put into effect the instructions of a legate sent *a latere* from Rome. It may even be that Urban himself in 1098 had conferred on the Great Count nothing more than the formal title of legate, and had granted him few, if any, powers greater than those which a few years later were assumed by Henry I of England. If this be so, the confirmation of privileges accorded to Roger by the anti-pope Anacletus II could hardly have included legatine powers. Certainly, during his reign, Roger the Great would make wide claims in this connexion, but while it would be rash to be dogmatic on so controverted a subject it seems probable that King Roger did not here inherit any specially privileged position from his father.[48] At all events, among the numerous concessions made to Roger by Innocent II at the moment of the pope's defeat in 1139, there is no mention of any legatine authority being vested in the Sicilian king.[49]

Like Henry I, however, Roger was always resolutely opposed to allowing any papal intervention in his dominions. He would suffer no papal legate to enter his territory, remarks John of Salisbury, except at his request or with his permission.[50] In this he followed the example both of William the Conqueror and Henry I, but he was more successful than they were and his acts were more provocative. For Roger here made no distinction between Sicily and his dominions of the Italian mainland, thus barring papal legates from entering Apulia where the pope had large and recognized feudal rights. He seems, moreover, to have been able to maintain his position with great consistency during the numerous disputes which inevitably ensued, and in 1149 Eugenius III was forced to give formal recognition to the claim that no papal legate should enter Sicily unless requested to do so by Roger.[51]

---

[46] Cf. Curtis, *Roger of Sicily*, Appendix 'A'.   [47] *Regesta Pontificum*, VIII, No. 104, p. 30.
[48] Ménager, in *Cahiers* (Poitiers), II, p. 318.
[49] *Regesta Pontificum*, VIII, No. 159, p. 42; Falco Benev., s.a. 1139.
[50] John of Salisbury, *Historia Pontificalis*, p. 66.
[51] *Regesta Pontificum*, VIII, No. 172, p. 45; Romuald, s.a. 1149.

As in England, too, even more acute tension was created in the matter of the appointment of prelates, and in the Sicilian kingdom this raised problems of exceptional complexity. After his coronation in 1130, Roger made or confirmed at his own pleasure episcopal appointments at Syracuse, Agrigento and Mazzara.[52] In 1131 he caused the Church of Lipari-Patti to be raised to the status of a bishopric, and he likewise demanded that Cefalú should be erected into an episcopal see.[53] Nor were such acts confined to Sicily, for similar arrangements were made on the king's behalf at Capua, Melfi and Chieti.[54] All these acts were moreover confirmed at Roger's request by Anacletus, who furthermore, on the king's demand, gave to the archbishop of Palermo permission to consecrate several of Roger's bishops. At the same time he raised the see of Messina to the status of an archbishopric.[55] The long wars that followed Roger's coronation during the schism of Anacletus were thus of cardinal importance to the Sicilian Church, for Innocent steadfastly refused to consecrate any of these prelates.[56] Nor would he do so even at the time of his surrender at Mignano. After 1139, therefore, there remained both in Sicily and on the mainland no less than fifteen bishops who were styled *electi*[57] – prelates who had been appointed by King Roger but who had been refused consecration by the legitimate pope. Great was the indignation at Rome. The king, it was said, 'instead of allowing any freedom of election named in advance the candidates to be elected, thus disposing of all episcopal offices as if they were palace appointments.'[58] But despite an uneasy compromise effected between the pope and the king in 1150,[59] these conditions do not seem to have been substantially changed during the remainder of King Roger's reign.

The matter was moreover complicated by another controversy. In the past the Sicilian bishoprics had all been directly subjected to Rome, whereas Roger now wished to introduce into Sicily a provincial organization subject in the first instance to the metropolitan direction of Palermo.[60] In this way he hoped (like Henry I with Canterbury) to be able to use a metropolitan see as a means of exercising his own dominance over the Sicilian Church, and he would thus

[52] *Regesta Pontificum*, VIII, No. 137, p. 37. Cf. Jordan, in *Moyen Age*, XXV, p. 32.

[53] Jaffé-Lowenfeld, No. 8422; Collura, Nos 42, 43.

[54] Cf. Curtis, *op. cit.*, p. 275.   [55] Jaffé-Lowenfeld, No. 8433.

[56] *Regesta Pontificum*, VIII, No. 164, p. 43.

[57] Cf. Curtis, *op. cit.*, p. 275.

[58] John of Salisbury, *Historia Pontificalis*, p. 65.

[59] *Ibid.*, p. 67.

[60] *Ibid.*, pp. 67, 68.

have been able to place the archbishopric of Palermo as a barrier between Rome and his own secular authority. Thus arose a new series of disputes with the papacy. After his surrender at Mignano, Innocent may have accorded to Roger the title of king, but he never yielded on the matter of the direct subjection of the Sicilian bishoprics to Rome. And his successors, particularly Eugenius III, would, in the same spirit, refuse to make other bishoprics the suffragans of Palermo.[61] Indeed, the matter was not to be finally settled during Roger's life. But two years after his death, by a concordat ratified at Benevento in 1156, a provincial constitution was at last given to the Sicilian Church, and Palermo was finally recognized as a metropolitan see.[62]

Throughout his reign as king, Roger maintained over the Church in all his dominions a control which was both strict and consistently exercised. In 1132, for instance, he promised the chief men of Bari that he would not appoint a stranger to be their bishop,[63] and three years later he could be seen settling a dispute between John, the bishop he had established at Patti, and Philip, the prior of St Philip of Argiro.[64] Again, in 1136 he confirmed to the churches of St Cosma in Cefalú and St John of Rocella their independence from the abbey of Holy Trinity Mileto, whilst in 1139 he ratified the union of the sees of Troina and Messina.[65] Then in 1141 the king was regulating the affairs of St Mary of Nardo near Lecce,[66] and during the next year he seems to have been particularly active in ecclesiastical affairs. In the spring of 1142, while still at Palermo, he settled a dispute between the church of St Nicholas and the abbey of Galati near Patti, and in passing over to Italy he gave judgement at Capua in a plea between the monastery of St Laurence in that city and John bishop of Aversa.[67] Such acts forcibly illustrate a policy directed towards extending the royal authority over the Sicilian Church at the expense of the papacy. And in 1151 Roger felt himself strong enough to have his son William crowned as king and as his successor by the archbishop of Palermo without any previous consultation with the pope.[68]

It is easy to appreciate the feelings of outrage with which Roger's ecclesiastical policy was received at Rome, where the papacy still cherished Hildebrandine traditions, and was, during these very years, being continuously

---

[61] Cf. Caspar, *op. cit.*, pp. 412 et sqq.
[62] Watterich, *Vitae*, pp. 352–5; also bull of Hadrian IV, *Pat. Lat.*, 188, col. 1471.
[63] *Cod. Dipl. Bari*, V, pp. 137, 138.   [64] Collura, No. 48.   [65] Collura, No. 50.
[66] Ughelli, *Italia Sacra*, I, p. 1045; cf. Chalandon, *Domination*, II, p. 107.
[67] Chalandon, *Domination*, II, pp. 108, 113.
[68] John of Salisbury, *Historia Pontificalis*, p. 69.

subjected to the stimulating and intransigent influence of St Bernard. 'The king,' said John of Salisbury, 'after the manner of tyrants, had reduced the Church in his dominions to slavery.'[69] Nor was it only in the matter of papal legates or episcopal appointments or even solely with the royal intrusion into ecclesiastical administration that the king of Sicily would come to be regarded in a special sense as the 'terror of the Church'. In all these matters a parallel could be found in the acts of Henry I, but there was always in the Sicilian kingdom a subtle difference in temper and a heightened emphasis in the royal opposition to the papacy.

VII

Both Henry I and Roger the Great were ruthless in extending their secular authority at the expense of the Church, but the background to their controversies with the papacy was in each case distinct. The Norman Conquest had brought England more directly into the political structure of Latin Christendom of which the pope continued always to be recognized as the spiritual head. Indeed, the fact that the Anglo-Norman kingdom had been established in some measure by papal favour was never wholly forgotten even during the reign of Henry I either in London or at Rome. Certainly the Normans had here followed their usual practice of harnessing older traditions to their service, but these had served in England to strengthen and not to weaken the original connexion. The Anglo-Norman realm owed much to great Italian ecclesiastics such as Lanfranc and Anselm, but the two notable archbishops of Canterbury were on the whole dutiful supporters of the papacy. An even greater debt was incurred by the Normans in England to Anglo-Saxon traditions. But here too it was a Christian legacy which the Normans seized, and it contributed to the efflorescence of spiritual life in England which marked the twelfth century. In Anglo-Norman England there was, in short, a clash between the Crown and the papacy on questions of administration. But there was never any question that the Church in England was an integral part of Latin Christendom, and to that extent subject to papal direction.[70]

The situation in Sicily was different. There the Norman kingdom had been established not by the favour of the papacy but in its despite, and the eclecticism which developed in the Norman South was of a wholly different character from the conditions in the North. Once again it was part of the Norman

---

[69] John of Salisbury, *Historia Pontificalis*, p. 65.
[70] Cf. Douglas, *William the Conqueror*, chap. 13; and *Norman Achievement, passim.*

policy to develop earlier traditions to their own advantage, but here those traditions were for the most part not those of the Latin West. Roger, for instance, was anxious to conciliate his Greek subjects. He himself understood Greek,[71] and he was indifferent to the points at issue between the Greek and the Roman Churches. In this way he came to be a notable benefactor to some of the basilican monasteries in his dominions. He made lavish grants to the Greek abbeys of St Maria del Patir, St Nicholas 'de Casalis' near Rossano, and St Salvatore 'de Lingua' near Messina.[72] Perhaps it was not without reason that King Roger was reputed to have delighted in the religious eloquence of a certain Greek prelate variously named as Theophano, or Filippo, who was also credited with having been at one time archbishop of Taormina.[73]

More significant is it that this Norman king of Sicily should have ordered ecclesiastical disputes in his realm to be tried by Greek officials of his court, as was the case in 1142 when Philip the protonotary gave judgement in a plea between a certain Geoffrey the Frank and Gerard bishop elect of Messina.[74] But the most notable illustration of Roger's Greek sympathies and their ecclesiastical connotations came in 1143 when he accepted with enthusiasm the dedication of the *History of the Patriarchates*, a work which had been written by one Neilos Doxopatros, a Greek priest in Palermo who had long been resident at Constantinople.[75] In this book the author sets out with emphasis the claims of Constantinople against the primacy of Rome, and Roger not only received these arguments with sympathy but showed consistent favour to Neilos himself.[76] In all this there was certainly a political motive which, so far as ecclesiastical politics were concerned, set Roger apart from any other ruler in the West. Henry I, for instance, might savagely dispute with the papacy the relative powers of the king and pope within Western Christendom, but here both pope and king would be regarded as essential powers within the Western Church which they professed to serve. Roger, on the other hand, was not reluctant to associate himself, against the Roman primacy, with a schism in the Church Universal.

Yet more revolutionary in the eyes of contemporaries was the policy adopted by Roger towards Islam. This was the age of crusades when Christendom

[71] Herval, in *Studi Ruggeriani*, p. 84.
[72] Collura, No. 57.
[73] Herval, *op. cit.*, pp. 85, 86.
[74] Cusa, *Diplomi Greci*, pp. 302–6; Collura, No. 67.
[75] Herval, *op. cit.*, p. 85.
[76] Chalandon, *Domination*, II, pp. 104, 110.

considered itself to be at war with Islam, but already Roger had shown himself indifferent to religious considerations in the acquisition and administration of the empire he had won in North Africa. And now the same tolerance and favour were shown towards his Moslem subjects at home, many of whom were welcomed into his intimacy.[77] Indeed his court was to contain many officials with Arab titles, and to be presided over by an 'Emir of Emirs',[78] and probably in 1137 King Roger entered cordial correspondence with the Fatimite caliph Al Hafiz.[79]

These contacts are most frequently cited in connexion with the efflorescence of literature and art in the Norman kingdom of Sicily to which the Greek and Arab subjects of King Roger the Great made so notable a contribution.[80] But it was their ecclesiastical implications which most forcibly affected the sentiments of contemporaries. Some parallel to Roger's conduct towards Moslems may perhaps be found in the earlier Norman government of Antioch by Tancred, though assuredly not to his attitude towards the Greeks.[81] But among his contemporary rulers in the West, Roger was unique, and for this reason throughout his reign he became the object of ever increasing mistrust and apprehension. Not only did he seem to be a promoter of schism, but during the very years when St Bernard was urging Western Christendom to undertake the Second Crusade Roger might almost be regarded as an ally of the Saracens. Perhaps, they said, he might himself have renounced the true Faith for the sake of Islam.[82] For could not the muezzin be heard in the streets of Palermo, and was there not already a harem in the Ziza? He was 'half a pagan',[83] and an enemy of the Church whose power he strove to weaken and whose unity he sought to destroy.

The overtones in these loud invectives are not to be heard without misgiving, yet in the conditions of the mid-twelfth century they are not difficult to explain, for at that time no ruler in the West displayed such open cynicism in his complete indifference to ecclesiastical loyalties. His administration was not only ruthless in its efficiency, it was also exclusively secular in its aims,

[77] Cf. Amari, *Storia Musulmani*, III, pp. 537 et sqq.; A. de Stefano, *Cultura in Sicilia*, pp. 5–28.
[78] See above, chaps 3 and 5.
[79] M. Canard, in *Studi Ruggeriani*, I, pp. 126–46.
[80] See below, chap. 6.
[81] See below, chap. 10.
[82] Letters of St Bernard, *Pat. Lat.*, 182, *passim*; Otto of Freising, *Chronica*, VII, c. 28; Falco Benev., s.a. 1130. Cf. Wieruszowski, *op. cit.*, pp. 53–79.
[83] *Annalista Saxo*, s.a. 1154.

and anticlerical in most of its consequences. Here in fact was a direct challenge to the political values and beliefs still prevailing, and venerated, in Christendom. None the less, a close comparison can still be made in this respect between Roger and Henry I of England. It is true that the Anglo-Norman king never ceased to proclaim the Christian basis of his power whatever may have been his personal sentiments, or to operate ostensibly within the accepted Christian conventions of the Latin Church. But what he achieved at the expense of the Church in the area of centralized administration might perhaps be estimated by reflecting that after the weakness of Stephen's reign, it needed the murder of an archbishop of Canterbury in his own cathedral before the earlier conditions could in some measure be restored.

Thus while Roger might be paradoxically termed the first modern ruler in medieval Europe, the contribution of Henry I to this same development is not to be ignored because of the more deceptive manner in which it was expressed. It was in Norman tracts composed in Rouen or York, and not at Palermo, that the overriding sanctity of kingly power was most forcibly expressed.[84] And the consequences of this might be the reverse of religious: they might lead to results strictly similar to those which were being prepared more openly in the Norman South. For if a king in either of the Norman realms could be accorded autonomy in the control of both the spiritual and temporal activities of his subjects, once again the way was opened for the proclamation of the modern secular state.

[84] Douglas, *Norman Achievement*, pp. 146, 172.

Chapter 8
THE MIND OF THE WEST

I

The Norman impact upon Europe between 1100 and 1154 was not confined to politics and government. It extended also into the sphere of culture, where its results were both durable and far-reaching. This was the more surprising since the Normans themselves produced few exponents of the arts and sciences, and singularly few writers or scholars of outstanding excellence. Crude and sometimes brutal, violent and astute, their genius lay in rulership and in the consolidation of power. But in the realms they ruled, there took place an astonishing cultural revival that was noteworthy even in an age which, throughout Latin Christendom, was marked by an efflorescence of literature, legal learning, scholarship and the arts – a revival to which the term 'twelfth-century renaissance' has been legitimately applied.

The brilliant contributions offered from the Norman kingdoms to the varied achievements of this renaissance were truly remarkable, but they were made for the most part by the peoples whom the Normans ruled rather than by the Normans themselves. The strange consequences which might ensue from the action of rulers who were stimulators of work by others rather than themselves creators can be illustrated by reference to familiar architecture. No buildings of this age are more deservedly famous than the Cathedral of Durham which continues to delight, and the Cathedral of Monreale which never fails to excite an astonished wonder. No two edifices could, moreover, be more different in general appearance. But neither of them would have been possible apart from the consolidation of the Norman kingdoms which took place between 1100 and 1154. To move from St Bartholomew the Great in London to the *Cappella Palatina* in Palermo is to travel into a different world. But both those worlds had been formed under Norman direction. In the sphere of culture it would seem that what was achieved during this brilliant period in the kingdoms governed by the Normans depended in large measure upon traditions which were not their own.

Henry I's England could provide a further example, for he had consolidated under Norman rule a kingdom which was already ancient when it had been conquered by his father. The older notion that Anglo-Saxon England was culturally decadent on the eve of the Norman conquest derives from a famous passage in the chronicle of William of Malmesbury which was to be elaborated in turn by John Milton and Thomas Carlyle and which is still reiterated in some quarters.[1] But today this opinion would be rejected by most scholars, and the productions of England in respect of the arts and sciences during the earlier half of the eleventh century should by no means be despised. Anglo-Saxon embroidery and metal work was then highly regarded, and the English coinage of that period can still be admired. Moreover, in the middle of the eleventh century Anglo-Saxon England was still continuing to produce a vernacular literature that was without parallel in Western Europe. England, before the coming of the Normans, might perhaps be described as politically decadent, but that decadence had evidently not yet substantially affected the civilization which the Anglo-Saxons had produced but which they could no longer defend.[2] Certainly, the Norman kingdom consolidated by Henry I was built upon ancient foundations, and all its activities, cultural as well as governmental, owed much to the past.

None the less, learning and literature in England were to be profoundly affected by the establishment of the Norman political order. There can be no question that Henry I ruled in England over a kingdom which had been made more intimately than ever before an integral part of Latin Christendom, and this at a time when the Latin culture of Europe was undergoing its great revival. The results to England were indeed to be spectacular, both in loss and gain. The vernacular literature which had been produced in Saxon England was almost brought to an untimely end. Links can sometimes be found between the productions in Anglo-Saxon of the early eleventh century and the beginning of a literature in 'middle English' in the fourteenth,[3] but it remains generally true that in the interval, during the reigns of Henry I and his immediate successors, a transformation took place so that almost everything of distinction which was then thought and written in England was thought and written in Latin.

It is true that one of the recensions of the Anglo-Saxon Chronicle was continued in the vernacular until 1140, but its entries become less authoritative, and they stand alone. On the other hand, the reign of Henry I was marked by

---

[1] Will. Malms., sect. 245; Milton, *History of Britain* (1695), pp. 356, 357; Stubbs, *Constitutional History* (quoting Carlyle) (1891), I, p. 236.

[2] Darlington, in *History*, XXVIII (1912), pp. 1–13.

[3] R. W. Chambers, 'Continuity of English Prose', in his edition of *Nicholas Harpsfield's Life of More*.

a great revival in England of the Latin chronicle.[4] A distinguished list of outstanding names is easily made. There was, for instance, Eadmer, who not only wrote a general history of considerable value, but who also compiled a fine Latin life of his hero, St Anselm, archbishop of Canterbury. There was Simeon of Durham, whose extensive productions related not only to the north but also to the general history of England. Many lesser names could also be included, such as that of Ailred of Rievaulx, whose account of the Battle of the Standard (1138) included one of the finest contemporary appreciations of the corporate influence on Europe of the Normans, through whom 'fierce England fell captive, sumptuous Apulia was made to flourish anew, whilst far-famed Jerusalem and noble Antioch were brought to surrender'.[5] Other names might easily be added such as Henry of Huntingdon and the continuator of the chronicle ascribed to Florence of Worcester.

Eminent among this brilliant group of writers was William of Malmesbury, whose great *Deeds of the Kings* was finished in 1125, whilst its sequel, the *Modern History*, was written between 1140 and 1142.[6] These were, moreover, only the most important of his numerous productions, and he had some justification for his own claim to be the successor of Bede after a long interval, for with him and his fellows the writing of the Latin chronicle in England was brought to a new pitch of perfection. These historians wrote with penetration in the language common to the whole of the West, and they approached the problems of history in a manner which could command a general rather than a provincial interest. Yet even here something of the paradox implicit in the Norman contribution to European culture can be detected. Many of these men had at least one English parent,[7] and most of them were concerned to picture England as their *patria*. They extolled the Norman regime which they served; they were conscious of their part in a revival which stretched all over the Latin world; but they wrote of England as of a country which they regarded as their own.

None the less, the transition symbolized in their work is very notable, and it was exhibited with even greater clarity in other quarters. Men from England were to make their essential contribution to the diverse productions of Latin Europe during this age. But their work was not specifically addressed to the kingdom from which they came, and they regarded their labour as part of a larger enterprise common to the whole of Latin Christendom. Thus

[4] Douglas, *English Historical Documents*, II, esp. pp. 97–102.
[5] *Chronicles of Stephen*, ed. Howlett, II, pp. 318–19.
[6] Will. Malms., I, pp. lx–cxlvii.   [7] Darlington, *Anglo-Norman Historians* (1947).

although such men as Robert of Hereford, Walcher of Malvern and Anselm abbot of Bury St Edmunds will demand citation in different connexions,[8] they may here be noted as sharing in certain common characteristics. They all wrote in Latin; they all travelled extensively in Europe; and they all received most of their instruction and much of their inspiration from overseas. In all these respects they represented the conditions which had come to dominate English learning during the earlier decades of the twelfth century.

No better examples of the consequences of these changed conditions could be found than in the careers and productions of Adelard of Bath and John of Salisbury.[9] Adelard of Bath flourished in the time of Henry I, and he received his training in scholarship not in the West Country from which he came but in the schools of France, notably Tours and Laon. Afterwards he travelled widely, visiting Norman Sicily before 1109, and his journeys probably extended into Syria. The inspiration he received from his travels was derived mainly from his contacts with Greek and Arabic learning, and his own production was truly remarkable both for its quality and its range. His writings extended from trigonometry to astrology, and from Greek philosophy to the elements of applied chemistry. He translated from the Arabic versions of both the *Elements* of Euclid and the important astronomical tables of Al Khwarizmi. He also possessed an adequate, though not an extensive, knowledge of Greek. His mathematical skills have attracted admiration, and while in philosophy he might be regarded as a pupil of Plato, he has also been claimed as the first Latin writer of the Middle Ages to cite Aristotelian physics. Such a man from Anglo-Norman England was an ornament to the flourishing European learning in his day. It is therefore highly significant that he was a member of the court of King Henry I, and probably an official in the royal exchequer.[10] His career in scholarship must have been made to some extent under the patronage of the Norman king.

Equally illuminating is the career of John of Salisbury.[11] He was born about 1120 and survived until 1180, and he has been saluted as the 'leading figure in English scholarship for thirty years'. His production too was large and varied, though unlike that of Adelard more literary than scientific. Perhaps his most notable book was his *Policraticus* or 'Courtiers Trifles and Philosophers' Footprints', wherein his wide-ranging erudition was employed in a

[8] See below, pp. 151, 152.
[9] Haskins, *Medieval Science*, chap. II.
[10] R. L. Poole, *Exchequer*, pp. 51–3.
[11] C. C. J. Webb, *John of Salisbury* (1932).

constructive criticism of the principles and practices of government. He also wrote admirable biographies of St Anselm and St Thomas Becket, whilst his *Historia Pontificalis* is an illuminating series of memoirs of the papal court where he was resident for many years. John of Salisbury has been the subject of an extensive literature,[12] but he may be commemorated as illustrating the transformed temper of English scholarship in his time. His fine humanism was notable even in that age, inasmuch as nothing human failed to interest him. He was moreover well versed in the classics and he wrote with a feeling for formal perfection that was wholly admirable. Like all the greater English scholars of that period he was a widely travelled man. He received his formal education in the schools of northern France, and remained a cosmopolitan scholar. 'I have ten times passed the chain of the Alps,' he wrote in 1159. 'I have twice traversed Apulia.'[13] He was indeed a moving witness to the community of minds among the Latin-writing and Latin-speaking clerical world of the twelfth century[14] – the world into which England had been brought under Norman rule in the time of King Henry I.

II

To ensure that England should make an outstanding contribution to the corporate culture of Western Europe in the twelfth century was not the least of the Norman achievements, but it was matched by what they accomplished in the South, where the results which flowed from the establishment of their Sicilian kingdom were equally important and even more spectacular. The various influences from so many quarters which contributed to the character of the Sicilian realm of Roger the Great have already been noted in connexion with the development of secular and ecclesiastical government under him.[15] They were, however, to be displayed even more notably in the propagation of the arts and sciences, and in the production of works of learning and literature. And it was precisely here that the Sicilian Norman kingdom would produce its most profound effects on Latin Christendom during the twelfth-century renaissance.

In the middle of the twelfth century the Norman kingdom in the South was marked by an eclectic and highly sophisticated civilization which was

[12] C. Brooke, *Twelfth-Century Renaissance*, pp. 53–74.
[13] Cf. Douglas, *Development of Medieval Europe*, p. 275.
[14] C. Brooke, *op. cit.*, p. 74.
[15] Above, chaps 6 and 7.

then unique in Western Europe. Scholars and writers from all over the Latin West, and particularly from Italy and Provence, mingled in Norman Sicily with Islamic writers who represented the Moslem population from whom the island had so recently been taken. And there were also Greek-speaking men of letters who had continued to flourish in Apulia and Calabria under Byzantine rule, and who now came with their fellows to the royal Norman court to foster the connexion between Sicily and the Eastern empire.[16] The intellectual and artistic revival which began under Roger the Great in the Norman South was thus derived from Latin, Greek and Arabic traditions. This was indeed the 'glory of Trinacria the three cornered island'[17] in the twelfth century, and especially in its middle decades.

To isolate these elements would, however, not be easy, any more than it would be easy to separate the Frankish, Greek and Moslem contributions to the characteristic buildings of Norman Sicily, such as the Cathedral at Cefalú or, at Palermo, the Palatine chapel with its wonderful mosaics and pointed arches, or the church of the Eremiti with its oriental domes and its structure in the form of the Cross. It is true that there is little in Palermo to compare with the unequivocal romanesque magnificence of St Nicholas at Bari, but the speech of northern France was heard, and may well have been predominant, at Roger's court. Nor was this the only importation from the Norman North. Echoes of the *Song of Roland*, so clamant and so haunting, coloured many of the traditions of the Norman South, and later legends of Charlemagne actually caused the 'Peers of France' on their way from the Holy Land to give two mountains in Sicily the names of Roland and Oliver.[18]

As in England, though with less distinction, the Latin impact on Norman Sicily could also be illustrated in contemporary Latin chronicles. The traditions earlier established by William of Apulia and Geoffrey Malaterra were sustained in the time of Roger the Great.[19] Just across his northern frontier, Falco of Benevento wrote a hostile history of the Norman realm,[20] and within the Norman kingdom Alexander abbot of Telese completed before 1144 his admiring account of the acts and achievements of King Roger.[21] Assuredly

---

[16] A. de Stefano, *Cultura in Sicilia* (1954); R. Herval, 'Eclecticisme intellectuelle à la cour de Roger II', *Studi Ruggeriani*, I, pp. 73–104.

[17] Jamison, *Eugenius*, p. xvi.

[18] C. Curtis, *op. cit.*, pp. 405, 406.

[19] Cf. E. Paratore, in *Studi Ruggeriani*, I, pp. 167–82.

[20] I, pp. 161 et sqq.; cf. Chalandon, *Domination*, I, pp. xli–xlvi.

[21] I, pp. 85–148; cf. Chalandon, *Domination*, I, pp. xlvi–xlix.

this production in the South was not comparable in quality with the historical work that had been completed in the Anglo-Norman kingdom, but it was not negligible, and it would be continued. Thus Romuald, archbishop of Salerno from 1153 to 1181, won fame as an historian,[22] and equally distinguished was the work known as the *Book of the Kingdom of Sicily*,[23] traditionally attributed to a certain Hugo Falcandus who apparently came from Normandy late in the twelfth century, although its author may possibly have been none other than the emir Eugenius who began his career under Roger the Great and continued it under his successors.[24] In any case, it is a remarkable production, illustrating the history of Sicilian kingdom in the latter half of the twelfth century with plentiful references to its earlier development.

The distinguishing character of the civilization developed in the kingdom of Roger the Great did not, however, come from the North, or even, in the main, from the Latin world at all. Geographically, Sicily is ideally placed to act as a bridgehead between Greek and Latin culture, and Roger the Great was eager to seize the opportunities which had been offered him. In many parts of the kingdom, such as Apulia and Calabria, there was a large Greek-speaking population and in the numerous basilican monasteries there were fine libraries containing many Greek books of biblical and theological learning. The importance of this to the developing relations between the spiritual and temporal authorities in the Norman South has already been noted, particularly in connexion with the controversial works of Neilos Doxopatros,[25] but during the earlier half of the twelfth century there was undoubtedly an influx of Greek books of all types from Constantinople into Calabria and Sicily; and the new libraries of San Salvatore near Messina and S. Maria del Patir in Rossano are said to have been particularly enriched.[26] It was therefore in especially favourable conditions that King Roger exercised his patronage of Greek scholarship and sponsored a revival which was to reach its climax in the years immediately following his death. Latin versions of the *Optics* of Euclid and of Aristotle's *Logic* were already in circulation in Sicily between 1154 and 1160.[27] Thus was the work of Sicilian translators from Greek into Latin beginning to affect the mind of Europe.

---

[22] Muratori (ed.), *Script. Ital.*, VII, pp. 1–246; cf. Chalandon, *Domination*, I, xlix–lii.

[23] Siragusa (ed.), *Scrittori*; cf. Chalandon, *Domination*, I, pp. lii–lxi.

[24] Jamison, *Eugenius*, pp. 177–278.

[25] See above, p. 137.

[26] Herval, *op. cit.*, p. 24; Haskins, *Medieval Science*, p. 142.

[27] Haskins, *Twelfth-Century Renaissance*, p. 293.

The two most familiar names are those of Henry 'Aristippus' and his younger contemporary Eugenius the emir.[28] Both produced most of their work after 1154, but it was under Roger the Great that they first rose to eminence. Henry 'Aristippus' has often been considered to have been of Greek stock, but he was more probably a Norman secular clerk, and is particularly noteworthy for his renderings into Latin of the Platonic dialogues of the Meno and the Phaedo in translations which were not to be superseded until the fifteenth century. He became archdeacon of Catania in 1156 and died in 1162. Eugenius the emir, who was born about 1130, belonged by contrast to a Greek family that had settled in Palermo. Greek was thus his native language, and between 1158 and 1162 he composed some twenty-four poems in his mother-tongue. But he had already made himself proficient in Latin, and very early in life he took part with 'Aristippus' in the preparation of a translation from Greek into Latin of the *Almagest* of Ptolemy. He had also become keenly interested in the problems of physics, chronology and mathematics, and with this stimulus he added a knowledge of Arabic to his other skills. Thus equipped, he translated into Latin the Arabic version of the original Greek text of the *Optics* of Ptolemy. He was to survive to an advanced age, and he may be viewed as a link between the Greek and Arabic elements in Sicilian civilization in the kingdom of Roger the Great.

The Arabic influence on the Norman kingdom in the South has been plentifully illustrated in the work of modern historians, who have properly seen in it one of the most remarkable phenomena in the growth of medieval Europe.[29] Even to contemporaries it was a matter of wonder and surprise. Thus some thirty years after Roger's death Ibn Athir, the Moslem historian, wrote of him:

> He adopted the customs of Moslem kings with regard to the officers he appointed to his court. Here he departed from the usual practice of the Franks who did not comprehend the functions of such officials. Roger, moreover, always treated Moslems with great honour. He was familiar with many of them, and favoured them even against the Franks.[30]

Similar eulogies could be found in the works of contemporary Arab poets such as Ibn Baroum, Abd ar Rahman and Abd al Daw, with whom Roger was on terms of friendship, whilst Omar ibn Hassan voiced his gratitude for

[28] Jamison, *Eugenius, passim.*
[29] Cf. Amari, *Musulmani, passim.*
[30] Amari, *Bibl. Arabo-Sicula*, I, p. 433.

the protection he had received from the Sicilian king.[31] It is small wonder that these Moslem poets repaid with eulogies the favour they received. 'The face of this king,' it was said, 'shines on the darkness. The sun might be envious of him for he has pitched his tent where the Gemini rise.' The hyperbole has an oriental tone which is reproduced in the descriptions given of the dwellings of this Norman ruler. 'Behold the Palace of the king,' cries Ibn Omar, a commentator of the Koran. 'It is there that joy dismounts to make her dwelling.'[32] 'Oh Favara,' writes Abd ar Rahman, 'palace of two seas. You display all that man could desire for a life of pleasure amid splendid surroundings. Love may sate itself beside your lakes, and passion make its joyful dwelling beside your streams.'[33] The whole atmosphere is that of the palace of a sultan with its sumptuous decorations, its harem, and its unrestrained luxury.

Many of the consequences of the favour which King Roger showed to his Moslem subjects, and of the welcome he extended to Arab craftsmen and scholars, have survived to this day. Thus Palermo in his time was famous for the products of its Moslem weavers, and Roger not only sustained them but in 1147 brought in Greek weavers from Dalmatia to enrich their work from Byzantine traditions.[34] Undoubtedly Greek artists under Norman direction also made a dominant contribution to the great churches which came to adorn Palermo at this time, but few would deny some Saracenic features in the *Cappella Palatina* which was built in 1132, in the Martorana which arose in 1136, or in the fortress of the Ziza which seems to have been completed in 1154. Arabic studies, too, particularly in science and mathematics, were vigorously pursued in Sicily between 1130 and 1154 under the king's encouragement.[35] Roger himself, it is said, was particularly interested in geography, and certainly it was at his command that one of the great works of Arab learning, the *Geography of al Idrisi* (Edrisi), was undertaken, and at last completed in 1154 'for the comfort of those who wish to go round the world'. The king's share in this enterprise, and particularly in the great map with the Arabic commentary which accompanied it, was apparently very large, inasmuch as he called to his court many Arab travellers to supply him with additional information. As a result, the work was eventually to be styled the

---

31 Herval, *op. cit.*, pp. 90–110.
32 Quoted Herval, *op. cit.*, p. 92.
33 *Ibid.*, p. 94.
34 Curtis, *op. cit.*, p. 400; Arnold (ed.), *Legacy of Islam*, p. 169.
35 Stefano, *Cultura in Sicilia*, pp. 12–24.

'Royal Book' and dedicated with lavish praise to the 'great King whom Heaven has loaded with glory and power'.[36]

It was at all events yet another example of the patronage offered by Roger the Great to the tripartite culture which marked his Sicilian reign and which made Palermo 'the happy city of the three-fold speech'. The range of that revival to which so many men of such diverse origins contributed included the constructive work of Greeks from Apulia and Calabria, of Moslems from Sicily, Spain and North Africa, and of Latin scholars from the Italian main-land, and many others came from even further afield to share in the stimulus inspired by this corporate endeavour. It extended over the fields of classical learning and philology. It embraced mathematics and science. And it pro-duced translations from the Greek and the Arabic which were to have lasting influence. When, moreover, it is recalled that an important group of New Testament manuscripts can be traced to scribes at Roger's court, some further indication of the scale of this activity is supplied. The intellectual interests and productions of Sicily under its first Norman king were in truth astonish-ing.[37]

III

The Normans, therefore, albeit themselves seldom interested or creative in the things of the mind, were none the less able between 1100 and 1154 to establish conditions in which such interests might be fostered in the realms they ruled. Was there in this respect also a connexion between the Norman realms of the North and of the South, and did those kingdoms, either separ-ately or together, exercise during these decades a special or individual influ-ence on the renaissance within Latin Christendom which was to reach its climax before the twelfth century had closed?

There is of course no question of England before 1154 having the same direct contacts with the Greek and Moslem worlds of culture which were enjoyed in the Norman kingdom of the South. But in the time of Henry I the Anglo-Norman realm was made a part of Latin Christendom, and, as such, it established new European connexions just at a time when, owing to Norman action, the Mediterranean was once again becoming the centre of Europe's cultural gravity after a long decline.[38] It is not surprising, therefore,

[36] Arnold, *op. cit.*, pp. 89–92; V-F. Gabrieli, in *Studi Ruggeriani*, pp. 115–25.
[37] Haskins, *Medieval Science*, p. 143.
[38] Southern, *Making of the Middle Ages*, p. xi.

that a closer relationship should have developed between the Normans of the North and of the South. Men such as Robert of Selby, Thomas Brown and Henry of Blois bishop of Winchester were familiar figures at the courts both of Henry I and Roger the Great, and while their influence was mainly exercised on matters of government and administration, it also extended into the fields of literature and the arts.[39] The great Anglo-Norman historian, Ordericus Vitalis, writing about 1142, was already fully aware of this. It is astonishing how conscious he was of the unity of the Norman world in his time, and how well informed he was about achievements of the Normans in Italy and Sicily.

These connexions are particularly interesting in respect of the extension of Greek culture into the West.[40] What has been described as the 'natural link between the Norman empires in Sicily and England' explains for instance the powerful effects of Byzantine example on English painting in the early half of the twelfth century.[41] Thus the work of the *scriptorium* at Winchester in the time of Bishop Henry of Blois shows the Byzantine influence on the craftsmen he employed, and there can be little doubt that this was derived through the medium of Sicily. The decorations of the famous Winchester bible for instance recall the frescoes at Monreale,[42] and still more notable is the similarity between the illustrations in the psalter prepared for Henry of Blois about 1150 and the mosaics in the church of the Martorana in Palermo which had been given to the Virgin by the emir George of Antioch in 1143. The wall-paintings in the chapel of St Anselm in Canterbury Cathedral can be compared both as to subjects and treatment with some of the most famous mosaics in the *Cappella Palatina* erected by Roger the Great in his Sicilian capital.[43] Such interconnexions can be traced even in the region of popular folklore. The Normans, it would seem, brought with them Celtic legends from Britain to the South, since before the twelfth century had closed it was apparently believed in some quarters that King Arthur of the Round Table had found his last resting-place under Mount Etna.[44]

Equally important, and more complex, are the problems raised in respect of the transmission of Arabic science to the West during this period. The

[39] Haskins, *Renaissance of Twelfth Century*, p. 61.

[40] M. V. Anastos, 'Byzantine Influence on Latin Thought', *Twelfth Century Europe*, pp. 131–59.

[41] C. Brooke, *op. cit.*, pp. 146 et sqq.   [42] Demus, *Mosaics of Norman Sicily*, p. 451.

[43] Brooke, *op. cit.*, Plates 115, 116, 117, 118 – a superb sequence.

[44] Curtis, *op. cit.*, p. 405.

essential and dominant part played by Moslem Spain has long been recognized, and it was clearly by way of the Iberian peninsula that most of Arabic
science known to Latin Christendom in the twelfth century was derived.
However, a large part of the scientific knowledge of twelfth-century Spain
had been acquired from Arabic translations of Greek and Latin texts, such
as Greek versions of works of Ptolemy and Euclid and Latin renderings of
fragments from Aristotle and Hippocrates.[45] Thus, while pride of place must
certainly be given to the schools of Toledo, Palermo had the advantage of
direct contact with the Greek East, and direct knowledge of the works of
Greek science and philosophy which were known in Spain only through
Arabic translations and summaries.[46]

Any precise assessment of the relative importance of Spain and Sicily in
the transmission of Arabic science would be impossible here, but the situation in England is particularly relevant.[47] Moslem science came to England
in the earlier half of the twelfth century mainly through the medium of a
converted Spanish Jew called Peter Alfonsi who sometime after 1106 was
physician to Henry I. Closely associated with him were men such as Robert
of Hereford, who was particularly interested in Arabic studies of chronology,
and Walcher of Malvern, who introduced England to the use of the astro-
labe.[48] Most notable of all, however, was Adelard of Bath. It is usually
assumed that Adelard derived the bulk of his scientific interests and knowledge from Spain. But his travels through other lands, however, and particularly through Sicily, are well recorded, while it is not known for certain
whether he ever personally visited Spain.[49]

IV

After 1154 the influence exercised as from the Norman kingdoms on the
mind of Europe began rapidly to diminish, and as a specific factor in the
history of European culture it would soon cease to exist.[50] At the same time
notable changes began to appear in the cultural interests of the West.

It would for instance be easy to exaggerate such modifications as took place
in the character of the 'twelfth-century renaissance' during the latter half of

---

[45] Haskins, *Medieval Science*, pp. 2–19.   [46] *Ibid.*, p. 159.
[47] Southern, 'The Place of England in the Twelfth-Century Renaissance', *History*, XLV
(1960), pp. 201–16.   [48] *Ibid.*, pp. 210–11.
[49] Haskins, *Medieval Science*, pp. 20–41.
[50] Below, pp. 214–17.

the twelfth century, but undoubtedly some significant alterations of emphasis can be detected. Letters, for example, began to move from epic towards romance.[51] The standard literature of feudal society, the *Chanson de Geste*, began to give way to romantic fantasies devoted to Tristan or Lancelot or King Arthur.[52] There still remained, of course, the imperishable poetry of the *Song of Roland*, but in a literary world dominated by Eleanor of Aquitaine, the wife of the first Angevin king in Norman England, men were beginning to respond more readily to the fascinations of chivalry and courtly love than to the inspirations of the Holy War. A comparable transition can be observed in religious art.[53] In representations of the Crucifixion, the formal Christ crowned and triumphant in death begins to give way to the dying figure racked by all the attributes of pain, and realizing the extreme limits of human suffering. Thus, too, was the theme of the Virgin and Child also affected. The child enthroned on his mother's knee and blessing the world gradually began to give place to the laughing, playful or even caressing child dear to later medieval piety. And the so-called 'Gothic' churches soon to arise all over the West can be contrasted with the massive 'romanesque' edifices with their great rounded arches which were characteristic of the earlier half of the twelfth century.

Although these transitions began during the period when Norman influence on the West was rapidly declining, the consequences of what had been achieved for Europe in the Norman realms between 1100 and 1154 continued to be felt during the ensuing decades with results that were sometimes surprising, and even contradictory. Thus the *Chansons de Geste* obviously reflected better than stories of King Arthur and the Holy Grail the aggressive spirit of a warrior people that had imposed a king upon England, captured Palermo, and, with Bohemund, stormed the walls of Antioch. But at the same time it must be remembered that Geoffrey of Monmouth, from whom so many of the Arthurian legends were derived, finished his *History* before 1140 in the Norman North. Similarly, some of the later transformations in religious art were likewise foreshadowed in Norman England. One of the earliest expressions of the developing cult of Our Lady is, for instance, to be found in the writings of Anselm, abbot of Bury St Edmunds from 1121 to 1148,[54] the nephew of the great archbishop who bore the same name.

51 Southern, *Making of the Middle Ages*, chap. V.
52 C. Dawson, *Medieval Essays*, pp. 175–84, 193, 199.
53 Southern, *Middle Ages*, chap. V; Brooke, *op. cit.*, 90–106.
54 Douglas, *Feudal Documents from Bury St Edmunds*, pp. cxxxv–cxxxvii.

And this same abbot was particularly influential in the early propagation of the 'Miracles of the Virgin' which later achieved such influential popularity.[55]

Similarly, one of the most authoritative recent contributions[56] to the controversies respecting the origins of 'Gothic' architecture lays emphasis on the fact that the pointed arch came to Western Europe from the East, and mainly through the medium of the Moslem world; and no visitor today to the *Cappella Palatina* in Palermo can doubt the part played by the Norman kingdom of Sicily to the process. Nor in this matter is the Norman realm in the North to be disregarded. Some indications of the new style have been seen even in Durham. And it has also been suggested that Adelard of Bath, who was interested both in Greek applied mathematics and in Arabic architecture, may have had some part in solving the technical problems connected with the construction of the new high vaults, and may thus have been one of the agents responsible for the introduction of 'Gothic' architecture into the West.[57] Even in the sphere of learning the same problems could be posed. It would be singularly foolish to credit the Normans with any direct influence either in creating the earliest of the great medieval universities towards the end of the twelfth century or with the rapid development of theological erudition in the thirteenth. None the less, if scholastic theology owed much to the study of formal logic, note should be taken of the Aristotelian studies which were practised in Sicily between 1130 and 1154. And in any account of the early history of universities in Western Europe reference must be made to the organized school of medicine which flourished at Salerno in the time of Roger the Great.[58]

The contribution made to the developing culture of Latin Christendom by the efflorescence of scholarship and art between 1100 and 1154 among the peoples governed by the Normans was very large and widely spread. It covered all the nascent aspirations which were lambent during that formative period, and it was made by men who were outstanding even in that adventurous age. The 'renaissance of the twelfth century', viewed as a whole, would certainly have been very different, and less rich, apart from the work of such as Adelard of Bath in science, of John of Salisbury the humanist, and of the Greek and Arabic scholars and translators who surrounded Henricus Aristippus and

[55] Southern, in *Medieval and Renaissance Studies*, IV (1958), pp. 176–216; *History*, XLV, pp. 211–13.

[56] J. H. Harvey, in *Antiquaries Journal*, XLVIII, pt i (1968), pp. 89–99.

[57] Brooke, *op. cit.*, pp. 102–3.

[58] Haskins, *Medieval Science*, pp. 153–91; *Renaissance of the Twelfth Century*, p. 293.

Eugenius the emir in the Sicilian kingdom of Roger the Great. Assuredly, the intellectual and artistic achievements in the Norman realms during the earlier half of the twelfth century had enriched the mind of the West.

The Norman influence on Europe as displayed between 1100 and 1154 was manifestly pervasive and profound. It enhanced the strength of the West and at the same time modified its temper and its political structure. The great Norman kingdoms which were then established were a source of power, and within those kingdoms new trends of thought were developed and new principles of governmental organization which might disturb what had hitherto been the accepted relations between the spiritual and temporal authorities in Latin Christendom. The great access of power attained by the West during these years gave a new turn to the relations between Rome and Constantinople, and between Western Europe and the Eastern empire, and a new era inevitably opened in the confrontation between Christendom and Islam. Thus had the stage been set for the crusades.

PART THREE

THE NORMANS IN
THE WORLD'S DEBATE

Chapter 9
CRUSADING ORIGINS

I

Nowhere was the Norman impact upon the course of European history to be more notably displayed than in the inception of the crusades, and in their conduct during the earlier half of the twelfth century.[1] However, just as Norman policy in this matter underwent great modifications during these decades, so also were both the origins and the consequences of the Crusades themselves to be both varied and complex. Today scholars seem to be as sharply divided as were their predecessors as to how the crusades should best be interpreted. To some the crusades appear as what they professed to be – a sincere effort on the part of Western Christendom to rescue the Holy Places of Palestine from infidel hands. Others would seek to explain them by reference to the advance of the Seljuk Turks, whose conquests not only imperilled the pilgrim routes to Syria but so menaced the power of the Christian emperor at Constantinople that he was eager and able to attract mercenaries from the West. By others again, the whole movement has been regarded as a reflexion of papal policy which, in its turn, has been very diversly judged. Finally, more strictly economic causes have been adduced to explain this outpouring of Western men, and the crusades have also been more crudely envisaged as essentially a colonizing venture by predatory Western warriors.

Doubtless there is some truth in all of these contrasting interpretations, a further distinction being among those who regard the crusades as essentially a part of the development of Europe, and those who view them rather as an episode in the history of the Moslem world. Equally noteworthy, and certainly more provocative of discord, is the cleavage between those who treat the crusades primarily, if not exclusively, as the product of political and economic forces, and those who still believed that the dominating crusading

[1] All studies of the crusades are primarily indebted to S. Runciman, *History of the Crusades*. Admirable summaries of recent interpretations are given in J. J. Saunders, *Aspects of the Crusades* (1962); in T. S. R. Boase, 'Recent Developments in Crusading Historiography', *History* (1937); and in P. Rousset, *Les Origines et caractères de la première Croisade* (1945). Reference may be made to the review of Rousset's book by J. L. La Monte in *Speculum*, XXIII (1948), and to Giles Constable's criticism of that review in *Traditio*, IX (1953). See also J. L. La Monte, 'Some Problems of Crusading Historiography', *Speculum*, XV (1940).

impulse was genuinely religious. Edward Gibbon has given a finely balanced opinion of the chiefs and soldiers who marched to the Holy Sepulchre:

> I will dare to affirm that *all* were prompted by the spirit of enthusiasm, the belief of merit, the hope of reward, and the assurance of divine aid. But I am equally persuaded that in *many* it was not the sole, that in *some* it was not the leading principle of action.[2]

But in the changed circumstances of the modern world, historians evidently find it hard to achieve Gibbons's critical and scholarly detachment on this matter. As a result, it might almost seem as if the long debate about the crusades must now either continue with a repetition of outworn controversies or end in a stalemate of suspended judgement.

Perhaps for this reason it has recently been suggested that 'if we are to get at the essential meaning of the crusades another dimension is needed',[3] and that this new dimension may be provided by reference to the Normans.[4] After all, the Normans during this period have been displayed as placed at the very centre of those forces which would be most directly implicated in the crusades.[5] They had special relations both with the papacy and with Constantinople. They had come to control the central Mediterranean, and they could exercise political and economic pressure alike on Islam and on Eastern and Western Christendom. In Sicily, moreover, they had already shown themselves as prominent exponents and exploiters of the notion of a Holy War. New light may perhaps, therefore, be thrown on some of the general problems of crusading history, and their implications for Europe, if these are re-examined in relation to Norman political action between 1095 and 1154.

II

The inception of the crusades is normally referred to the speech or speeches which Pope Urban II made to a great assembly at Clermont near Montpellier on 27 November 1095. According to the various surviving accounts,[6] the pope fervently lamented the sufferings endured by Eastern Christians at the

---

[2] Gibbon, *Decline and Fall*, VI, p. 271.
[3] G. Barraclough, in *New York Review of Books*, 21 May 1970.
[4] Cf. Barraclough, *op. cit.*, with special reference to Douglas, *Norman Achievement*.
[5] Douglas, *Norman Achievement*, chaps V, VI and VII.
[6] Of these, the chief are Fulcher of Chartres (*Gesta Francorum*, I, c. 4); Baudri of Dol (*Hist. Hierosolimitana*, I, c. 4); Robert the Monk (*Hist. Hierosolimitana*, I, c. 1 and 2); and Guibert

hands of their Moslem enemies. He expressed his horror at the desecration of the Holy Sepulchre by infidels, and at the hardships endured by Christian pilgrims to Jerusalem. Finally, he is said to have called on the warriors to unite in a war to recapture the Holy Places from the enemies of Christ. The Church would moreover protect the property of all those who went on such a crusade, and the pope as Vicar of Christ promised remission of sins by way of Indulgence to all those who, being penitent, expiated their offences by undertaking this sacred task.[7] The pope's speech produced an astonishing effect on his audience. It was greeted with shouts of *Deus Vult* – it is God's will – and hundreds of those present forthwith took the crusader's vow.

It is a moving description, but there is some danger of over-simplification, for assuredly the policy of Urban II was only one of many factors which promoted the crusade.[8] The pope's exhortations were doubtless sincere, and they were certainly influential, but the setting of the crusading movement (though not its ultimate inspiration) had in fact been formed by a revolution in power politics which had taken place during the previous decades. It had been created when the political balance of the Mediterranean world was transformed by the armed advance of the Seljuk Turks through Asia Minor and Syria, and by the contemporary conquests made by the Normans in Apulia, Calabria and Sicily.[9] The new era in the relations between Christendom and Islam had been foreshadowed in the spring and summer of 1071. On 19 August of that year the emperor Romanus IV was utterly defeated by Alp Arslan, the great Turkish leader, at Manzikert.[10] It was the greatest single disaster ever suffered by Byzantium before 1204, and was to rob the Eastern empire of its fairest provinces. But as a misfortune it did not stand

---

of Nogent (*Hist. Hierosolimitana*, II, c. I). Some thirty years later, William of Malmesbury set down his own account which he claimed to be derived from eye-witnesses (*Gesta Regum*, pp. 393–8). See further 'The Speech of Urban II at Clermont', *Amer. Hist. Rev.*, XI (1906), cf. D. Munro, in *Amer. Hist. Rev.*, XXVII (1922), pp. 70–3.

[7] Villey (*Croisade*, pp. 142–55) claims that this was the first instance of a plenary indulgence to be found in Canon Law. This is doubtless correct, but it might be interesting to consider how far Urban II advanced in this matter beyond the acts of Leo IX (Douglas, *Norman Achievement*, pp. 99–101), and how far his own action was surpassed by Eugenius III in 1145. Cf. Constable in *Traditio*, IX (1953).

[8] See in particular C. Erdmann's great book, *Die Entstehung des Kreuzzugsgedankens* (1935), which many will consider the most important single contribution that has ever been made to the study of Crusading origins.

[9] C. Cahen, in Setton and Baldwin, *Crusades*, I, chap. 5; Runciman, *op. cit.*, I, pp. 58–66; Douglas, *Norman Achievement*, pp. 53–67.   [10] C. Cahen, in *Byzantion*, IX (1914).

alone. Four months before the battle of Manzikert – on 16 April[11] – the conquests of the Normans in southern Italy had culminated in the capture of Bari, and the rule of Byzantium over Apulia and Calabria was brought to an end.

The full consequences of these momentous events were, however, only slowly to be disclosed. The interests of Alp Arslan, and his successor Malik Shah, were directed chiefly towards the East, and in due course the Turkish dominions were stretched almost to the borders of China. But Turkish armies were also active in the West. In the year of Manzikert, Atziz ibn Abaq captured Jerusalem,[12] and gradually all Syria including Damascus fell into Turkish hands. Further to the north, other conquests were made. Antioch was finally lost to the Turks in 1085,[13] and parts of Asia Minor began to pass under their control. Certainly, the Eastern empire might feel itself in peril. And during these same years events of almost equal importance had taken place in the West. The Christian empire of Constantinople had never been able to regain Sicily from Islam. But by 1091 – four years before the Council of Clermont – this feat had been accomplished when the conquest of the island had been completed by the Normans who had recently wrested Apulia and Calabria from Byzantine rule.[14]

A great redistribution of political power had in fact been consummated. In the East a new authority had arisen which claimed the support of all Moslems. It had already supplanted the Abassid dynasty at Baghdad, and was challenging the Fatimite rulers at Cairo. And these same Seljuk Turks were now firmly establishing themselves in Syria and Asia Minor. All Europe was bound to be affected by such changes, the more especially as they occurred just at a time when Latin Christendom was beginning to achieve a new unity under papal leadership, and when the central Mediterranean was passing under the rule of the Christian power now established by the Normans in Sicily. Appeals from Constantinople for aid against the Moslem enemy therefore had wide repercussions in the West.[15]

The developing crisis entailed both secular and ecclesiastical consequences. The papacy was not only concerned to defend the Christians in the East, it

[11] Ann. Bar., s.a. 1068–71; Will. Apul., vv. 486–570; Malaterra, II, c. 40.
[12] Runciman, *op. cit.*, I, pp. 75, 76. Jerusalem was, however, to be retaken by the Fatimites before it was finally captured by the Christians in 1099.
[13] Halphen, *Barbares*.   [14] Malaterra, IV, c. 2; Chalandon, *Domination*, I, pp. 327–54.
[15] On the vexed question of the acts of Alexis I in 1095, see D. C. Munro, 'Did Alexis ask for aid at the Council of Piacenza?', *Amer. Hist. Rev.*, XXVII (1922). See also Charanis, 'Byzantium, the West and the origin of the First Crusade', *Byzantion*, XIX (1945).

was also eager to bring the see of Constantinople once again under the control of Rome, and thus to restore the unity between the Eastern and Western Churches which had been threatened since the so-called 'Schism of Caerularius' in 1059.[16] This policy would certainly be resisted both by the patriarch of Constantinople and by the emperor on whom he depended. Before the First Crusade was launched, then, an anti-Byzantine element had been intruded into crusading policy through the cooperation between the papacy and the Normans. The Normans needed papal sanction to preserve from Byzantium their conquests in Italy and Sicily. The papacy required Norman support not only against the emperors in Germany, but also against the see of Constantinople with its pretensions to independence in the East.

III

It is against this political background involving Rome, Constantinople and Norman Sicily that the implications of Urban's action at the Council of Clermont must in the first instance be judged. But the crusade he preached must also be regarded as one of the products of the revival in the Western Church which was taking place during these years.[17] The resurgence of the papacy with the moral support of Cluniac monasteries, and with the material assistance of the Normans,[18] was an essential part of that reformation. And it was the papacy thus strengthened which was to take the lead in the crusade. The two movements were in fact inseparably interconnected. In the great ecclesiastical councils of 1096, for example, by far the greater part of the business was devoted to the reforms. At Piacenza the whole reforming programme was outlined in considerable detail, and at the Council of Clermont itself the matter of the crusade which formed the basis of the pope's concluding exhortation was represented in only one of the surviving canons.[19]

The papacy could never have set in motion so wide a movement from Latin Christendom towards the East if its own prestige had not recently been vastly enhanced. Nor could it have done so had the official reform of the hierarchy of the Church not been matched by a corresponding outburst of religious

[16] This was clearly one of the chief aims of Gregory VII. See his letters in Jaffé, *Monumenta Gregoriana*, pp. 64, 69, 111, 144, 150, 163, and cf. Runciman, *Eastern Schism*, pp. 59–62.
[17] Cf. Fliche, *Réforme grégorienne*, 2 vols (1924, 1925).
[18] For the Norman contribution to the emancipation of the papacy, see Douglas, *Norman Achievement*, pp. 130–5. For Cluny and its influence, see Gieysztor, in *Medievalia et Humanistica*, VI, pp. 24–6.
[19] Hefele-Leclerc, V (1), pp. 399–405.

fervour throughout the West. It was in response to a peace-movement which for long had enjoyed popular support that the Council of Clermont proclaimed a weekly truce from all fighting among Christians, and gave special protection to those who took refuge by wayside crosses.[20] Numerous monastic orders were also established at this time, such as the congregation of Fontevrault, or the Carthusian Order founded in 1084 by St Bruno, who was to end his days as a hermit in Norman Italy.[21] All these new orders, which were sustained by popular enthusiasm, were inspired by a desire for eremitical seclusion or for increased asceticism. They may also have reflected a sentiment which was spreading through the Christian West – a sense that to attain holiness it was necessary to renounce by penitence, or expiation, or prayer, a world that was full of violence, obscenity and sin.

The most vivid expression of this religious zeal was to be found in the pilgrimages which had come to play an ever increasing part in the life of Latin Christendom.[22] They were made in particular to the basilicas of Rome, to the shrine of St James at Compostella, and especially to the sacred sites in Palestine. The movement spread so rapidly during the latter half of the eleventh century that streams of pilgrims of all ages and classes, and of both sexes, travelling either singly or in large companies, were moving southward and eastward from Western Europe to return at last, if fortune favoured them, with tales of wonder which would excite the respect and the admiration of their fellows who had stayed at home. The personal motives of these pilgrims were certainly varied, but they all had one general aim: they wished to pay reverence to the holiness of particular shrines, and they desired to say their prayers at the sacred places indicated to them by their piety. And among all of these places there towered in solitary eminence 'Jerusalem the Golden', the scene of the passion of Our Lord, and most especially the Holy Sepulchre where His Body had rested for three days before He rose from the dead.

It was to a society thus strangely moved that Urban II in 1096 proclaimed the Holy War, and the success of his appeal depended directly upon these enthusiasms which had already become lambent in the West. The idea of a Holy War had been slow in developing, but during the latter half of the eleventh century the growing consciousness in Latin Christendom of its common and militant purpose created a climate of opinion more favourable

[20] L. C. McKinney, 'The people and public opinion in the eleventh-century peace movement', *Speculum*, V (1930). [21] Knowles, *Monastic Order*, pp. 191–208. [22] Cf. Runciman, *Crusades*, I, chap. III; Alphandéry and Dupront, *La Chrétienté et l'idée de Croisade*, I, chap. 1 and *passim*.

than ever before to the waging of war on behalf of religion.[23] And both the papacy and the Normans were ready to exploit the notion to their own advantage. Thus the aristocracies of the West were constantly summoned by the papacy to fight for the cause of the Church as interpreted by Rome. Spiritual blessings might in this way be invoked not only on Christians fighting the Moors in Spain, but on all those who would ensure that any Christian conquests there made would be subjected to the papacy. A Holy War might be proclaimed from Rome against Christian emperors such as Henry IV in the West, and Alexis I in the East.[24] The exploitation of the same ideas by the Normans was equally assiduous. According to their apologists, the Normans in the South were 'especially favoured by God', and their leaders were actually made on numerous occasions to address their troops before battle in language more appropriate to sermons. We should not be surprised, therefore, to hear that celestial warriors were sometimes seen in the sky assisting the Normans during their battles, or that a descending flight of singing angels had welcomed the Norman capture of Palermo from the Moslems.[25]

We are already in the atmosphere of the First Crusade – an atmosphere of signs and wonders – of the discovery of the Holy Lance or of the Divine participation in the Great Battle of Antioch. After the capture of Malta by Roger the Great Count in 1089, the Christian inhabitants of the island apparently came out to greet the Norman victor with crosses in their hands and chanting *Christe eleison*. Small wonder that the same Roger was constrained to describe himself in his charters as 'the champion of the Christians', 'strong in the favour of God', 'girt with the heavenly sword and adorned with the helmet and spear of celestial hope'.[26] Before ever Urban preached the crusade at the Council of Clermont, the papacy in conjunction with the Normans had made Latin Europe familiar with the conception of the Holy War as a matter of practical politics.

IV

Even this does not, however, fully account for the sense of urgency prevailing in the West at the end of the eleventh century. The religious war between

---

[23] Douglas, *Norman Achievement*, pp. 93–101.   [24] *Ibid.*, pp. 99–100; Rousset, *op. cit.*, pp. 44–7.
[25] Amatus, VI, cc. 19, 20; Douglas, *op. cit.*, pp. 103, 104.
[26] Charters in this sense will be found in Caspar, *op. cit.*, p. 632, and in Jordan, *Moyen Age*, XXXIII, p. 240.

Christendom and Islam had started in Spain even before it began in Syria, and there at this time a new era of tension was beginning. The first phase of the *reconquista* had culminated in the capture of Toledo by Alphonzo VI of Castille in 1085, and in the same year the Christians suffered their disastrous defeat at Zalaca, after which the victors were summoned to prayer beside mounds of decapitated Christian heads.[27] In one sense, therefore, the crusades might almost be regarded as a diversion which drew off Moslem strength to the East so that the Christians could achieve more enduring triumphs in the West.[28] But of far greater effect on Latin Christendom was the threat to the pilgrimages to Syria which had come to play a vivid part in the Christian life of the West. Clearly the maintenance of the pilgrimages depended directly on the political stability of the Eastern empire, and on the tolerance of Moslem rulers.[29] But both these conditions now began to be affected by the Turkish conquests, and there is no doubt that the hardships suffered by the pilgrims excited in the West a widespread indignation which was susceptible to ruthless exploitation.[30]

The way was thus prepared for the savage propaganda which reached its climax before the opening of the twelfth century. Detailed descriptions were circulated of the tortures said to have been inflicted on the pilgrims with 'unspeakable cruelty', and men were told to remember the 'thousands' who had 'suffered vile deaths'. To those acquainted with twentieth-century wartime broadcasts, the accent is familiar, and the whole formed part of a wider-based invective expressed, for instance, by Robert the Monk against 'the accursed race' that was so practised in murder and rape, and so addicted to the persecution of all the children of Christ.[31] The polemical literature produced at this time was in fact astonishing both in its character and scope. The so-called 'crusading bull' attributed to Sergius IV (1009–12), with its invitation to 'kill the sons of Hagar', was in fact concocted at the abbey of Moissac in 1096.[32] Elsewhere, too, the Moslems were denounced as idolators addicted to all sorts of excesses and sexual malpractices, whilst Mahomet was held up to hatred and scorn as a monster of ill-conceived depravity.[33] All

[27] Douglas, *op. cit.*, p. 161.
[28] See the interesting allusion to Spain in William of Malmesbury's report of Urban II's speech (*Gesta Regum*, p. 395).
[29] Cf. Runciman, in Setton and Baldwin, *Crusades*, I, pp. 68–70.
[30] Guibert of Nogent, *op. cit.*, II, c. 1.
[31] Robert the Monk, *op. cit.*, I, c. 2.   [32] Gieysztor, *op. cit.*
[33] N. Daniel, *Islam and the West: the Making of an Image* (1960). Cf. D. C. Munro, in *Speculum*, VI (1931).

these diatribes were based upon ignorance, most of them were pure fiction, and not a few of them were frankly disgusting. Nothing, it would seem, was too fantastic to be reported or believed, for 'it is safe to speak evil of one whose malignity exceeds any evil that can be spoken'.[34]

Such was the background to the passionate declarations of Urban and his followers.

> Of Holy Jerusalem we dare not speak. . . . This very city in which Christ suffered for us because our sins demanded it, has been reduced to the pollution of paganism. . . . Who now serves the church of the Blessed Mary in the valley of Josaphat where she herself was buried? And some of you have seen with your own eyes to what abominations the Lord's Sepulchre has been given over. . . . And yet in that place rested the Lord; there he died for us; there he was buried. . . . Most beloved brethren, if you reverence the source of that holiness and glory, if you cherish the shrines which are the marks of His footprints on earth . . . you should strive with your utmost efforts to cleanse the Holy City and the glory of the Sepulchre by every means in your power.[35]

During the ensuing months the pope himself and his numerous emissaries carried the message of Clermont all over Western Europe. Countries as far removed as Scotland and Denmark were affected, but it was France and to a lesser degree the Rhineland where the pope's call was received with most enthusiasm. The success of the appeal was reflected in almost all the principal chronicles of the time, and can be found even in legal documents. Charters for the abbeys of Saint-Père de Chartres and Saint Père de Puys record transactions made in connexion with the expedition in order that men might fight to rescue the Holy Sepulchre of Our Lord. And two brothers sold their lands because they wished to go to Jerusalem 'not only as pilgrims but also in order that with God's help they might destroy in the Holy City the mad and wicked rage of the pagans'.[36]

A long and complicated political development seems here to be reaching its consummation, and between 1087 and 1096 the progress was very rapid. Although the earlier orientation of papal policy had been directed towards Constantinople rather than Jerusalem, with the object of reuniting the whole

[34] Guibert of Nogent, *op. cit.*, I, c. 1.
[35] Baudri of Dol, *op. cit.*, I, c. 4.
[36] *Cart. S. Père Chartres*, II, p. 428; *Cart. S. Victeur Mersellies*, I, p. 27.

Church under the ruler of Rome, with Urban II there is a change of emphasis. In the report of Urban's speech given by Robert the Monk, it is Jerusalem, 'the navel of the world', which calls aloud for deliverance, and for Guibert of Nogent the rescue of the Holy Sepulchre is the most holy object of the Crusade.[37] Urban II had in fact given expression to a transformation of papal policy from an effort to assist the Churches in the East into the propagation of a religious war against Islam. In short, the reforming papacy, having advanced with Norman assistance to a new position of political authority in Latin Christendom, was preaching the Holy War which the Normans had previously proclaimed in connexion with their Sicilian venture. All that remained was for the pope to nominate Adhemar bishop of Puys as his representative on the crusade, and to select 15 August 1096 as the day when the great expedition should set out for the East. It was certainly appropriate that among the eight chief leaders of the First Crusade five should have been Normans or with Norman connexions and that among them there should have been both a son and a son-in-law of William the Conqueror.

V

Neither the inception of the crusade nor its character, however, can be fully explained without some reference to the gales of religious emotion which swept over so many of the humbler folk of Western Europe at this time as a result of crusading propaganda. The wickedness of the world might perhaps be expiated by spectacular expressions of popular devotion or in corporate acts of public penance. As a result, in the scattered villages of France and the Rhineland, or among the struggling populations in the new towns, men were impelled to undertake for the sake of their souls the long journey of Christian rescue to Palestine.[38] And their enthusiasm was further strengthened by the widespread dissemination at this time of a vivid apocalyptic teaching. The hope that the Second Coming of Christ was imminent has always been current among certain groups of Christians, but it seems to have become especially prevalent during the last quarter of the eleventh century. And it was now further stimulated by a sedulously fostered belief that the final act in the great drama of Earth and Heaven would soon be opened by the appearance of Anti-Christ himself, who would seek to dominate the world, and only after long warfare would be destroyed by the Christians under the leadership

[37] Guibert of Nogent, *op. cit.*, II, c. 1.
[38] Alphandéry and Dupront, *op. cit.*, *passim*.

of some great warrior hero. Then, and only then, would the kingdom of God be restored and all things be made new.[39]

It is tempting to dismiss these effusions as trivial or irrelevant. But the political influence which they exercised was not negligible. Their effect was not confined to the uninstructed, but was felt also among the learned and even among the directors of policy. Urban himself urged the crusade on the grounds that men should make haste in their preparations to resist Anti-Christ, whose coming is 'almost at hand'. For as the Scriptures have taught us, he added, Anti-Christ will first capture the Mount of Olives, and then occupy the Holy City. And it is there that he must be overthrown by the servants of God.[40]

The effect of such chiliastic preaching was enhanced by the fact that while the crusade proper was proclaimed to the higher ranks of society by Urban and his bishops, the message was often carried to the populace by very different means. A horde of *prophetae* now arose, preaching the crusade as the prelude to the creation of a new social order, or perhaps even of the end of the world itself. Some of these men were sincere, if unbalanced, zealots, such as the famous Peter the Hermit from Amiens,[41] whose sanctity was hardly in dispute, or the more sophisticated Robert Arbrissel, the founder of Fonte-vrault, who likewise declared that Anti-Christ was at hand.[42] And alongside of such men there were many others who could be described as crazed fanatics, or the victims of megalomania: self-styled prophets of the Most High, claiming special graces from Heaven or even to be themselves the reincarnation of the Son of God. It was such men who seized the occasion of the crusade to inflame the passions of a proletarian population which was already materially distressed and emotionally disturbed. Nothing was lacking which modern broadcasting propaganda would have supplied – there were atrocity stories, over-simplification, inflammatory denunciation, and all the hopes and fears that might be raised by prophecies of the end of the world. For Anti-Christ was even now approaching. Signs in the heavens, famines and pestilences on earth testified to his advent. If he could be overcome by the capture of the

[39] These beliefs, so strangely compounded of hopes and fears, were of long ancestry. They had received fresh currency from an influential treatise, *De Ortu Antichristi*, which Adso of Toul had composed late in the tenth century (Migne, *Pat. Lat.*, Vol. 137).

[40] Guibert of Nogent, *op. cit.*, II, c. 1. This might be read in connexion with the *Ludus Antichristi* which was written about 1160 at the Bavarian abbey of Tegernsee.

[41] On him, see generally H. Hagenmeyer, *Le Vrai et le Faux sur Pierre l'Hermite* (Paris, 1183).

[42] Alphandéry and Dupront, *op. cit.*, p. 40.

earthly Jerusalem, then a heavenly Jerusalem might descend for men, and the poor would inherit the earth.[43]

During the early months of 1096 large companies of men and even of women began spontaneously to form in north-eastern France and in the Rhineland. Inspired by emotions which were compelling if ill-defined, they began moving slowly towards Syria under the leadership of self-appointed messengers from Heaven. A few lesser knights might be found among them, but for the most part they were untrained, and often unarmed, serfs, who had fled from their manors, or journeymen who had failed to make a living in the towns. They were joined also by a rabble of outcasts, petty thieves and brigands, who hoped that the expedition might provide plentiful opportunities for plunder. What most characterized all these companies was their complete lack of discipline. They were a menace to every city and to every land, Christian or Moslem, through which they passed. Their messianic fervour was fierce, uncontrolled and ruthless. They would surely attain Jerusalem, and in the process not only enrich themselves but also destroy all the friends of Anti-Christ at home and abroad. In fact they behaved with bestial cruelty towards both Jews and Moslems, and their passage through Europe and beyond was marked by wholesale looting and depredation. It is not, therefore, surprising that the large 'popular' expeditions associated, for example, with Peter the Hermit, Folkmar and Gottschalk all met with disaster, and were repelled after much carnage on both sides by the opposition they encountered not only from Turks and Moslems, but also from the Christians in such countries as Bohemia and Hungary where they had looted and devastated.[44]

This was, of course, far removed from the policy of either the papacy or of the Normans, for both these parties, albeit for different reasons, contemplated effective military expeditions conducted by trained warriors under recognized leadership and with defined objectives. But Urban II and his Norman supporters had unleashed forces that were beyond their control, and unwillingly inspired movements which might bring atrocities to the East and subversion to the West. It would need all the authority and expertise of the military leaders of the crusade, and particularly of the Normans, to rescue the crusading movement from the confusion which threatened it, and even

[43] Alphandéry and Dupront, *op. cit.*, *passim*, and esp. pp. 43–81. N. Cohen, *The Pursuit of the Millennium*, may also be consulted, but only with caution.
[44] Runciman, *Crusades*, I, pp. 121–33; F. Duncalf, in Setton and Baldwin, *Crusades*, I, pp. 256–65.

so the savage chiliasm which had already been so disastrously displayed was to exercise its influence on the crusade proper when it was launched.

In these circumstances the great expeditions of the Holy War, as preached by the papacy and as supported by the Normans, were initiated and organized. Slowly they proceeded eastward to Constantinople, either by the land route down the valley of the Danube or across the Adriatic from Norman Bari. Then more slowly still did they carry their war against the Turks through Asia Minor and on to Palestine. And these baronial armies too were composed of many divergent elements. There were magnates such as Raymond count of Toulouse and Geoffrey of Bouillon who, with their followers, were inspired chiefly by a desire to rescue the Holy Places from Islam, and with them should probably be placed Robert duke of Normandy, the eldest son of William the Conqueror. There were others such as Bohemund, the Norman from south Italy, who were mainly interested in gaining lands for themselves at the expense either of the Turks or of the Eastern empire. And there was a disorderly rabble of outcasts and zealots devoid of military experience and prone to every atrocity. The interplay of these forces was to give to the First Crusade its special character, and the clash between them appropriately reached its first climax during the critical months of 1099 which witnessed the foundation of the Norman principality of Antioch.

Chapter 10

THE NORMAN PRINCIPALITY
OF ANTIOCH

I

The First Crusade was influenced at every turn by the Normans. The under-taking in its initial stages had been assisted by their interested interpretation of the Holy War. And now the Normans were not only the chief military contribution to the success of the crusade, but they were also, before its close, to establish a powerful Norman state in the East. Only a very shrewd observer could, however, have anticipated any of these results in the spring of 1097 when the crusading armies began to assemble at Constantinople. For the Normans represented but one element in these great expeditions from the West.[1] There was also, for instance, the large force led from the Netherlands and the Rhineland by Godfrey de Bouillon duke of Lower Lorraine, with his two brothers, Eustace III count of Boulogne and Baldwin, later to be king of Jerusalem. This force had started as early as 15 August 1096, travelling by the land route through Hungary and past Belgrade, and about the same time there came the army of Hugh of Vermandois, younger brother of the French king, who came through Lyons and Rome, and then on by way of Bari, overseas to Durazzo. Raymond of Saint Giles count of Toulouse brought a very large contingent from southern France over the Alps to the head of the Adriatic, and then onwards by land through Split and Dubrovnik. It was a miscellaneous company that had been collected at Byzantium, and some chroniclers were astonished at its character. 'Who ever heard such a mixture of languages in a single army?' asked one. 'Had not the Welshman left his hunting?' exclaimed another. 'The Scot his native lice, the Dane his drinking and the Norwegian his raw fish?'[2] Such was the assemblage which the Normans joined.

They had come in two large contingents. One of these was under the command of Robert duke of Normandy, the eldest son of William the Con-queror, with Stephen count of Blois, who had married Adela, the Con-queror's daughter.[3] These moved southward through Pontarlier, and, having

[1] Runciman, *Crusades*, I, pp. 143–71. [2] Will. Malms., II, p. 329.
[3] On all that concerned Duke Robert, see C. W. David, *Robert Curthose* (1920).

crossed the Alps, took the pilgrim route to Rome and on to Monte Cassino, joining a very large force of Normans from all over south Italy who were at that time besieging Amalfi.

It was at this point that the second Norman army for the Crusade was formed.[4] Its leader was Bohemund of Taranto, who took the crusader's oath outside Amalfi in June 1096. The elder brother of Roger Borsa duke of Apulia, against whom he was in constant war, Bohemund's motives on this occasion may be partly explained by reference to his earlier career, for he had fought in the Balkans with his father, Robert Guiscard, and was well aware that there were rich prizes to be won in the East. He was also moved by the challenge to his pride offered by the spectacle of so many Normans who had come from north of the Alps. 'Are we not also French?' he is reported to have said. 'Did not our ancestors come from France? Should our cousins and brothers set out without us on the road to martyrdom and Paradise?'[5]

The sincerity of such declarations may well be questioned, but there was undoubtedly a certain unity of sentiment among all the Normans who took part in the First Crusade. Bohemund and Robert were later to act in fairly close concert, and Robert was to linger in southern Italy for many months before crossing the Adriatic, being treated with deference and lavish hospitality by Roger Borsa during the whole winter of 1096–7. The Norman duke of Apulia regarded the duke of Normandy as his 'natural lord'.[6]

The two Norman contingents on the crusade shared many common characteristics. It was not so much those who had profited by the Norman conquests in England and Italy who felt impelled to take up the Cross, but more often those whose careers in the conquered lands had been placed in jeopardy and who now saw in these expeditions an opportunity of retrieving their fortunes. The well-established Norman rulers thus viewed the project without enthusiasm. They were consolidating their dominions and were not to be diverted from the task. William Rufus did not allow any of his bishops to attend the Council of Clermont, and his brother Henry I later discouraged the preaching of the crusade in England.[7] Roger, the Great Count, who was in 1096 by far the strongest of the rulers in the south, showed no zeal for the crusade, and one Arab writer asserts that he refused to participate because his doing so might damage his trade with the Moslems in North

---

[4] Cf. Jamison, in *Essays . . . M. K. Pope* (1939), pp. 183–208.

[5] Robert the Monk, Bk II, chap. 3.

[6] Fulcher of Chartres, Bk I, chap. 2.　　　　　　　　　　　[7] Ord. Vit., IV, p. 211.

Africa.[8] It was, therefore, perhaps natural that very few of the Norman barons of Sicily took the Cross, though two of them, Roger of Barneville[9] and Robert of Sourdeval,[10] both originally from the Cotentin, were notable both in themselves and for their exploits. The two principal Norman leaders in the crusade, though distinguished, had achieved no great political success at home. Robert duke of Normandy had been singularly unsuccessful in his dealings with his younger brother King William II before he pawned his duchy to go on the crusade. And Bohemund, who as the eldest son of Robert Guiscard must have expected to succeed his father as duke of Apulia, had been unable to prevent the title passing to his younger brother, Roger Borsa. Clearly he had to win a new title for himself.

A similar situation confronted many of their followers.[11] The spectacular career of Odo bishop of Bayeux was in sharp decline when he left for the East with Duke Robert, only to die at Palermo on the way, and his companion, Ralph of Gael, had been banished from England when he forfeited the earldom of Norfolk after the rebellion of 1075. Arnulf of Hesdins, who had wide lands in England in 1086 at the time when the Domesday Book was compiled, had lost all of them ten years later,[12] and there were a number of younger sons, such as Aubrey and Ivo of Grandmesnil, who clearly still had their way to make in the world. Many of the followers of Bohemund, too, had obviously jeopardized their Italian future by supporting him against Roger Borsa. Among these was young Tancred, his nephew,[13] and

---

[8] Ibn el Athir (Gabrieli (ed.), *Arab Historians of the Crusades*, p. 4) vividly describes the coarse vehemence with which Count Roger refused the request.

[9] Roger of Barneville (for whom see *Gesta*, p. 16; and also Hagenmeyer (ed.), *Gesta*, p. xxi n. 29) was a wealthy baron in Sicily who in 1094 had made large grants to the abbey of Lipari. He frequented Count Roger's court and witnessed some of his charters (P. Guillaume, *L'abbaye de Cava*, App. 'E', No. II; Jamison, *op. cit.*, p. 207). He was killed outside Antioch on 4 June 1098, and was buried with honour inside the city. He is commemorated in the *Chanson d'Antioche* (i, p. 255; ii, p. 140). See further, Hatem, *Poèmes épiques*, p. 217.

[10] Roger of Sourdeval had been an active agent in the Norman Conquest of Sicily. In 1094 he had witnessed one of Count Roger's charters, and in 1098 he was already well established at Antioch (cf. Jamison, *loc. cit.*).

[11] For the companions of Duke Robert on the crusade, see C. W. David, *op. cit.*, App. 'D', pp. 221–9.

[12] D.B., I, fols 45, 62, 65; *Liber de Hyda* (Rolls Series), pp. 301–2.

[13] Or perhaps his cousin. Emma, Tancred's mother, was either the daughter or the sister of Robert Guiscard, and Tancred was thus either the nephew or the cousin of Bohemund. Hagenmeyer, both in his edition of Ekkehard (pp. 329–30) and in his edition of *Gesta Francorum* (p. iv n. 19), argues strongly that Tancred was Bohemund's nephew, and this

Geoffrey of Montescaglioso, whose personal devotion to Bohemund was notorious. Herman of Canne, who was also on the expedition, had, with his brother Abagalard, been disinherited by their uncle Robert Guiscard, and had spent many years unsuccessfully striving to regain their lands. William of Grandmesnil and a certain Peter 'de Alpibus' did not join the expedition until it reached the Bosphorus, since they had, before 1096, been compelled to depart, defeated, from Italy to take refuge at Constantinople.[14] The Norman participation in the First Crusade could thus in one sense be described as the attempt at a third Norman conquest made by those men and those families who had failed to realize their ambitions through the conquests of England and Italy.

The natural leader in such a venture was Robert duke of Normandy, the eldest son of William the Conqueror, the more especially as his brother-in-law, Stephen count of Blois, was inadequate both on the bed and the battlefield, so failing to win the respect either of his wife or of his companions in arms.[15] But Duke Robert, though a brave and popular man, lacked the qualities of statesmanship, and his interest remained with his duchy in the North. The real architects of the third Norman conquest were thus to be Bohemund and Tancred. They were hard, unlovable, unscrupulous and intensely able men, subtle in their designs and ruthless in their acts. Of the two, Bohemund had the wider vision, while Tancred, who was his equal in duplicity, was the more practical and perhaps the more successful. Certainly they made a deep impression on their contemporaries. 'Bohemund and Tancred are mortal like all other men,' it was said, 'but their God loves them exceedingly, beyond all others, and therefore he grants them exceeding courage.'[16] Though both were personally repellent, they cannot be ignored, for apart from them the course of the crusades, and indeed the later development of medieval Europe, would have been, if not necessarily less happy, very different.

---

conclusion, which is supported by Ekkehard (*loc. cit.*), by Baudri of Dol (I, c. 8), by Guibert of Nogent (III, c. 2), and by Robert the Monk (c. 11), together with a considerable medieval tradition, is now generally accepted (see Runciman, *Crusades*, I, p. 155). On the other hand, Ralph of Caen (cc. 1 and 2) and Ordericus Vitalis (III, pp. 183, 456, 457) imply that Emma was Robert Guiscard's sister (see further Jamison, *op. cit.*, p. 196). The legend that Tancred had a Saracen father can be dismissed out of hand (see Nicholson, *Tancred*, pp. 4 et sqq.). Tancred's father was an obscure marquis named Odobonus, who probably came from north Italy, and later settled in Sicily.   [14] Jamison, *op. cit.*, pp. 198–207.
[15] *Gesta*, p. 63.   [16] *Gesta*, IX, c. 22.

The character of Bohemund I presents a fascinating problem to the historian. A hero to many of his contemporaries, he has been very diversely judged by posterity. One modern authority dismisses him as a 'swashbuckling scoundrel', whilst another salutes him as 'almost if not quite the greatest genius of his generation'.[17] In view of his violence and deceit it is tempting to regard him simply as a crude and predatory marauder. But his policies were not undiscriminating, and he was something of a visionary, since he dreamed of creating a great Asiatic empire. He has also been credited with 'innate military genius'.[18] Here, he was shrewd enough to learn from Byzantine theories of tactics, but it was his personal achievement to transform the defective means at his disposal into an efficient agent of war. Turkish tactics presented him with novel problems which he solved by novel methods. The strength of the Turks lay in their mobility and particularly in their skilled use of mounted archers. This threat he countered by a disciplined coordination in battle between his foot-soldiers and his mounted knights. The infantry should protect the flanks of the cavalry as they advanced, and at the same time manœuvre the Turks into a mass formation which would receive the irresistible charge of the mounted knights. Bohemund was undoubtedly the ablest general produced on the Christian side during the First Crusade.

Also beyond question is the strength of his personality. The fascinated horror he inspired in the young Byzantine princess, Anna Comnena, daughter of the emperor Alexis I, was always remembered by her, and described much later in a famous passage in her memoirs.[19] It is said also that when Bohemund was a prisoner at Sebastia in 1100 the ladies of the Danishmend Turkish court likewise fell under his spell.[20] But it was not only women that he dominated. So great was his prestige that during the crusade of 1101 the Lombards disastrously deflected the course of the crusaders into northeastern Anatolia in the fond hope that they might rescue their hero, and in 1102 a lock of his fair hair was being piously circulated among the Christians in Palestine.[21] These episodes, however, were surpassed during his journeys through Western Europe in 1105–6, when vast crowds collected to acclaim

[17] J. J. Saunders, *Aspects of the Crusades*, p. 21; E. Barker, in *Encyclopedia Britannica*, 11th edn, 'Crusades'.
[18] R. C. Smail, *Crusading Warfare*, pp. 202 et sqq.
[19] *Alexiad*, XIII, c. 10. Cf. Douglas, *Norman Achievement*, p. 65.
[20] Ord. Vit., IV, p. 144.
[21] Albert of Aix, VIII, c. 7.

the Christian champion, and men gazed on him 'as if he were Christ Him-self'.[22] Nor was his appeal only to the vulgar. Bohemund was notoriously lacking in wealth, but in 1106 he was given in marriage a daughter of the king of France, and when in 1107 he led his monstrous and ineffectual crusade against the Eastern empire, he received plenary spiritual support from the papacy.[23] The element of paradox was, indeed, to colour his career down to its close. After his defeat by the emperor Alexis in 1108, he retired to southern Italy to end his days in a discredited obscurity that was in marked contrast to his former renown. But no less than six of his successors in the East were to bear the nickname he had made so famous, and the Norman dynasty he founded in Syria would outlast both those in England and Sicily.

II

Bohemund sailed from Bari in October 1096 with well-armed and well-equipped forces that included not only Tancred, but also his cousins Richard and Rannulf, the sons of William 'of the Principate' count of Salerno.[24] Once across the Adriatic, however, the expedition loitered, and Bohemund did not reach Constantinople before April 1097. Nor was it until May that he was joined there by the other Norman army under Duke Robert. The situation in the capital had by that time become critical. During the spring of 1097 the crusading leaders, with one exception, took an oath of allegiance to the emperor Alexis, pledging themselves to restore to the empire any of the former imperial lands which they regained from the Turks. They did so, however, with varying degrees of reluctance. Stephen count of Blois, Robert of Normandy and Hugh of Vermandois made little difficulty, but Godfrey and his brothers put up a vigorous opposition, and Raymond of Toulouse, who in the event was the only crusader to take his oath seriously, hesitated for several weeks. It is even said that Tancred slipped secretly out of the capital lest he should be compelled to perform homage.[25]

Relations between the Crusaders and the Eastern emperor were evidently

[22] Ord. Vit., IV, pp. 142–4, 211–12.

[23] *Ibid.*, IV, p. 213.

[24] William 'of the Principate' was a younger brother of Robert Guiscard. His son Richard is alleged to have married a sister of Tancred. On the counts of Salerno and 'of the Principate', see L. R. Ménager, in *Quellen und Forschungen* (1954), pp. 67–73.

[25] *Gesta*, II. Ralph of Caen, c. xii.

delicate from the start, and they reflected a fundamental divergence of policy. For Alexis the purpose of these great expeditions from the West was to restore the lost provinces to an empire which he rightly claimed to be the chief secular bulwark of Christendom in the East. Many of the crusaders, on the other hand, had been taught to regard the Crusade as an armed pilgrimage by which they might mend their souls through the redemption of Jerusalem and the Holy Sepulchre. Others among them, inspired either by religious zeal or by hope of enrichment, were more simply concerned to wage with success a Holy War against Islam. This cleavage of sentiment between East and West was very deep, and it was to be ruthlessly exploited by interested parties either by reference to the schism between the two Churches or as a means of strengthening the claims of Western magnates to dominions in Syria. The case of Bohemund in 1097 was therefore of exceptional importance, for he had very recently been at war with the Eastern Empire. In 1082 his troops had threatened Constantinople[26] and now that he had arrived on the Bosphorus as a crusader his acts might well prove crucial. After a private interview with the Emperor Alexis, however, he took the oath of allegiance without demur, though he demanded that he should be given high command in the imperial army. To this request Alexis returned an evasive answer.[27]

The transactions between Bohemund and Alexis in 1097 were later to prove of great significance. The anonymous *Gesta Francorum* asserts that, in return for his oath, Bohemund was promised by Alexis 'lands beyond Antioch fifteen days' journey in length and eight in width provided that he would swear fealty with free consent'.[28] It is generally believed, however, that this passage was a later interpolation in a narrative which is usually very favourable to the Normans, and that it was inserted at Bohemund's instigation during 1106, when he was in Western Europe, in order to justify his seizure of Antioch and his projected crusade against Alexis.[29] It is difficult to see,

---

[26] See above, chap. 9.　　　　　　　　　　[27] Runciman, *Crusades*, I, p. 158.

[28] *Gesta*, p. 12.

[29] See the fundamental article by A. C. Krey, in *Essays . . . Munro*, pp. 57–78. A conclusion which has been accepted by Professor Claude Cahen (*Syrie du Nord*, p. 8), by Sir Steven Runciman (*op. cit.*, II, p. 47), and, albeit with some reservations, by F. Duncalf (in Setton and Baldwin, *Crusades*, I, p. 287) is assuredly not lightly to be assailed. I may, however, venture the personal opinion that the arguments advanced by Miss Evelyn Jamison (*Essays . . . M. K. Pope*, pp. 183–208) have perhaps not been given full weight. Miss Jamison had, moreover, earlier suggested that the *Gesta* was brought to Western Europe not by Bohemund in 1106 but by Duke Robert in 1101 (Brit. Acad. *Proceedings*, XXIV (1938), pp. 279–80).

however, why an oath by Bohemund should figure in a propagandist interpolation, and it is still more remarkable that the passage in question does not in fact mention Antioch at all, but only lands beyond it. Is it conceivable that Alexis in 1097 did actually contemplate setting up the Norman leader in a frontier fief which might buttress Antioch against the Turks to the East, and particularly against Aleppo? These are plausible speculations, but in view of the character of the evidence it would be rash to assert that any secret treaty of this nature was ever made between Alexis and Bohemund when the latter was at Constantinople in 1097.

Before the crusade had reached the walls of Antioch, Bohemund had already won for himself a dominant place among its leaders. It was he who more than anyone else warded off disaster at the battle of Dorylaem in July 1097,[30] and now his qualities of leadership were to be faced by a more severe test. The long siege of Antioch which lasted from October 1097 to June 1098 inflicted great hardships on the crusaders. Sickness became rife and food supplies began to run out. By Christmas 1097 actual famine threatened, and Bohemund conducted a raiding expedition into the fertile valley of the Orontes in the hope of bringing back provisions.[31] It was certainly Bohemund who at this time did most to raise the sagging spirits of the crusaders. There were even some who attempted to desert,[32] and Baldwin from Boulogne, who had quarrelled with Tancred at the time of the capture of Tarsus, left for the East to establish himself in due course as count of Edessa. Then in February 1097, Taticius, the representative of the emperor Alexis, left for Byzantine.[33] By May, therefore, matters seemed desperate, and now the crusaders, demoralized and impoverished, were suddenly called upon to face a relieving Moslem force led by Ridwan emir of Aleppo. Once again it was Bohemund who saved the situation by beating off the attack, and soon his pertinacity was to be rewarded. On 3 June, aided by treachery from within the walls, he led the final assault on Antioch in company with

[30] *Gesta*, III, c. 9. Cf. Smail, *Crusading Warfare*, pp. 168, 169.

[31] Ralph of Caen, c. 53; cf. Setton and Baldwin, *Crusades*, I, p. 311.

[32] Including a certain 'William the Carpenter', who was ignominiously brought back by Tancred. He spent the whole of the night 'in my lord Bohemund's tent lying on the ground like a piece of rubbish'. The following morning Bohemund rated him: 'You miserable disgrace to the whole Frankish army . . . you blot on the people of Gaul. . . . You loathsome lout, why did you run off so shamefully? I suppose you wanted to betray the knights of Christ.' (*Gesta*, VI, c. 15.)

[33] *Gesta*, IX, c. 27; *Alexiad*, XI, c. 4. These give different versions of the motives of Taticius and the influence of Bohemund.

Raymond of Toulouse, and by nightfall, after an appalling massacre, the city was in Christian hands.[34]

III

The following weeks saw the first crisis in the establishment of the Norman power in Syria, and the rapid succession of events which now took place formed a significant pattern round the person of Bohemund. It had long been known that Kerbogha, the Atabeg of Mosul, was intending to rescue Antioch, and his large army appeared before the walls only three days after the capture of the city by the Christians. The besiegers thus became the besieged, and found themselves in dire peril. The crusaders felt themselves outmatched, their forces appeared inadequate, and already their food supplies began again to fail. Once more desertions took place, and this time from important magnates such as Aubrey and William of Grandmesnil and Stephen of Blois, the son-in-law of William the Conqueror.[35] The one remaining hope for the Christians seemed to lie with the Eastern emperor, who was advancing to their help. But Alexis was actually persuaded that all was lost in Antioch, and he turned back northwards.[36] It was an act with far-reaching consequences. Not without reason did the Christians in Antioch consider themselves to have been betrayed, and Alexis was never to be forgiven. The bitterness against Byzantium which informs so many of the Latin chroniclers of the First Crusade is thus in part explained, and no single event did more to promote, at the expense of the Eastern Empire, the establishment of an independent Norman state in northern Syria.

In the meantime, however, it was necessary to seek encouragement from the supernatural, and it was forthcoming. On 10 June 1098 a certain Peter Bartholomew, a pilgrim of low repute, announced that St Andrew had appeared to him in a vision and told him that the Holy Lance which pierced our Saviour's side was to be found in the church of St Peter at Antioch, and that with this weapon in their possession the Christians could be victorious over all their foes.[37] There is no reason to doubt the sincerity of Peter Bartholomew, who later offered to go through fire to prove his honesty and perished in the attempt. But his assertions about St Andrew and other visions

34 *Gesta*, VIII, c. 20; Fulcher of Chartres, I, cc. 7 and 8; Ralph of Caen, c. 67.
35 *Gesta*, IX, c. 23; Ralph of Caen, c. 79; Ord. Vit., IV, p. 118.
36 *Gesta*, IX, c. 27.
37 Runciman, 'The Holy Lance found at Antioch', *Analecta Bollandiana*, LXVII (1950).

which he reported were at first received with some scepticism, particularly by Adhemar bishop of le Puys, the papal legate, and Arnulf of Cioches, chaplain to Duke Robert of Normandy. Some of the crusaders on their passage to the East may even have seen the Holy Lance that was preserved in the church at Constantinople, and a few may perhaps have been told how, long ago, Otto the Great of Germany had carried the Holy Lance with him when he advanced to his great victory over the pagan Hungarians at the battle of Lechfeld in 955. Nevertheless, on 15 June 1099 the sacred relic was found under the floor of St Peter's Cathedral in harassed Christian Antioch.

The discovery of the Holy Lance entailed considerable political consequences. To many sincere men, and notably to Raymond count of Toulouse and his followers, it seemed that God was at last taking pity on His champions, and their spirits rose. Elsewhere, the results were less pleasant. The horde of savage vagabonds following the crusade had become particularly unmanageable during the long siege of Antioch. They are described as roaming about half-naked, feeding on roots and herbs and murdering with torture any infidel that fell into their hands. It was even reported that they were wont to disinter the bodies of dead Turks in order to mutilate them, and that they actually practised cannibalism.[38] Much exaggeration may here be suspected, but there is no doubt that the activities of these fanatical ruffians were further stimulated by the finding of the Holy Lance, and their conduct presented a serious problem to the crusading leaders. Even Bohemund found it difficult to control them. But Bohemund was none the less to be the chief beneficiary from the miracle in which, incidentally, he did not believe.

For undoubtedly the rising morale of the crusaders in the city helped him to attain the greatest military success of his career. The story of the 'Great Battle of Antioch'[39] which so fired the imaginations of contemporaries and afterwards of posterity, needs no re-telling. On 28 June 1099 the Christians sallied out of Antioch carrying the Holy Lance with them, and they routed the army of Kerbogha. It was a triumph as complete as it was unexpected. Men afterwards asserted that they had seen heavenly warriors fighting for the Christians in the sky, but the chief secular architect of the victory was manifestly Bohemund, whose skilled combination of his footmen and

[38] The fullest description is in the *Chanson d'Antioche*. See Hatem, *Poèmes épiques*, pp. 195–7.
[39] *Gesta*, IX, cc. 28, 29; Albert of Aix, IV, cc. 47–56; Setton and Baldwin, *op. cit.*, I, pp. 322–3.

mounted knights in action was directly responsible for the Moslem defeat.[40] Small wonder that he returned to Antioch with vastly increased prestige, or that he now began actively to implement his long-cherished plan to seize the great city for himself. Naturally, his ambitions provoked opposition from some of the other crusading leaders, and particularly from Raymond of Toulouse, who for long refused to surrender the city to the Normans. Pressure was, however, increasingly brought to bear on the count to depart for Jerusalem in order to rescue the Holy Sepulchre, and at length Peter of Narbonne bishop of Albara declared to the delight of the zealots that if Raymond would not lead them he would give the Holy Lance to the people so that they could proceed to Jerusalem with Christ Himself as their leader.[41] As a result of this, Raymond count of Toulouse departed southward into Tripoli in January 1099, leaving Bohemund and the Normans in possession of Antioch. A new era in crusading history had opened.

IV

The expedition which Raymond of Toulouse led southward from Antioch was, in due course, to be joined by Duke Robert of Normandy and by Tancred. After much fighting it was to capture Jerusalem on 15 July 1099 and on 15 August to win a decisive victory at Ascalon over a relieving Moslem force which had advanced from Egypt. Meanwhile, Arnulf of Cioches, chaplain to Robert of Normandy, had been made patriarch of Jerusalem,[42] and a new secular government had been given to the city. Godfrey 'de Bouillon', the brother of that Baldwin from Boulogne who had been established at Edessa, was, to the chagrin of Raymond of Toulouse, chosen on 22 July 1099 to be 'Advocate of the Holy Sepulchre'. He had, it was said, refused to wear a crown of gold where his Saviour had worn a crown of thorns.[43] But on his death, some twelve months later, Baldwin himself moved down from the north to be crowned on Christmas Day 1100, after long controversy, as the first crusading king of Jerusalem.[44] At the same time, Edessa passed to a kinsman of the new king, Baldwin 'of Le

---

[40] Smail, *op. cit.*, pp. 173, 174.

[41] Raymond of Aguilers, c. 14; Nicholson, *Tancred*, p. 75.

[42] On him, see David, *op. cit.*, App. 'C'. The family to which he belonged may be represented among the tenants-in-chief in Domesday Book. See Douglas, 'The Domesday Tenant of Hawling', Bristol and Glos. Arch. Soc. *Trans.*, LXXXIX (1966), pp. 28–31.

[43] Raymond of Aguilers, c. 20. Cf. Runciman, *op. cit.*, I, p. 292.

[44] Runciman, *op. cit.*, I, pp. 315–26.

Bourg', count of Bethel, who would reign there as count until in 1117 and succeed Baldwin I as king of Jerusalem.

In all these momentous events the Normans played a significant part. Indeed, if Duke Robert had not departed for home in the late summer of 1100 he might eventually have been a strong candidate for election as king of Jerusalem.[45] Both he and Tancred had distinguished themselves in the campaigns which led to the capture of the Holy City, and more particularly in the decisive battle of Ascalon. Tancred had, moreover, been responsible for the original seizure of Bethlehem when he planted his standard on the Church of the Nativity.[46] Afterwards he took his full share in the final assault of Jerusalem itself. During the appalling massacre which followed the capture of the city, his flag floated over the Al Aqsa mosque, though it did not prevent[47] the slaughter of those who had taken refuge in the building. Later, Tancred shared in the election of Godfrey of Bouillon as the first crusading governor of Jerusalem, and he was deeply implicated in the controversies which resulted in Arnulf of Cioches being supplanted by the papal legate Daimbert of Pisa as patriarch of Jerusalem.[48] And Bohemund was to be invited in vain by Daimbert to withstand the coming of Baldwin from Edessa to Jerusalem for his crowning.[49] But, speaking generally, Norman interests at this time were being concentrated on northern Syria rather than on Palestine. It was from Antioch that the influence of the Normans was now to be exercised, and in such a manner as to give a new turn to the whole crusading movement.

The seizure of Antioch by Bohemund was a direct challenge to Byzantium from the Normans. For the recovery of the city with its dependencies had been a primary objective of the Eastern emperor in his propagation of the crusade. Bohemund was therefore quick to exploit the schism between the Eastern and Western Churches in order to strengthen his own position. The famous Letter of the Princes was written in August 1098, shortly after the Christian victory over Kerborgha, and it was undoubtedly concocted by Bohemund. It called for a transformation of papal policy and invited the pope to come in person to Antioch to give effect to the change.

We have driven out the Turks and the pagans, but we have not been able to conquer the heretics: the Greeks, the Armenians, the Syrians and the

[45] Ord. Vit., IV, p. 65.   [46] Fulcher of Chartres, c. 15; Albert of Aix, V, cc. 44, 45.
[47] *Gesta*, X, c. 38.   [48] Ralph of Caen, cc. 135, 136.
[49] Albert of Aix, VI, c. 27; Will. Tyre, X, c. 2; Bohemund had been taken prisoner before he received Daimbert's letter.

Jacobites. Come then our beloved Father and Chief – seated on the chair that was established by Blessed Peter [i.e. at Antioch] . . . your authority, and our valour, will extirpate heresy of every kind.[50]

The attempt to utilize the tension between the Churches in order to secure papal support against Byzantium for Norman separatist ambitions in Syria could hardly have been more clearly expressed. And soon yet more drastic steps were taken in the same direction. Bishops of the Latin allegiance were set up at Tarsus, Artah and Mamistra; and in 1100, at the instigation of Bohemund, Bernard of Valence was established as Patriarch of Antioch. Thus was the Eastern schism brought a stage nearer, and once again the process was made to favour Norman policy.[51] In return for supporting Daimbert of Pisa at Jerusalem, Bohemund now received from the papal legate official recognition of his title of prince of Antioch.[52]

Inevitably, therefore, the Norman principality of Antioch had from the first to be defended from the Eastern emperor, and this in part explains why its early history was so precarious. In August 1100 Bohemund himself was for a time removed from the scene. Seeking to stabilise his northern frontier, he advanced towards Armenia and was captured by the emir of Sebastia, so that for more than three years Antioch was to be ruled in his absence by his nephew Tancred.[53] This astonishing young man – he was only some twenty-five years of age – had already demonstrated his ability. He had distinguished himself, for instance, in the campaigns during 1099 in Palestine.[54] But his own ambitions evidently lay elsewhere. In the summer of 1100 he had therefore moved northwards with a small force of twenty-four knights, and with these he acquired an important group of lordships in Galilee.[55] Thus it was as 'prince of Galilee' that he was now elected to act as regent in Antioch for his uncle Bohemund. His vigorous conduct of its affairs began, moreover, at once to produce notable results.

[50] Text in Hagenmeyer, *Kreuzzugsbriefe*, pp. 161–5.
[51] Cahen, *Syrie du Nord*, pp. 305–10; Runciman, *Eastern Schism*, pp. 92, 93.
[52] Fulcher of Chartres, I, cc. 33, 34; Albert of Aix, VII, cc. 6–8; Cahen, *op. cit.*, p. 224. The homage alleged to have been given by Bohemund to Daimbert was perhaps cunningly contrived by the former to obviate the necessity of offering allegiance to any secular ruler who might be established in Jerusalem. Daimbert and Bohemund seem to have been together in Jerusalem on this occasion from 21 December 1099 to New Year's Day 1100.
[53] Albert of Aix, VII, cc. 27, 28; Fulcher of Chartres, I, c. 35.
[54] Above, p. 179.
[55] Ralph of Caen, c. 39; Will. Tyre, IX, c. 13.

By the beginning of 1102 he had taken possession of the essential port of Lattakieh, and he was extending his authority towards Aleppo.[56]

Evil days were, however, now coming upon Antioch. In 1104 the crusaders in the East suffered their first serious reverse in Syria when a united Christian force was heavily defeated in an attempt to take Harran, the great stronghold between Edessa and the Euphrates. Baldwin of le Bourg, then Lord of Edessa, and his kinsman, Joscelin I of Courtenay, were captured while their Norman allies Bohemund and Tancred came back with diminished strength to Antioch.[56a] The legend of the invincibility of the Franks was in fact being dissipated, and for Norman Antioch the situation was especially critical. For the Norman principality had to face not only the Turks, who were now flushed with success, but also the troops of the Eastern emperor, who at this time occupied the whole of Cilicia. In these circumstances Bohemund, now released from captivity, decided that the only hope for the Norman state in Syria lay in reinforcements from Europe. He therefore decided to appeal in person for help from Latin Christendom, and in the autumn of 1104 he departed for the West.[57]

Bohemund's visit to the West brought to a new climax all the changes which the Normans were effecting in the crusading movement as a whole. Not only did he become at once a hero to the whole of Latin Christendom, and not only was he given a daughter of the king of France in marriage, but he persuaded an influential section of Western opinion that the proper object for crusading attack should be not Jerusalem but Constantinople. Moreover, he managed to convert Pope Paschal II himself to this policy. That was the meaning of his spectacular appeal in the cathedral of Chartres in April 1106, when he called on the knights of Latin Christendom to support him in an onslaught on the Eastern empire.[58] The response was to be gratifying. It is true that his negotiations with Archbishop Anselm of Canterbury brought him no help from King Henry I of England,[59] but Bohemund travelled widely, certainly through Flanders, probably to Angers and Bourges and perhaps even as far as northern Spain.[60] His main support came, however, from Normandy, from northern France and from southern Italy. Among the leaders who accompanied him in the force which he

---

56 Röhricht, *Regesta*, No. 36. Cf. Nicholson, *Tancred*, pp. 120–5; Cahen, *op. cit.*, pp. 229–30.
56a Cahen, *op. cit.*, pp. 236, 237; Ralph of Caen, c. 153.
57 Yewdale, *Bohemund*, pp. 101, 102.
58 Suger, *Vita Ludovici*, p. 22; Ord. Vit., IV, p. 213.
59 Eadmer, *Hist. Novorum*, pp. 179, 180.   60 Yewdale, *op. cit.*, pp. 111, 112.

eventually took from Brindisi across the Adriatic and onwards towards Constantinople were, for instance, Hugh de Puiset, *Vicomte* of Chartres, Ralph and Jocelyn from Pont Échanfré, near Bernay, Robert of Montfort-sur-Risle and Robert from Vieuxpont-sur-Dives.[61]

But more important was the close association of the papacy with the venture. The expedition which Bohemund led in 1107 against the emperor Alexis was in every essential sense a crusade. It was blessed by the papacy; its members were fortified by the papal indulgence; a papal legate accompanied the troops and Bohemund fought under a papal banner.[62] His utter defeat and humiliation by Alexis (who used Turkish mercenaries against the Normans) was thus felt as a reverse throughout Western Christendom, and it enlarged yet further the cleavage between the East and West. As for Bohemund, his surrender was almost unconditional. He formally ceded his rights in Antioch to the emperor and then departed to his Apulian estates to end his days in disappointment on 6 March 1111.[63] It was an astonishing end to a spectacular career. And it left the future of Norman Antioch in the hands of Tancred.

IV

The more one contemplates the achievements of Tancred the more remarkable do they appear. In 1100, when still in his middle twenties, he came to rule over a recently founded and precarious principality at a time of crisis, and not only restored order but also enlarged the boundaries of Norman authority.[64] Later, when Bohemund had departed to Europe, even harder tasks, and greater responsibilities, confronted him. At the end of 1104 his famous uncle had left for Europe in something like despair. The Greeks had overrun Cilicia and seized control of Tarsus, Mamistra and part of Lattakieh. The Turks, encouraged by their victory at Harran, had advanced across the Orontes under the leadership of Ridwan of Aleppo. Nor was this all. For Bertrand, the son of Raymond of Toulouse, the old enemy of the Normans, was establishing himself in Tripoli, while Baldwin I who, despite Bohemund's efforts, had become king of Jerusalem in 1100, was now extending his ambitions towards Syria. The future of Antioch must indeed have

61 Ord. Vit., IV, pp. 213, 240.
62 Yewdale, *op. cit.*, pp. 107, 108, and the authorities there cited.
63 Runciman, *Crusades*, II, p. 51.
64 Above, pp. 171-2.

appeared grim. Yet in four years all this was to be changed. Tancred always kept clearly in mind what should be the main objectives of Norman policy in Syria. His enemies were the Greeks to the north, the Moslems to the east and the rival crusading princes to the south. And as a result of Tancred's wars between 1104 and 1108[65] all these foes had been checked. The king of Jerusalem and Bertrand were kept from interfering in Norman affairs; Greeks were driven out of Cilicia and Lattakieh, and Ridwan and his allies were beaten back eastwards towards Aleppo.

By 1108 the Norman principality of Antioch had not only been firmly re-established but its strength had been vastly increased. Its influence could now be extended far beyond its own boundaries. Thus in the absence of Baldwin of le Bourg, after Harran, Tancred was able to take possession also of Edessa, and in due course he installed there as his vassal his cousin Richard of Salerno, the son of William count of the principate and the grandson of Tancred of Hauteville.[66] So the greater part of northern Syria fell at last to the house of Hauteville, and Norman rule now stretched from Lattakieh in the west to beyond Tarsus in the north, to cover in the south a substantial part of northern Tripoli and to extend eastward right across the Euphrates to beyond Edessa. It was a vast region, and in 1108 it was ruled by a grandson of Robert Guiscard, with the assistance of one of Guiscard's nephews. The extent of Norman expansion in the early twelfth century could hardly be better illustrated. Indeed, it is hard to escape the impression that if Tancred had not died young, the Normans under his leadership might have captured Aleppo itself and thus altered the whole future course of the crusades.

The achievement of Tancred is easier to describe than to explain. He was not by origin a man of wealth, nor did he ever hold any exalted position in Italy. He thus had few resources at his disposal when he arrived in the East. Indeed, after his first establishment in Galilee he seems to have relied for the most part on the support of native Syrian and Greek Christians, whom he strove to conciliate at Haifa and Tiberias. There must, however, have been a wonderful strength of character in this young man when he came to the regency of Antioch, and only his spectacular success during the next three years could have ensured the continuance of his rule. The return of Bohemund in 1103 caused a short break in his personal fortunes, but after his formidable uncle had left for Europe his advance was constant. His rising

[65] For details, see Cahen, *op. cit.*, pp. 241–9.
[66] Runciman, *Crusades*, II, p. 112.

reputation was marked by his marriage in 1106 to Cecilia, daughter of the king of France by Bertrada of Montfort,[67] and the imposing list of his vassals in 1110 given by Albert of Aix[68] is itself testimony to the authority attained: Hugh of Cantalou and William of Albini, lords of Tarsus and Mamistra; the bishops of Tarsus and Albara; Roger of Montmorin and Roger of Vieuxpont. To these might be added representatives of the families of Sourdeval and Saint-Lô, of Chevreuil, of Barneville and of Le Ferté Fresnel. The majority of these belonged to families still flourishing in the Norman dominions to the north and south of Europe. Together with Richard of Salerno, his vassal at Edessa, they formed around Tancred, the Norman ruler of Antioch, a feudal court that was truly impressive.

The feudal barons who supported Tancred constituted a primary source of his strength. They came for the most part directly from southern Italy, and it is not surprising therefore that the feudal structure of Norman Syria came to conform more closely to that which had been established in the Norman kingdoms in the West rather than to the arrangements which had been made elsewhere in feudal Europe.[69] In particular, as in Norman England and Norman Sicily, the number of knights owed for military service to the prince from his tenants-in-chief in return for their holdings (the *servitium debitum*) was in each case strictly specified by means of an individual bargain, formally recorded, and bore no automatic relation to the size of the fief.[70] As in England and Sicily too, the prince seems here to have played little part in the subinfeudation of the rear-vassals, which was left to his tenants-in-chief. But the institution of liege-homage and the heredity of all fiefs seem to have been established from an early date.[71] Obviously, the feudal organization of Norman Antioch presented special features proper to the conditions prevailing in a crusader state, but the resemblances there to be found with Norman feudalism elsewhere are certainly not to be ignored.

There are some feudal contrasts to be observed between Norman Antioch and the Latin kingdom of Jerusalem. But like his Norman contemporaries in England and Sicily, Tancred did not depend exclusively on feudal contracts for the government of his principality, or for the extension of its power. It

[67] *Ibid.*, II, pp. 29, 48.
[68] Albert of Aix, VII, c. 14; Nicholson, *Tancred*, pp. 215, 216; Grousset, *Croisades*, I, p. 486.
[69] Cf. Cahen, *op. cit.*, pp. 527–34.
[70] For this as exemplified in England, see the classical essay by J. H. Round, *Feudal England*, pp. 225–317.
[71] Cahen, *op. cit.*, pp. 527–34.

was for instance in his time that the great officials such as the constables, the chamberlains and the chancellors, whose functions were modelled on the Norman states of Europe, rose to power in Norman Syria, and the administration of Norman Antioch would come more and more to depend upon them.[72] In his wars, too, Tancred relied to a large extent on the mercenary troops which he attracted to his service by the promise of plunder, and whom he rewarded, also, out of the loot which he had himself obtained. Arab writers state that he was exceptionally generous to his soldiers, and on the whole they served him well.[73] It was with their support that he was able successfully to implement against all his opponents a calculating and unscrupulous policy that was throughout dictated by self-interest.

Thus in 1100 he had intrigued with Daimbert to prevent the succession of Baldwin I as king of Jerusalem, and showed himself completely indifferent to the lamentable fate of the crusading expedition of 1101. In 1102 he refused to contribute to the ransom of his uncle Bohemund, whose release was bound to circumscribe his own ambitions. He took no steps towards bringing Baldwin of Le Bourg out of captivity, and when at last Baldwin achieved freedom in 1108 Tancred opposed his reinstatement at Edessa unless he became the vassal of the Norman ruler of Antioch. In this he was ultimately unsuccessful. Nor, despite his seizure of Tortosa, could he prevent Bertrand, the son of Raymond of Toulouse, from occupying the greater part of the province of Tripoli, which in 1112 would pass to Bertrand's son, Pons, who reigned there as count until 1134. These civil wars had lamentable consequences, for in them Christians sought for Turkish allies in their struggles against each other, and it was this situation which was directly responsible for the failure of the crusaders to take advantage of Moslem disunity between 1109 and 1112.[74]

VI

Troubles faced Tancred during the closing years of his short life, but up to the time of his death he remained by far the most powerful ruler in northern Syria. His success was partly due to his clear-cut perception of the paramount importance of sea-power for the survival of the Latin states in the East.

---

[72] *Ibid.*, pp. 452–5.

[73] Nicholson, *op. cit.*, p. 228; Smail, *op. cit.*, p. 93. Tancred in youth had himself served for pay.

[74] Stevenson, *Crusaders in the East*, pp. 81–95.

Apart from the county of Edessa, which was always somewhat isolated, the Christian conquests never stretched further eastward than the frontiers of hostile Aleppo in the north, and in the south they hardly extended beyond the Jordan, or to the borders of Moslem, if friendly, Damascus. As a result, this narrow strip of territory needed to be constantly sustained from the sea. This had been apparent from the beginning of the enterprise. During the First Crusade the land forces received important help from Italian and Byzantine fleets, and in March 1099 English ships under the command of Edgar Atheling, the Saxon prince, had sailed into the harbour of Saint-Simeon to cooperate in the siege of Antioch.[75] Similarly, after the Latin states had been established, it was essential for them to exercise effective control over the coastal towns. But neither the rulers of Antioch nor the kings of Jerusalem possessed navies, so they were forced to depend on the fleets of others.

Bohemund and Tancred appreciated this situation from a very early date. Indeed, Antioch was in this respect particularly vulnerable, since the harbours of Lattakieh and Saint Simeon, which were essential to its defence, were subject to attack not only by Moslem fleets but more particularly by the ships of the Eastern empire. Tancred's constant preoccupation with these ports was thus fully justified. But since neither he nor his uncle had ships of their own, they were forced to rely on the great Italian cities which exacted a heavy price for the assistance they provided. The very first charter which Bohemund is known to have issued at Antioch was the grant of 14 July 1098 which gave to the Genoese and their fleet the church of St John, a market and many houses in the city.[76] Three years later Tancred not only confirmed and enlarged these gifts, but added a third of the harbour dues of Saint-Simeon and half of those in Lattakieh.[77] Finally, he made a grant to the Pisans in Antioch and Lattakieh, specifically in return for the help they had given him against the Greeks.[78] Much of Tancred's success was undoubtedly due to this maritime policy which was to be continued by his successors. And it was partly for this reason that in 1111, on the death of Bohemund, he was able to refuse out of hand the demand of the emperor Alexis that he should hold Antioch as a vassal of the Eastern empire.[79]

---

[75] Ord. Vit., IV, pp. 70–2; Runciman, *Crusades*, I, pp. 227, 228. But see also David, *Robert Curthose*, pp. 237, 330.

[76] Röhricht, *Regesta*, No. 12; Hagenmeyer, *Kreuzzugsbriefe*, Nos 13 and 14.

[77] Röhricht, *Regesta*, No. 35.   [78] *Ibid.*, No. 53.

[79] *Ibid.* Cf. Setton and Baldwin, *Crusades*, I, p. 401.

Meanwhile a similar policy was being pursued in the kingdom of Jerusalem in such a way as to modify the Norman fortunes. There, too, reliance was placed on the Italian cities rather than on the Eastern empire. As early as June 1100 Godfrey, advocate of the Holy Sepulchre, granted to the Venetians freedom of trade together with a church and a market in all the cities he controlled. They were also to have a third of any town they helped to capture, and were promised the whole of Tripoli when it should be captured if they would pay sufficient tribute for it. Again, in 1111 Baldwin I is said to have given the Venetians houses in Acre, and later charters gave them property in Ascalon in return for military service. During the same period the Genoese were also receiving favour from the kings of Jerusalem, as when in 1105 Baldwin I granted them privileges in Acre, Tortosa and Caesarea.[80] Finally, the Pisans were to profit by the reign of their own archbishop, Daimbert, who became patriarch of Jerusalem in 1099.

As a result of these activities, the ports of Haifa, Arsuf, Caesarea, Sidon and Tripoli, together with Lattakieh and Saint-Simeon, all passed into Christian hands before the death of Tancred in 1112.[81] It was a great achievement, for it enabled the Latin states to survive during the first critical period of their establishment. And the manner in which it was accomplished entailed lasting consequences for the future fortunes of the Normans in the East. The Italian cities had been firmly established in the Levant, and a counterbalance had thus been set up against the Byzantine navy which was a special peril to Norman Antioch. On the other hand, when at a later date Norman naval power was extended from Sicily into the eastern Mediterranean, then Genoa, Pisa and Constantinople would alike find themselves faced with a new and a formidable rival on the sea.

Throughout his career, Tancred relied as much upon statesmanship as upon force to attain his ends. His early rule in Galilee was marked by exceptional mildness, and in particular by toleration of the ritual and practices of existing Christian communities of oriental origin. He never practised that intransigence towards heretics which Bohemund for his own reasons saw fit to display, and this was to prove of special importance when he came to rule over Antioch, for the city, and the countryside which it controlled, contained not only a large Moslem population (which had suffered severely during the sack of the town in 1098) but also large communities of Greek and Armenian Christians who had flourished during the long years of

[80] See La Monte, *Feudal Monarchy in the Latin Kingdom of Jerusalem*, App. 'D'.
[81] *Ibid.*

Byzantine rule. These Tancred strove successfully to placate at the same time as he showed himself reasonably generous towards the Latin Church. He sustained the Latin hierarchy in the principality under the leadership of a Latin patriarch, and he founded churches in Nazareth, Mount Tabor and Tiberias, making also substantial grants to the monastery of Our Lady in the valley of Jehosophat.[82]

All this represented a policy of conciliation, and it is even possible that this may have extended to his Moslem subjects. Later tradition alleged that he knew Arabic,[83] and among the most curious relics of his rule are coins which represent him in a headdress that looks like a turban, surrounded by an inscription in Greek letters.[84] Tancred's rule was certainly not oppressive and it appears to have been readily accepted. No rebellion marked his administration of Antioch, and at the end of his reign his subjects rallied to his support during the critical campaign of 1111. His government of Antioch seems in its details to have been remarkably efficient,[85] and alike in its feudal organization and its administrative practice it reflected developments in the Norman states of Europe rather than those deriving from Lorraine or Provence which were to be displayed to some extent in the other crusading states.[86] In all these ways Tancred's government seems most notably to have fostered the interests of the principality whose power he so vastly increased. Self-regarding, secular and ruthless, he served the welfare of those he ruled, and he established on sure foundations the Norman state in Syria.

VII

Tancred died in December 1112 at the early age of thirty-six or thirty-seven.[87] On his death-bed he is said to have made certain dispositions which were substantially to affect the future.[88] His widow, Cecilia of France, was to marry Pons, the son of Bertrand count of Tripoli. Until Bohemund, the infant son of Bohemund I, should come to Syria, Antioch was to be ruled by Roger of Salerno, the son of Richard of the principate, once lord of

---

[82] Röhricht, *Regesta*, No. 36; Will. Tyre, IX, c. 13.

[83] *Historia Belli Sacri*, c. 67.

[84] Nicholson, *op. cit.*, pp. 6–8; Archer and Kingsford, *Crusades*, p. 145 and Plate.

[85] Cahen, *op. cit.*, pp. 435 et sqq.

[86] Runciman, *op. cit.*, I, *passim*.

[87] Stevenson, *op. cit.*, pp. 94, 95. [88] Will. Tyre, c. 8.

Edessa. Thus the cohesion of the Norman and Hauteville interest in Syria was safeguarded, and in the event Roger of Salerno was to reap the full benefit of Tancred's achievement. He dominated his Christian neighbours in Tripoli and Edessa and in 1115 defeated at Tel Danith, across the Orontes, a large Turkish force which was threatening his principality.[89] So complete was this victory that if it had been followed up, Aleppo itself might have fallen to the Normans. But Roger was content to have safeguarded his own territory, and it is impossible to avoid the impression that the aggressive vigour which had created the Norman power in Syria had departed with the death of Tancred. The Norman state of Antioch was never stronger or more feared than it was between 1112 and 1119 at the time of Roger of Salerno,[90] but Norman policy seemed to be turning away from expansion, and degenerating into a defensive effort to preserve earlier conquests or inherited possessions.[91]

The decline in the influence of Norman Antioch was enhanced by a series of crises respecting the succession. In 1119 Roger of Salerno, together with many of his troops, perished at the hands of the Turks near Sar-Meda, after a terrible battle known later as the 'Field of Blood'.[92] Baldwin II, now king of Jerusalem, thereupon took over the administration of Antioch on behalf of his daughter Alice, the wife of Bohemund II. In 1126, Bohemund II himself arrived from Italy to claim his inheritance. But he only survived until 1130, when he was killed in Cilicia by the troops of Zenghi. He left as his heiress his daughter Constance, who was then only nine years old. Her marriage therefore became a political issue of immediate urgency.[93] The Eastern emperor was naturally directly concerned, as were also Baldwin II and Fulk count of Anjou, who in August 1131 succeeded to the kingship in Jerusalem. At the same time Alice, the redoubtable widow of Bohemund II, seized the opportunity to try to regain the influence she had lost.

The matter was also of deep interest to Roger, the new Norman king of Sicily. For Roger the Great, who had so recently achieved royalty, had never ceased to assert his right of succession to the kingdom of Jerusalem in virtue of the treaties made in 1113 on the occasion of the childless marriage of his mother Adelaide to King Baldwin I.[94] And he could also put forward a claim

[89] Runciman, *op. cit.*, II, pp. 131–3.

[90] Cahen, *op. cit.*, pp. 275–83.

[91] Stevenson, *op. cit.*, p. 95.

[92] Runciman, *op. cit.*, II, pp. 149–52.

[93] Setton and Baldwin, *op. cit.*, I, pp. 436, 437. [94] Above, chap. 2.

to Antioch itself. Before he left for Syria in 1126, Bohemund II is alleged to have appointed William duke of Apulia as his heir. There is some confusion about these arrangements, but it is certain that when William died without issue in 1127, Roger of Sicily, who succeeded him in the duchy of Apulia, also claimed any rights which Bohemund II might have acquired in Antioch. And after Bohemund's death he determined to seize them.[95]

It is little wonder, therefore, that the negotiations respecting the marriage of the child Constance were long and acrimonious. At length, however, the successful claimant was not, as might have been expected, Manuel, son of the Byzantine emperor John II Comnenus, but Raymond 'of Poitiers', son William IX duke of Aquitaine.[96] Thus once again the Norman world found itself to be generally involved. For the choice challenged the Syrian claims which were already being put forward by King Roger of Sicily. Moreover, Raymond himself was at this very time established at the English court of King Henry I, whose daughter was the wife of Geoffrey of Anjou, son of King Fulk of Jerusalem, and who was to be the mother of Henry II, king of England.

After considerable adventures[97] Raymond at length arrived in Syria to claim his child-bride and his principality. But between 1119 and 1139 the power of Antioch had been sapped by these continual disputes as to the succession, and Raymond was in no position to resist the attacks which must inevitably be made upon him. Thus he had at once to face the hostility of the Eastern emperor, whose son had been rebuffed, and whose claims on Antioch had never been abrogated. The expeditions of John Comnenus against Antioch were in fact to be most damaging. Of one of them it is said:

> He first took Tarsus and Mamistra and numerous strongholds and a vast expanse of land. After expelling the Catholic bishops in these cities and replacing them with heretics, he besieged Antioch. And although it was his duty to ward off the nearby infidels by uniting the Christian forces, none the less it was with the aid of infidels that he strove to destroy the Christians.[98]

The account is of course biased, but it must, none the less, be remembered that the emperor's campaigns against Antioch were undertaken at a time

[95] Chalandon, *Domination*, I, pp. 380–1.
[96] Setton and Baldwin, *op. cit.*, I, p. 437.
[97] Roger actually tried to kidnap him on his way from London to Antioch.
[98] Otto of Freising, *Chronicle*, VII, c. 28.

when Zenghi was beginning his counter-attack against the Christians. At all events, they were at first successful against the Norman principality. In 1138, after a siege, the emperor made a ceremonious entry into Antioch, and the Greek imperial flag flew once again over the city.[99] All that Bohemund and Tancred had contended for seemed to have been lost, for at different times both Raymond and his immediate successor recognized both the emperor and the king of Jerusalem as their suzerains.

It would, however, be easy to exaggerate the decline in the political influence of the Norman principality during these unfortunate years. Roger of Salerno never recognized any overlord, and the regency of King Baldwin II was first sanctioned by the High Court of Antioch and later exercised by him specifically as the guardian of his granddaughter, Constance. Similarly, Fulk of Anjou king of Jerusalem, acted as regent in Antioch only in virtue of the relationship to Constance, whose aunt he had married. And more notably still, the barons of Antioch showed such effective hostility to John Comnenus in 1138 that the emperor was forced to leave Antioch very soon after his triumphant entry into the city.[100] Finally, on the death of Raymond of Poitiers in 1149, neither Constance nor her greater vassals thought it necessary to ask anyone's leave in respect of her remarriage. In fact, she took as her second husband not a nominee from Constantinople, but Rainald of Châtillon, near Auxerre, a knight of middle rank, who would administer Antioch in the name of his wife. Her daughter, Maria, was in due course to marry the emperor Manuel Comnenus.[101]

Despite occasional concessions enforced by circumstances, the claims of Antioch to be independent were never abandoned, and they were normally enforced. Even Raymond of Poitiers, who was sometimes compelled to bow to Constantinople or Jerusalem, could still style himself *Princeps Antiocheni regni*,[102] and Jocelyn of Edessa acknowledged his vassalage to the ruler of Antioch, *teste Raimundo Antichae principe regnante*.[103] Bohemund and Tancred had in short created a strong military state which could vindicate its autonomy, and which would outlast the kingdom of Jerusalem itself. Norman Antioch always remained the most powerful of the Latin states of the East and in other conditions it might have developed into a kingdom as strong

[99] Will. Tyre, XIV, c. 30; Ord. Vit., V, pp. 99–101.
[100] *Ibid.*
[101] Runciman, *op. cit.*, II, pp. 358–60.
[102] Röhricht, *Regesta*, No. 194.
[103] *Ibid.*, No. 206.

and as efficient as that of Roger the Great in Sicily or Henry I in England. Constant wars, the difficulties in the succession, and the ultimate substitution of a French for a Norman dynasty were, however, to prevent this. Thus it was that during the years which separated the death of Bohemund II in 1130 from the opening of the Second Crusade in 1147, the Norman impact on the crusading movement came to be made less from Norman Antioch than from Norman Sicily. The future lay with St Bernard and Roger the Great.

Chapter 11

ROGER THE GREAT AND ST BERNARD

I

Between 1146 and 1154 the crusading movement was drastically modified, and the Norman influence upon it changed. The long disputes over the succession at Antioch and the decline of the principality had taken place during the same years as there had risen to power a dominant Norman kingdom in the Mediterranean. Moreover, these two developments were themselves contemporary with the achievement by Islam of a new unity in Syria under the leadership of Zenghi of Mosul. The Moslem counter-offensive against the Christians was beginning, and it obtained its first great success with Zenghi's final capture of Edessa in December 1144. That event profoundly affected public opinion both in the East and in the West. Throughout Islam it was hailed as the beginning of the recovery of Syria from the Franks, and after his death in 1146 Zenghi passed on his prestige to his son Nureddin, who was in every way qualified to carry on the work of his father as a champion of the Faith.[1]

In the West too the effects of the capture of Edessa were specially to be felt. The Latin states of Syria were all menaced, and the Norman princi-pality was particularly involved. Raymond prince of Antioch, who was also overlord of Edessa, therefore sponsored an urgent appeal to Pope Eugenius III, begging that the 'unconquerable Strength of the Franks'[2] might be mobilized against Islam. As a consequence, on 1 December 1145, Eugenius, who was then in exile from Rome owing to the rebellion of Arnold of Brescia, issued his famous bull, *Quantum praedecessores*.[3] It was addressed to Louis VII of France and called on him and on all the princes and the faithful in his realm to go to the rescue of the Churches in the East. This Christian duty would, moreover, be recompensed by specific religious rewards. The families and

---

[1] Stevenson, *Crusaders in the East*, pp. 87–152.

[2] Otto of Freising, *Two Cities*, VII, c. 33. The pope, who was exiled from Rome by Arnold of Brescia, was at the same time informed of the exploits of a great Christian hero in the Far East. Thus did Prester John enter into Western history (cf. Runciman, *Crusades*, II, p. 467).

[3] Text in *Pat. Lat.*, 180, col. 1065; and *Rec. Hist. Franc.*, XV, p. 429.

possessions of those taking part would be protected, and at the same time the Crusading Indulgence was clarified and extended. After invoking the sanction of 'Almighty God, and of St Peter chief of the Apostles', the pope continued:

> By the authority vested in us by God, we grant such remission of sins and absolution . . . that whoever will faithfully begin, and complete such a holy journey, or will die on it, will obtain remission of all his sins which he will have confessed with a humble and a contrite heart, and will receive the fruit of eternal reward from the Remunerator of all things.

The bull was proclaimed afresh at the French royal court at Vesalay on 31 March 1146 amid scenes of intense enthusiasm. And the result was the inception of the so-called Second Crusade.[4]

As it developed, moreover, the Second Crusade became far wider in scope than the First. The original impulse had been given by a Moslem threat in Syria, and the papal appeal had been directed in the first instance to France. But the resulting campaigns spread over all the frontiers of Europe until it must have seemed as if Christendom had determined to make a united onslaught against all its infidel foes. It was indeed a new and striking phenomenon of the Holy War that so many scattered expeditions should have been undertaken between 1146 and 1149, and all professedly inspired by the same pious motives.[5] The simultaneous eruption of all this activity suggests a closer coordination of crusading endeavour than anything that had been attempted in 1096. And the explanation will be found first in the preaching of St Bernard, and secondly in the more precise definition of papal crusading policy that was achieved at this time.[6]

The Second Crusade, unlike the First, was to attract the personal participation of many of the most powerful rulers of the West.[7] The most enthusiastic of these was Louis VII of France,[8] and his example would be followed

---

[4] It would be pedantic to discard the term 'Second Crusade', though there were many expeditions between it and the 'First Crusade'. On everything connected with the Second Crusade I am particularly indebted to a notable article by Professor Giles Constable in *Traditio*, IX (1953), pp. 213–79. See also V. G. Berry, in Setton and Baldwin, *op. cit.*, I, chap. XV, and Runciman, *op. cit.*, II, pp. 247–88.

[5] Constable, *op. cit.*, p. 215 n. 8.   [6] Below, Chap. 9.

[7] On what here follows, see Constable, *op. cit.*, pp. 213, 214, 276, and the authorities there cited.

[8] He was genuinely religious; he had sins to expiate; and he desired to exalt the Christian prestige of French royalty. See Pacaut, *Louis VII*, pp. 46, 47.

by Amadeus III of Savoy. East of the Rhine,[9] the emperor Conrad III of Hohenstauffen was to decide for his own reasons to join the crusade. During these years, therefore, great armies from France and Germany would move eastward overland to Constantinople,[10] and then onwards to their fate in Asia Minor and Syria. And similar action took place elsewhere. Alphonzo-Henriques, king of Portugal, advanced towards Santorem and in due course, with the aid of ships and sailors from England, wrested Lisbon from the Moors.[11] Meanwhile, a combined force from Barcelona and Genoa attacked Minorca, and in 1147 a great expedition under Alphonzo VII of Castille swept across Aragon to capture Tortosa.[12] Far to the north, too, magnates such as Henry the Lion and Archbishop Adalbert of Bremen crossed the Elbe to make repeated attacks against the heathen Wends, while campaigns were initiated from Poland against the Slavs.[13] Here indeed was a concourse of crusading princes that had no parallel in the First Crusade. And the absence of the Norman rulers of England and Sicily from this illustrious company will immediately be noted.

A similar contrast can be discovered in the attitude of the Eastern emperor at this time. Unlike Alexis I, Manuel I in 1146 had made no appeal to the West, for at that time he had little to fear from Islam. Moreover, the initiation of the new crusade owed much to Raymond of Antioch, and the independence of the Norman principality was an abiding affront to Byzantium. Manuel had also good reason to recall the misfortunes that had befallen the empire at the time of the First Crusade, and the disaster which nearly overtook Constantinople at the hands of Bohemund I. He had thus no desire to welcome crusaders from the West. Indeed between 1146 and 1154 he would discover his chief foe not in Nureddin, the champion of Islam, but in the Norman king of Sicily. For Roger had not only inherited a tradition of bitter enmity against the Eastern empire, but he was even now challenging the naval interests of Byzantium in the eastern Mediterranean. Here, moreover, Manuel might expect to find some sympathy within the crusade itself, since

[9] See H. Cosack, *Entschluss zum Kreuzzug*; and Berry, in Setton and Baldwin, *op. cit.*, I, p. 474.

[10] They were to be followed by a naval expedition led by Alphonzo of Toulouse from Provence to the coasts of Palestine.

[11] C. W. David (ed.), *De Expugnatione Lyboniensi*.

[12] The poem *Chronicon Adefonsis Imperatoris* (*España Sagrada*, XXI, 398) gives a full account of this crusading campaign of Alphonzo VII, 'who made the trumpets of salvation sound throughout all the regions of the world'.

[13] Constable, *op. cit.*, p. 244.

Conrad from Germany had also good reason to regard the Sicilian king as an enemy and as a usurper.[14]

A new pattern of politics was thus being superimposed on the crusade. If Manuel was right to fear that Constantinople might be sacked by Western crusaders, so also was Roger justified in thinking that the crusade might be turned against Sicily with the support of the emperor at Constantinople. A chronicler remarked that if Manuel could have induced Louis VII to join with Conrad and himself in a war against Sicily, he would have given the French king half his treasure.[15] This was not to happen, but the special position which Roger would occupy in the impending crusade was already indicated in 1146. The support of the king of Sicily might well prove essential to the success of any crusading effort in the East. At the same time, Roger was the central figure in a complex of controversial relationships which involved Conrad III, the German pope Eugenius, the French king and the Eastern emperor. But even more significant was the problem of what would be Roger's personal reaction to the stimulated enthusiasm which was once again impelling Western Christendom towards a war of religion. The course and the consequences of the 'Second Crusade' – its astonishing development and its final failure – were to be determined in large measure by the inter-action between the inspiration given by St Bernard and the secular policy pursued by Roger the Great.

II

Roger had for long years sustained claims to the kingdom of Jerusalem by virtue of the second marriage of his mother,[16] and to the principality of Antioch in his capacity as the successor to William duke of Apulia. But the influence which he would exercise on the crusade would be determined more by strategic than by dynastic factors. In 1146 Roger had been king for sixteen years, and had brought to their triumphant conclusion his long wars of survival and conquest. There was no ruler in Italy who could dispute his dominion over Capua, Apulia and Calabria, while from Sicily, where he was supreme, he had steadily extended his authority along the North African coast. His widespread dominions were defended not only by Saracen mercenaries but by great fleets which the Norman rulers of Sicily had created for

[14] Cf. Wieruszowski, in Setton and Baldwin, *op. cit.*, II, pp. 2–12.
[15] Odo of Deuil, p. 83; Otto of Freising, *Gesta Friderici*, I, c. 24; *Annales Cavenses*, s.a. 1147.
[16] See above, pp. 13, 14.

their service during the past fifty years. Roger was already in control of the Mediterranean, and no expedition through the inland sea could take place without his cooperation. The implication of this with regard to any crusading activity that might be developed in Syria or Spain was clearly appreciated by the Sicilian king.

The capture of Edessa by Zenghi in 1144 not only menaced the existence of the Latin states in Syria but increased their dependence on sea power. The failure of the crusaders ever to cut the communications between Baghdad and Moslem Egypt meant that their enemies, now further strengthened by their possession of an Edessan base, could always be reinforced from the landward side. Christian domination of the sea, and control of the Syrian sea ports which gave access to it, thus became once again essential to the survival of the crusading states. In the past this had been achieved by the help of the Italian maritime cities, and their assistance was once again urgently needed. But while these Italian republics were firmly established in the Levant,[17] their own dominance on the sea had by 1146 been circumscribed by the development of Norman naval power under Roger the Great, and their interests might well clash with his. Both Pisa and Genoa were to some extent dependent on the Straits of Messina, which were firmly in Norman hands, and if Venice was wedded to the sea, the marriage might prove unproductive should Roger obtain control of both shores of the Adriatic. The success of the Second Crusade in the East evidently depended on the effective deployment of Christian naval power in the Mediterranean, and to achieve such united action the participation of King Roger would certainly be needed.

III

Roger the Great was thus deeply implicated in the Second Crusade, but he had little to do with its original initiation, and he had scant sympathy with most of the motives which inspired it. The real architects of the Second Crusade were Pope Eugenius III and St Bernard. In one respect, Eugenius might here be said to have been merely following in the steps of his predecessors, and particularly in those of Urban II. On the other hand, *Quantum Praedecessores* was perhaps the first crusading bull ever issued, for Urban II is not known to have issued any bull in this connexion, and all that we know of his acts in this respect is derived from the various reports of his famous

[17] Cf. La Monte, *Feudal Monarchy*, pp. 226 et sqq.

speech, and from one of the canons of the Council of Clermont.[18] Eugenius is moreover considered by many scholars to have given a wider definition of the crusading indulgence than had ever been offered before,[19] and thus he has been credited with making a fundamental advance in papal policy towards the crusades. His bull of 1145 'set the pattern for the juridical development of the crusade as an institution in European history'.[20]

The matter is not, however, wholly clear,[21] and whatever may have been the later implications of the acts of Eugenius III in 1145, their immediate consequences were only to be effected through the work of others. Thus the support given to the project by Louis VII in 1146 was essential, and it was in that same year that St Bernard began his preaching which was to inflame the whole of the West.[22] Then, and only then, did enthusiasm begin to spread widely, but the zeal which was now engendered was intense. Most of the chroniclers of the time grow lyrical in describing the multitudes who in France and Flanders dedicated themselves to the venture. St Bernard himself shared in this exhuberance. Writing to the pope, he exclaimed: 'Towns and castles are so emptied that one may scarcely find one man among seven women.'[23] Such statements should be received with proper caution. But there can be no doubt that the saint's preaching was eagerly welcomed, and miracles were observed to mark his journeys. The results were speedily apparent. In France, for example, an immediate response to the call came from the bishops of Noyon, Langres and Lisieux and from the counts of Perche, Nevers and Soissons,[24] and these were evidently members of a large company.

---

[18] Hefele-Leclerc, VIII, pp. 399–405.

[19] Urban, it is said, remitted only the temporal punishment inflicted on the repentant sinner by the Church on earth, whereas Eugenius, by invoking the power of the Keys, as the successor of St Peter, included for the first time absolution from the temporal punishment which is imposed by God in Purgatory for every sin in addition to the ecclesiastical discipline. See A. Gottlob, *Kreuzablass und Almosenablass* (1906), pp. 199–200, and the illuminating discussion of the whole vexed question given by Constable, *op. cit.*, pp. 244–54.

[20] Constable, *op. cit.*, p. 253.

[21] It may be noted, however, that Eugenius made reference to 'the remission of sins which our predecessors established'. The matter may here be left in suspense.

[22] Berry, in Setton and Baldwin, *op. cit.*, pp. 447–76; Pacaut, *Louis VII*, pp. 44–8.

[23] *Letters*, ed. Scott-James, Ep. 323, p. 399.

[24] Berry, in Setton and Baldwin, *op. cit.*, pp. 447–76.

Even more influential were the letters which St Bernard continued to send throughout Latin Christendom. They certainly did not lack vigour:

> Now is the acceptable time. Now is the day of abundant salvation. . . . What are you doing you mighty men of valour . . .? Your land is well known to be rich in young and vigorous men. . . . Gird yourselves therefore like men and take up your arms with joy for Christ's sal in order to take vengeance on the heathen and to curb the nations. . . . You have here a cause which you can fight without danger to your souls – a cause in which to die may give salvation.[25]

Or again:

> Why do you hesitate, you servants of the Cross? Receive the sign of the Cross, and to all of you who have confessed your sins with contrite heart, the Sovereign Pontiff . . . offers a full remission of sins. Receive this gift, and seize this opportunity which will not come again.[26]

Nor was it only to warriors that the appeal was made. An even cruder commercial argument could be used:

> You who are merchants, men quick to seek a bargain, let me point out the advantages of this great opportunity. Do not miss it. Take up the sign of the Cross and you will find indulgence for all the sins you humbly confess. The cost is small: the reward is great.[27]

Thus did St Bernard write in praise of the 'new warfare', and he could even assert that the heathen should be offered the alternative of baptism or extermination.

> We utterly forbid that for any reason whatever a truce should be made with these peoples either for money or tribute until such time as by God's help they shall either have been converted or wiped out.[28]

This grim conclusion, so characteristic of ideological wars, was in keeping with much of the propaganda which marked the First Crusade, and the same overtones of popular prophecy could once again be heard. Shortly before his death in 1134, St Norbert, the founder of Premontré, assured the doubting that the end of the world would come 'in this generation'[29] whilst Otto of Freising was convinced that the advent of Anti-Christ was at hand.[30] For the

[25] *Letters*, ed. Scott-James, Ep. 391, pp. 461–3. [26] *Ibid.*, Ep. 391, p. 464.
[27] *Ibid.*, Ep. 391, p. 462. [28] *Ibid.*, Ep. 394, p. 467.
[29] *Ibid.*, Ep. 59, p. 86. [30] Otto of Freising, *Two Cities*, VIII, c. 7.

masses, signs and wonders again multiplied to indicate his coming. But while it would be rash to minimize the persistence of chiliastic sentiment in Western Europe during the earlier half of the twelfth century, or the degree to which it might be exploited by the unscrupulous, none the less the Second Crusade was less marked than the First by popular fanaticism. St Bernard addressed himself in the main not to the masses but to men in authority. Himself a conformist to the social order to which he belonged, he was anxious to curb these self-styled 'prophets' who were eager, as in the past, to provoke the mob to violence and atrocities.

Perhaps for this reason the Second Crusade was also less disfigured than the First by persecutions of the Jews. Anti-Semitic feeling was very strong both in France and England, and Peter the Venerable, abbot of Cluny asked:

> Why should not the Jews contribute more than anyone else to the Holy War? Robbers as they are, this is the time to make them disgorge.[31]

In the Rhineland a yet more serious situation was threatened when a wandering monk named Rodulf preached a pogrom to a population that had been inflamed by rumours of an alleged ritual murder of a Christian boy in Norwich two years previously.[32] But against all this St Bernard set his face. His denunciations of Rodulf were numerous and stern,[33] and his letters contain frequent admonitions in the same sense. 'The Jews', he declared, 'are not to be persecuted, killed or put to flight.' . . . 'Is it not a far better triumph for the Church to convince and convert the Jews than to put them to the sword?'[34]

St Bernard's preaching was first directed towards France and Flanders. Soon, however, his message was carried across the Channel to England and to the remoter parts of Britain. There the result was as curious as it was remarkable. 'You would have thought', declared an Anglo-Norman chronicler, 'that England was drained of men. When so many, and of such importance, were everywhere setting out.'[35] This, however, is an exaggeration. It is true that William of Warenne, Roger of Montbrai, Walter FitzGilbert of Clare, Philip, son of Robert earl of Gloucester, and William Peveril of Dover, joined the venture. But some of these had good reasons for absenting

[31] Migne, *Pat. Lat.*, 189, col. 369.
[32] M. D. Anderson, *A Saint at Stake: the strange death of William of Norwich* (1964).
[33] Berry, in Setton and Baldwin, *op. cit.*, I, pp. 472–4.
[34] *Letters*, ed. Scott-James, Epp. 392, 393, pp. 464, 466.
[35] *Gesta Stephani*, ed. Potter, p. 127.

themselves from England at this time,[36] and, speaking generally, the response of the Anglo-Norman baronage to the call for the Second Crusade was luke-warm, or self-interested. A letter from Eugenius sent to Jocelyn bishop of Salisbury in November 1146[37] shows that men who had been dispossessed of their lands before the preaching of the crusade, either by King Stephen or by his opponents, had subsequently taken the Cross in Order to claim the ecclesiastical protection granted to the property of crusaders.[38] Similarly, the greater enthusiasm generated among sea-faring folk in the southern and eastern shires was produced by the hope that ancient traditions of piracy could be com-bined with such religious warfare as might result in the capture of Lisbon.[39]

But during the spring and the summer of 1146, St Bernard made his famous miracle-working journeys to the Rhineland, to Switzerland and into Germany. And in the late autumn he had his most notable personal triumph when he persuaded the emperor Conrad III to take the Cross and to lead an army in person for the relief of Edessa. St Bernard called this the 'miracle of miracles', and its political repercussions were immediately to be felt. For just as Eugenius had not wished Conrad to go on crusade so long as the emperor could be used against Arnold of Brescia in Rome, so also had Roger the Great hoped for Conrad's departure since this would rid him of his most formidable enemy in Europe. The Norman King of Sicily thus had every reason to be pleased at what had occurred. Moreover, the crusade to the East could not now be regarded as primarily the affair of the king of France with his allies. Unlike the First, the Second Crusade involved a joint effort to the East by great armies recruited from both sides of the Rhine. The crusade, in short, could no longer be claimed in any restricted sense to be the *Gesta Dei per Francos*. It was in fact a German charter which in 1147 was dated at the time 'when the whole Roman world swore together . . . for the expedition to Jerusalem'.[40]

IV

It was during these same months also that the scope of the crusade was vastly extended in the public opinion of the West. And here was perhaps the most striking result of the close association of St Bernard with the pope. St Bernard, who so vociferously preached the Holy War, never limited its

---

[36] Cf. *Complete Peerage*, XII (i), pp. 457, 458. Robert of Torigni, *Chronicles*, IV, p. 152.

[37] Lowenfeld, *Epp. Pontificum*, No. 200, pp. 103–4.

[38] Constable, *op. cit.*, p. 261. [39] David, *De Expugnatione*, pp. 5–6.

[40] *Monumenta Boica*, No. 7348, quoted by Constable, *op. cit.*, p. 240.

objectives to Syria and Palestine. All the campaigns against unbelievers were in his opinion of equal religious value, and they should all attract the same ecclesiastical support and the same spiritual rewards. And this view came more and more to pervade Latin Christendom. Thus chroniclers in England and Scotland were keenly interested in the wars in Spain and Portugal,[41] whilst German annalists, occupied in the first instance with their own eastern frontiers, were almost equally concerned with the fate of the Germans and French armies in Syria. Again, Odo of Deuil, whose main preoccupation was naturally with his own King Louis VII, found time to comment on the English and Flemish expedition to Lisbon, and Otto of Freising in his notable history mentions in the same context the efforts of the Christians against the Wends and Slavs, together with the campaigns in Spain and before Damascus.[42] It was perhaps a German writer who best summed up the matter when he said, 'It seemed advisable that one part of our forces should go to the East, that another should go to Spain, and that yet another should be armed against the heathen Slavs who are nearest to us.'[43] These writers did not even distinguish clearly between Moslems and pagans, and one of them actually referred to the Wends as Saracens. The Christian armies everywhere could be considered as brothers in a common enterprise. Were they not all inspired by the same motives, and did they not all wear with variations the same crusading badge?[44]

Of course, not all such sentiments should be taken at their face value. But they cannot be ignored, and what gave them substance were the official pronouncements of the Church. As early as the summer of 1146 Eugenius conferred all the crusading privileges, both spiritual and temporal, on the Christians fighting against the Moors in Spain, and he was eager from the start to sponsor the expeditions against the Wends and the heathen Slavs. When in April 1147 he addressed the second issue of his bull *Divina Dispensatione* 'to all the faithful', he at length brought these scattered enterprises under the same patronage, to be fortified by the same spiritual sanctions. He praised those who had joined the expedition to the East and then continued:

> The king of Spain also is powerfully armed against the Saracens of those regions over whom he has frequently triumphed. . . . Certain of you,

[41] David, *De Expugnatione, passim;* Gervase of Canterbury, pp. 137, 138; *Chronicom Melrose,* p. 34; Saxo Grammaticus, p. 376. Cf. Constable, *op. cit.,* pp. 218–26.

[42] *Chronicon,* I, cc. 35–47; *Gesta Friderici,* I, cc. 61–6.

[43] Helmold of Bosen, cited by Constable, *op. cit.,* p. 225.

[44] The form of badge worn against the Wends was a circle surmounted by a cross.

however, are anxious to participate in this holy work, and plan to go against the Slavs and other pagans in the north in order to subject them to the Christian religion. We recognize this devotion. And to all who have decided to go against the Slavs, and remain in a spirit of devotion, we grant the same remission of sins and the same temporal privileges as to the crusaders proceeding to Jerusalem.[45]

By the spring of 1147, therefore, the pope, with St Bernard and his supporters, had transformed the character of the crusade. It was no longer viewed primarily as an attempt to sustain the Latin states of Syria, or even to protect the Holy Places of Palestine. It was now consciously planned as a general Christian offensive against unbelievers everywhere. Moreover, all the acts of the heathen could be regarded as a punishment for Christian sins, and the Holy War was thus envisaged not only as an opportunity for individual penance, but as providing vicarious satisfaction for the sins of Christendom as a whole.[46] That is what gave the campaigns of 1146–8 their ecumenical significance. And that is what made the failure of those campaigns so damaging to Christian morale.

Never had the Holy War been more vigorously proclaimed by the papacy or more ardently preached than by St Bernard. Thousands throughout the West had been made vividly aware of the great endeavour to which Christendom was pledged. And at the end of it all, as Robert of Torigny declared, 'nothing worthy of note had been done and scarcely any project had succeeded.[47] No lasting results were obtained from the wars against the Wends and the Slavs. And the great armies which went to the East suffered utter humiliation. After bitter quarrels between each other, and with the Eastern empire, the French army was defeated in an engagement in the Cadmus mountains, and the Germans were routed at Dorylaeum. Finally, the whole crusade in the East, weakened by these reverses, failed miserably before Damascus, and the princes and barons came home separately and without honour. Twelve years after the proclamation of the Holy War by Eugenius III, only Lisbon and Tortosa remained in Christian hands as a result of all these immense endeavours. For John of Salisbury, and for many others, this

---

[45] *Pat. Lat.*, 180, col. 1203; Constable, *op. cit.*, p. 255.

[46] *Letters*, ed. Scott-James, Ep. 391, pp. 461–2; Alphandéry and Dupront, *L'Idée de Croisade*, I, pp. xx, 185.

[47] Robert of Torigny, in Howlett (ed.), *Chronicles of the Reign of Stephen*, IV, p. 154; Constable, *op. cit.*, p. 215.

was indeed a terrible disaster for all Christians everywhere. And men were naturally quick to ask how such a catastrophe could ever have taken place.[48]

In view of the pious exhortations which preceded the crusade, it was inevitable that many should find spiritual reasons for its failure.[49] 'God', declared the annalist of Wurzburg, 'permitted the Western Church to be thus afflicted in order to punish Christians for their sins.' And the same theme was developed by Gerhoh of Reichersburg while discoursing on Anti-Christ.[50] More precise explanations were also given. For some, the misfortunes which befell the crusaders came from 'the jealousy of princes and the wrangling of prelates'.[51] According to others, the Germans were reluctant to help the French, whilst the French found the Germans 'intolerable'.[52] Finally, French and Norman writers[53] were quick to blame Byzantium for the catastrophe. The emperor Manuel was denounced as a false friend and a secret enemy; the Greeks were hateful; and Constantinople was 'arrogant in her wealth, treacherous in her practices, and corrupt in her faith'.[54] The relative importance, or indeed the combined adequacy of these explanations offered for the failure of the Second Crusade, could in fact be endlessly debated. Certainly they must be assessed in close relation to the political developments which gave them substance. Most particularly must they be considered in connexion with the acts of Roger the Great.

V

No consideration of the Second Crusade can avoid the question how far the Norman king of Sicily was responsible for its collapse, and thus for what was widely felt to be a disaster for the whole of Christendom. In 1146 Roger was admirably placed to give decisive assistance to the crusade, and he had,

[48] John of Salisbury, *Historia Pontificalis*, cc. XVIII, XXIII–XXVII.

[49] Most of the citations which here follow will be found in Professor Constable's notable article.

[50] *Ann. Herbipolenses, Mon. Germ. Hist. SS.*, XVI, p. 3; Gerhoh of Reichersberg, *De Investigatione Anti-Christi, Mon. Germ. Hist. Libelli de Lite*, III, p. 376. Others found it more comfortable to discover the cause of God's anger not in their own sins but in these of the Crusaders (cf. Hen. Hunt., pp. 280–1).

[51] John of Salisbury, *Historia Pontificalis*, c. XXIV.

[52] Otto of Freising, *Two Cities*, VII, c. 6; Odo of Deuil, c. III, p. 43.

[53] Anti-Byzantine sentiment was less frequently expressed by German commentators (cf. Constable, *op. cit.*, pp. 272–3).

[54] Odo of Deuil, c. V, p. 87.

moreover, recently been its chief promoter. The bitter invective directed by St Bernard against Roger at the time of his coronation had been discontinued after the king's pact with the papacy at Mignano in 1139. Later, too, Roger had permitted Cistercian monks to settle in Sicily. The saint could now therefore actually address the man whose 'tyranny' he had denounced, as 'one whose Fame had come to spread over the world' so that 'there is scarcely a corner of the earth where the glory of your name has not penetrated'.[55] It was doubtless satisfactory to both parties. But Roger could hardly be expected to respond with enthusiasm to the saint's crusading zeal. He ruled over an island which was largely Moslem in population, and both in Sicily and in North Africa he was already developing a policy of toleration that was beginning to yield notable results.[56] Personally indifferent to religion, and coldly calculating in his public relations, he was unlikely to be moved by St Bernard's emotional proclamation of the Holy War.

His crusading policy was further conditioned by the relations that had already developed between him and the other rulers in the West.[57] Conrad was his bitter enemy, and the departure of the German king probably prevented an imperial invasion of Apulia. In view of this, there could never be any question of Norman ships transporting German troops eastward from Italian ports. With Louis VII, however, the situation was different. Although the French king's wife, Eleanor, was a niece of Raymond of Antioch and thus opposed to any design that Roger may have had on the principality, relations between Sicily and France had been steadily improving since 1140, and Roger did not at first refuse naval assistance to the French crusade. For sentimental reasons, however, Louis VII preferred the route taken by the First Crusade, and so, after an interval of about a month, he followed the Germans on the way through Hungary to Constantinople. The Second Crusade was, therefore, like the First, to be land-based, and this was to prove a most serious handicap. 'Those who were destined to die chose the road through Greece.'[58]

There were, moreover, other more serious implications in the relation between Roger and Louis VII. Ever since 1140 there had been a party at the French court which considered that the chief obstacle to the success of Latin Christendom in the East was the Byzantine empire. And this party had always looked to the Sicilian king for leadership. Since Norman hostility to Byzantium was known to be of long standing, and it was now reinforced

[55] *Letters*, ed. Scott-James, Ep. 276, pp. 348, 349.   [56] See above, chap. 3.
[57] Otto of Freising, *Two Cities*, Bk VII, *passim*.   [58] Odo of Deuil, c. 1, p. 15.

by naval rivalry in the Mediterranean, Roger was well aware that he had many friends in the French crusading expedition, and partly for this reason he decided to act independently and with ruthless speed. At the very moment when the French and German armies were beginning to arrive at Constantinople, he launched a savage attack on the Eastern empire.

In the late summer or early autumn of 1147 a powerful fleet, consisting of many of the most formidable war vessels of the age, both biremes and triremes, was collected from all the ports of Apulia, and placed under the command of the emir George of Antioch. It set sail from Otranto, and proceeded across the Adriatic carrying a raiding force of considerable size. Corfu and Cephallonia were captured, and the expedition proceeded round the southern tip of Greece, ravaging the countryside in its progress, and setting up a garrison in the island of Cerigo to control the isthmus. In due course Thebes was reached. The town was sacked, and many hundreds of silkworkers were transported from there to Palermo in order to develop the silk-weaving industry in Sicily. The next victim was Athens, where considerable damage was done, and then the ships proceeded up the Gulf of Corinth. Both the Town and Acro-Corinth were looted. At last, early in 1148, the fleet sailed back to Sicily with such loads of plunder, including gold and silver treasure, that 'you would have thought that the vessels were freighters rather than ships of war'.[59]

This expedition was to affect the whole course of the crusade. Not only did it weaken the strongest Christian power in the East, but it exacerbated the tensions already existing among the crusaders, and sharpened their antagonism towards Byzantium. Thus before ever the French reached the Bosphorus there were some who urged Louis to turn back and seize the rich lands through which he had passed, and they added also that he should send messages to King Roger so that aided by the Norman fleet he could attack Constantinople itself.[60] When the French arrived at the outskirts of the city, this same action was passionately urged by Godfrey bishop of Langres, who pointed out how easily they could capture the city 'which was only Christian in name'. The bishop enlarged also on the vast amount of booty that could be obtained. It was indeed only after considerable debate that the French king decided to push on towards Syria.[61]

Roger's attack was also partly responsible for a most unfortunate development of Byzantine policy which now occurred. About this time, the emperor

[59] Chalandon, *Domination*, II, pp. 135–8; Caspar, *op. cit.*, pp. 374–85.
[60] Odo of Deuil, c. III, p. 59.   [61] *Ibid.*, c. IV, pp. 69–72.

made some sort of treaty with the Turks by which the latter could feel themselves at liberty to attack the crusaders without interference from Constantinople.[62] It is easy to see the bitterness that this caused, particularly among the French who had moved south to Ephesus and then suffered heavy losses from the Turks as they crossed over the mountains to take refuge in Attalia. Thus it was that 'the flowers of France withered before ever they could bloom at Damascus'.[63] And the emperor's contribution to the calamity was not easily to be forgotten. It is true that Manuel could argue that by the autumn of 1147 he had more to fear from the crusaders than from the Turks, and most of all from the Norman king of Sicily. But in the event the two navies which might have brought the crusade to success – those of Roger and Manuel – were throughout its course busily engaged in fighting each other.

Roger's war against the Eastern empire was to outlast the crusade itself. It forced the emperor to make alliances both with Conrad and with the Venetians in order that together they might withstand this 'dragon of the West, the common enemy of Christendom and the usurper of Sicily'.[64] The ensuing warfare, however, hardly merited so exalted a description. In 1149 Roger again raided the empire and his soldiers as a gesture fired burning arrows into the imperial palace outside Constantinople.[65] Manuel gained a more solid success when after many attempts he regained possession of Corfu.[66] Otherwise, all these hostilities were inconclusive. But in the meantime the crusade, which needed the support both of Manuel and Roger, had moved inexorably to its sorry conclusion. After their defeats in Asia Minor, the French and German forces were transported separately to Syria, and in company of the king of Jerusalem they moved to make their ill-considered assault on Damascus. There they found themselves divided by the mutual suspicions which had been fostered by the Sicilian king, and thus did they meet their final defeat.[67] Their return was inglorious. The French king with his wife Eleanor, after an attack by Byzantine ships, were rescued at sea by by the Normans and reached Calabria in July 1145.[68] Conrad, who dared not

[62] *Ibid.*, c. III, p. 55. But see the comments of Runciman in *Crusades*, II, pp. 274, 275.
[63] Odo of Deuil, c. VI, p. 119.
[64] Charter given by Manuel in 1148, cited by Chalandon, *Domination*, II, p. 138.
[65] Ibn Athir, in Amari, *Bibl. Arabo-Sicula*, p. 121.
[66] Chalandon, *Domination*, II, pp. 143–5.
[67] Runciman, *Crusades*, II, pp. 280–4. For an Islamic account by Ibn Al Qalanisi, see Gabrielli, *Arab Historians*, pp. 56–63.
[68] John of Salisbury, *Historia Pontificalis*, c. XXVIII. Louis had an interview with Roger at Potenza.

face the Norman navy, proceeded first to Constantinople and after an interval took the land route back to Germany.[69]

In the light of this record it is impossible not to regard Roger the Great as primarily responsible for the failure of the Second Crusade. It was not, however, confined to operations in the Levant, where Roger could exercise his full power. And even in the Mediterranean zone his influence needs to be carefully assessed. Certainly, the Christian armies in Syria had good reason to complain of his policy, but during these same years Roger was bringing to completion his own North African conquests with the capture of Tripoli on 15 June 1146 and that of the great Zirid metropolis of Al Mahdia in June 1148.[70] It was perhaps natural, therefore, that both Christian and Moslem writers should have been tempted to comment on these expeditions as if they were part of a Holy War. But it would be totally misleading to receive such declarations at their face value. Roger's African policy was dominated throughout by secular motives. Nor, as has been seen, was his government over the lands he conquered ever substantially influenced by religious considerations. It is hardly surprising that there seems no record that Roger's expeditions into Africa were ever actively sponsored by the papacy, or that his troops in these campaigns were ever accorded the crusaders' indulgence which was so widely conferred by Eugenius III during these years. Roger's wars in Africa between 1146 and 1148 were in fact part of the same endeavour which directed his great attack on the Eastern empire in 1147. Throughout, the overriding purpose of the Norman king was not to wage a religious war against Islam but to establish Norman dominance in the Mediterranean. In this endeavour he achieved spectacular success, but in so doing he inflicted irreparable damage on the Christian cause in the crusades.

VI

Although its ultimate consequences were only later to be fully disclosed, the specifically Norman contribution to the 'World's Debate' reached its conclusion with the death of Roger the Great in 1154. Already, however, that contribution had been revealed as both important and paradoxical. The Norman support of the papacy, and the Norman exploitation of the concept of the Holy War, gave to the crusading movement in its early stages an impetus

---

[69] Cf. Runciman, *Crusades*, II, p. 285.   [70] Above, pp. 55 et sqq.

which it might not otherwise have possessed, and much of the success attained by the armies of the West during the First Crusade was due to Norman generalship and Norman prowess in the field. But the influence of the Normans on the crusades was throughout determined by interests which were peculiar to themselves. No Norman ruler who was firmly established in the West, for instance, saw fit to make the journey to Syria. Thus the proposal that Count Roger I should participate in the First Crusade was rejected by him with coarse emphasis,[71] and during the first quarter of the twelfth century King Henry I of England was never tempted to qualify his secular interests in the North with any concern over the affairs of Palestine. Even Bohemund showed himself in the East less a crusader than as the heir to Robert Guiscard, and it was thus that he took his place alongside the other great Norman conquerors such as William of England and Roger the Great Count of Sicily. The Norman participation in the First Crusade reached its climax not at the Holy Sepulchre but at Antioch.

The establishment of the Norman principality of Antioch which was achieved at the expense not only of the Turks but also of Byzantium gave a new colour to the whole crusading movement. Henceforth such influence as had been exercised on the crusades by the Anglo-Norman kingdom now steadily declined, and the policy pursued by Bohemund and Tancred conformed more closely to that of the Norman rulers in Italy and Sicily. The very existence of Norman Antioch was an affront to Byzantium, which had never even recognized the Norman rule in Apulia or Calabria. And the Eastern empire was well aware that the Normans would always be ready to pose as the champions of Latin orthodoxy against the heresies of the Greeks. The division between Eastern and Western Europe was thus further enhanced. But at the same time the blatant territorial ambitions of Bohemund caused a certain disillusion in the West. Many might follow Bohemund in his attack on Alexis in 1106, but it is significant that after this 'crusade' against Constantinople, no great expedition to the Holy Land was planned in Europe until some forty years later when Latin Christendom was fired by the preaching of St Bernard.

King Roger's great attack on the Eastern empire in 1147 was thus in the tradition established by Bohemund. But it was conducted with infinitely larger resources, and the sentiments which animated his policy had by now been widely disseminated through the crusade. It is remarkable for instance that Odo of Deuil, speaking for the French about the misdeeds of the

[71] Cf. Gabrielli, *Arab Historians*, p. 4.

Eastern emperor, makes the bishop of Langres refer particularly to the wrongs which Byzantium had done to the Norman principality of Antioch.[72] There were indeed very many in the French force who welcomed Roger's attack of the emperor Manuel, and it was only the pious resolve of King Louis VII that prevented Constantinople from being sacked by Western crusaders in 1147 instead of in 1204. As it was, Roger, the Norman king of Sicily, did not destroy Byzantium. But he brought the Second Crusade to disaster.

The crusading movement as a whole was in fact never fully to recover from his acts. The greatest armies that had ever been sent from Western Europe to the Levant had suffered humiliating defeat. Nor was it only specific reverses that the Christians had to lament. There were also the great opportunities that had been missed. Never during the First Crusade had there been any possibility of coalescing the Christian endeavours in Spain and Syria into a united effort. But in the Second Crusade it was otherwise. That was what St Bernard and Pope Eugenius had envisaged, and that was what Roger, with his command of the Mediterranean and his African conquests, might have brought about. As it was, his policy was directed towards the destruction of the Eastern empire and the consolidation of his own power. Islam was thus saved from what might have been its greatest defeat at Christian hands – the loss of Aleppo and the permanent separation of Egypt from the Maghreb. With the union of Aleppo and Damascus under Nureddin in 1154, an uninterrupted Moslem dominion was created, stretching from Baghdad to Cairo. This effectively encircled the Latin states in the East and, despite all subsequent efforts, their ultimate fate could hardly be doubted.

Of almost equal importance was the damage to Christian morale caused by the wide and deep sense of failure which came to pervade the West.[73] There were even some who were led to question the spiritual leadership of Latin Christendom. St Bernard, the most renowned preacher of the age, had with all his authority promised God's blessing on the enterprise he extolled, and now this had degenerated into calamity. Similarly, Pope Eugenius III had offered, from the throne of St Peter, the most emphatic spiritual privileges to the crusaders, and now he had to lament 'the severe disaster to the Christian name which the Church has suffered in our time'.[74] How far this reaction against ecclesiastical authority was allowed to proceed is uncertain.

[72] Odo of Deuil, c. IV, p. 69–71.
[73] See Constable, *op. cit.*, pp. 266–76.
[74] Jaffé-Lowenfeld, No. 9347.

But it was evidently widespread. Thus John of Salisbury wrote that in 1148 Pope Eugenius hurried over the Alps from France into Italy:

> The more speedily (as some alleged) because news of the total destruction of the Christian armies in the East had reached him. And though in fact he would have been perfectly safe in France, he was unwilling at a time of such disaster to the French and German to remain in their midst.[75]

As for St Bernard, it is evident that he felt deeply the tragic situation into which he had been placed, and it is noteworthy that after 1149 there was a marked decrease in the number of Cistercian foundations.[76]

The impulse which had hitherto sustained the crusade had been irreparably impaired, and when in 1150 attempts were made in concert with St Bernard to promote a new expedition to the East, the response was lukewarm. Indeed, there now began to spread throughout the West a reaction against the whole crusading movement which was in due course to find expression in the denunciations of Albigensian heretics or in the mockeries of irreverent troubadors. The whole conception of the crusade was in fact beginning to change. Criticisms became more frequent; enthusiasm waned. It is true that the romantic exploits of Richard I were still to come, and that Louis, the sainted king, was to sail from Aigues Mortes to Egypt. But popular zeal had faded. The initial glory had departed. Never glad confident morning again.

For this transformation, Norman action between 1100 and 1154, and particularly during the reign of Roger the Great, must be held in large measure responsible. At the outset, the Normans had taken a lead in crusading warfare. But the territorial aggression which the Normans sponsored soon overcame the impulse to rescue the shrines. Crusading endeavours thus became progressively concerned more with the defence of the Latin states, such as Antioch, and less with the general war against Islam. At the same time, crusading policy came to be ever openly directed against the Eastern empire as well as against the Turks. At home, the transition was more subtle and more lasting. The crusades at their best were a reflexion of Latin Christendom. But the unity of Latin Christendom was now itself beginning to be threatened by the rise of self-sufficient secular states of which the kingdoms founded by the Normans were the most prominent. Thus not only the

---

[75] John of Salisbury, *Historia Pontificalis*, c. XVIII.
[76] Constable, *op. cit.*, p. 276.

initial success, but also the final failure, of the crusades owed much to the Normans. The crusading movement was complex in its origins, in its course, and in its consequences. But until 1154 it bore throughout a Norman imprint.

EPILOGUE

The Norman impact on the political and social growth of Europe during the earlier half of the twelfth century reached a term in 1154. On 26 February of that year, Roger the Great died at Palermo, and on 19 December Henry of Anjou was crowned at Westminster as the royal heir to the Anglo-Norman monarchy which had been ruled by his grandfather King Henry I. These events symbolized and were representative of changes of considerable magnitude. On 20 August of the previous year, St Bernard, who had for so long been the prophet of Latin Christendom, passed from the European scene, and some weeks earlier there had died Pope Eugenius III, who so consistently implemented the policies proclaimed by the saint. In 1152, Frederick Barbarossa succeeded the ineffective Conrad III as Emperor, and within four years he had not only restored order to a demoralized Germany, but inaugurated a policy which would carry the imperial power once again southward across the Alps, and eventually into the Norman kingdom of Sicily itself. Meanwhile the intellectual and artistic life of Latin Europe was developing on freshly individual lines. A new epoch was evidently opening.

Indeed, after 1154 it becomes progressively less appropriate to speak without serious qualification of any specifically Norman influence as continuing to operate on Europe at all. The consequences of policies powerfully pursued from London and Palermo would be widespread during the ensuing decades. But these policies became rapidly less and less dependent upon the Norman past. The contrast between Henry II and Henry I, kings of England, illuminates this. Henry I was a true son of William the Conqueror, and it was during his reign, and not before, that the full political and social consequences of the Norman Conquest of England began to be fully apparent. But with Henry II the situation was wholly different. Although this mother was a daughter of Henry I, his father had been a dominant count of Anjou, and it was as much an Angevin as a Norman element that he intruded into English politics. Both the constitutional changes that he effected in England, and the admirable political order which he imposed on his numerous fiefs overseas, derived in large measure from his outstanding personal qualities. And although he might at times recall that through his mother he was a great-grandson of William the Conqueror, he never forgot his Angevin ancestry, and his own temper could more properly be described as French rather than Norman.

This development in England was part of a wider movement which was taking place throughout what had been the Norman world, and it was apparent even in far-off Syria. The principality of Antioch founded by a son of Robert Guiscard and ruled successively by Bohemund and Tancred continued throughout the twelfth century to exercise a powerful influence on crusading history. But after the death of Tancred in 1112, and still more the death of Bohemund II in 1130, that influence became less definitely Norman as the succession passed in turn to the husbands of Constance, Raymond of Poitiers and Rainald of Châtillon, who were themselves not of Norman blood. As a result, after the death of Rainald in 1154, the impact of Antioch on crusading policy was to be Frankish and Syrian rather than Norman, and it was affected more and more by the power of the Sicilian kingdom now so firmly established in the central Mediterranean.

It was in fact in the Sicilian realm that this transition was to be most notably displayed. Roger the Great on occasion boasted of his Norman ancestry, and in one of his charters he actually made admiring reference to 'our Norman predecessors'. But he was only a lad at the time of his father's death, and he was brought up by his remarkable Italian mother with the aid of the Greek emir Christodoulos. Nor did he ever visit the Norman duchy in which, indeed, he would have felt a complete stranger. Moreover, during the twenty-four years he ruled as king, he presided over the most cosmo-politan court in Western Europe, where Greek and Moslem scholars and artists mingled with men from the West, and all alike enjoyed the patronage of a prince who was sympathetic to their work. Contemplating that sophis-ticated court, it comes almost as a shock to recall that this king, so versed in the manifold and contrasting cultures of his age, was actually the nephew of Robert Guiscard, the crude and brutal Norman conqueror of Apulia. The king's Norman father, Count Roger I, had effected the Norman conquest of Sicily, but after the royal reign of Roger the Great, the ever-spreading influence on Europe of the Norman Sicilian kingdom could no longer be described as exclusively, or even as predominantly, Norman.

Although these changes indicate the end of the direct Norman impact upon Europe, they should not be allowed to mask the enduring consequences of Norman action during the previous decades. The balance of power within Western Europe had been fundamentally altered. It is true that Frederick

Barbarossa would soon restore to the Germanic empire much of the dominance and more of the prestige which it had recently lost, but the great confederation of French fiefs ruled by the Angevin successor to the Norman kings of England continued to form an effective counterpoise in the West which would last until it was replaced by the rising power of the Capetian monarchy of France. In the South, too, the results on earlier Norman action were long to endure, even though the forms in which they were expressed were modified. The very fact that the whole of southern Italy together with Sicily had now been united into a single kingdom under Norman rule was a matter of vital moment to the whole of the West. If Sicilian policy in the future could no longer be styled as characteristically Norman, the political strength of the Norman Sicilian kingdom would steadily increase until it became a vital element in Western imperial power.

Of even more importance to the future would be the part played by the Normans between 1100 and 1154 in ensuring the eventual preponderance of Western over Eastern Europe. The Anglo-Norman realm, by linking England to a number of French fiefs, substantially increased the political resources of the West, and, in the South, the establishment of the new Norman kingdom in lands which had recently been under Greek or Moslem domination operated similarly. These achievements were particularly significant in that they took place at a time when the West was moving towards ecclesiastical cohesion under papal leadership. Indeed, in the crusades against Islam the Normans would themselves help to exploit the enthusiasms which had thus been engendered, and it was therefore of considerable importance to the future that the policy of the Norman Sicilian kingdom should have remained violently hostile to Byzantium, with results that were to prove disastrous to the Eastern empire as a rival to the West. For the consequential climax of Norman action in this field would not be displayed until 1204 when Constantinople was at last sacked by Western knights. In that same year Normandy would finally be separated from England and its individual influence on continental politics would cease. But the predominance of the Latin and Christian West in the civilization which until very recently was received by the world as characteristically European had by then been secured.

The Norman contribution to the history of Europe between 1100 and 1154 possessed a permanent importance as well as a particular interest. It was made during the years when Latin Christendom was attaining a new sense of political unity which would in its turn promote the formation of a European identity. In this process the Normans were intimately involved, and else-where too their acts would prove of enduring significance. The establishment of the Norman kingdoms during these decades was, for instance, a striking example of the permanent and inexorable connexion between mind and power and the men and institutions which were involved in these achievements were alike outstanding. They challenged the attention of contemporaries, and they have retained the interest of posterity. The questions which were then acutely raised in the Norman realms were among those which have remained of permanent interest to European men. They related to the most fundamental matters of faith and morals. They involved the rival claims of spiritual and temporal authority. They concerned such rights as might be asserted by the individual within the secular state. They impinged directly on the age-long and soul-stirring debate concerning those things which should be rendered to Caesar.

The ultimate consequences of these conditions were not even thus to be circumscribed. For the Normans of this age not only fostered the unity of Latin Christendom which would dominate medieval Europe. They also initiated in their kingdoms principles of government which eventually brought about its collapse. The efficient and rigorous administration of England under Henry I and Henry II, the purely secular government of Sicily under Roger the Great, foreshadowed developments which would out-last the medieval period itself. The modern absolute state, secular, centralized and aggressive, has a long and complicated ancestry stemming from pagan as well as Christian times. But there can be little doubt that in the Norman realms – in twelfth-century England and in twelfth-century Sicily – a significant stage was reached in its evolution. Here too would be raised vital issues of politics and ethics about which men have ever been ready to suffer and to die. The Norman impact upon Europe between 1100 and 1154 was made in a distant age, but some of the results of Norman action in that remote period are still alive among us today.

K.M of NORWAY

IRELAND

SCOTLAND

WALES

ENGLAND

London

SWEDEN

Elbe

Rhine

THE

EMPIRE

Danube

Reims

Paris

Loire

KINGDOM

OF

FRANCE

K.M of
LEON

Castile

Pyrenees

Marseilles

Barcelona

Corsica

Rome

Naples

ALMOR

Cordoba

Sardinia

Granada

MEDITERRA

SICI

Malta

AVIDES

Miles

0   500

NORTH   AFR

W. Bromage

EUROPE
c. 1100

Lands under
Norman rule

Lands under
Moslem rule

EASTERN EMPIRE

Durazzo

Danube

BLACK SEA

Caucasus

Constantinople

Smyrna

Athens

Crete

Cyprus

Antioch

Latakia

Aleppo

SELJUK

EMPIRE

Damascus

EAN SEA

Acre

Jerusalem

Alexandria

Cairo

FATIMITE CALIPHATE

C A

RED SEA

ARABIA

da

II The Kingdom of Roger the Great

III *The Crusading States of Syria circa 1140*

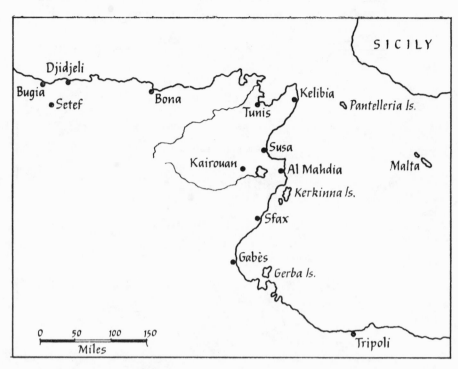

IV The African conquests of Roger the Great 1130–1154.

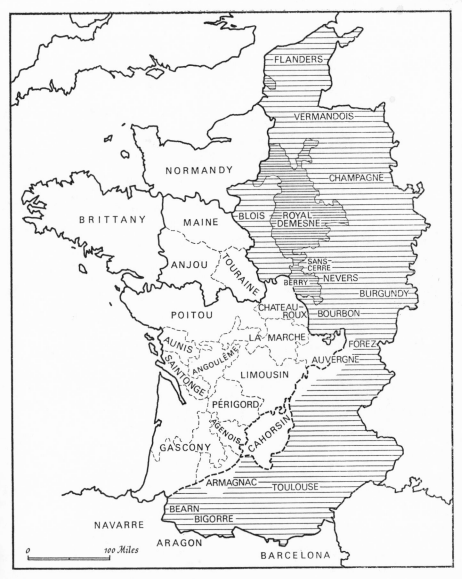

V *Continental Dominions of the King of England 1154–1160.*

SELECT GENEALOGIES

William the Conqueror
d.1087

Robert, Dk. of Normandy = Sibyl d. of
1087-1100   Geoffrey
            C. of Conversano

     William 'Clito'
       d.1127

Richard
d. about
1075

William II
K. of England
1087-1100

Henry I == (1) Matilda, d. of
K. of England   Malcolm III
1100-1135   K. of Scotland
Dk. of Normandy   (2) Adela d. of
1106-1135   Geoffrey
                C. of Louvain

Adela = Stephen
       C. of Blois

    Stephen
    K. of England
    1135-1184
    (See Table IV)

    Many others

William = Matilda
d.1120   d. of Fulk V
        C. of Aragon

Henry V = Matilda = **Geoffrey V**
Emperor   C. of Anjou
                 d.1151
               (See Table)

Henry II = Eleanor
Duke of Normandy   heiress to
Count of Anjou   Duchy of Aquitaine
Duke of Aquitaine
becomes
King of England
in 1154

❶ Kings of England

Tancred of Hautville

Sigelgaita
d. of Gisulf II
of Salerno

$=$ ROBERT GUISCARD
Duke of Apulia
C. of Calabria and
Sicily died 1085

(1) Judith d. of
William
C. of Evreux

(2) Eremberga d. of
William C. of Mortain

(3) Adelaide d. of
Manfred the Marquis

$=$ ROGER
Count of
Calabria and
Sicily
1085–1101

Alaine, d. of
Robert-le-Frison
C. of Flanders

$=$ ROGER BORSA
Duke of Apulia
1085–1111

WILLIAM
Duke of Apulia
1111–1127

Busila
= Carloman
K. of Hungary

d. = Rainulf
C. of Alife

d. = Ralph Maccabees
C. of Montescaglioso

Other
daughters

Constance
= Conrad, son
of Henry IV

Elvira of
Castille

$=$ ROGER
(3)
C. of Calabria 1105–1154
C. of Sicily 1105–1154
Duke of Apulia 1127–1154
Prince of Capua 1127–1154
King of Sicily 1130–1154

$=$ Beatrice of Rethel

Simon
(3)
C. of Calabria
and Sicily
1101–1105

WILLIAM
King of Sicily
1154–1186

Constance = Henry VI
K. of Sicily
Emperor
1190–1197

🄯 Rulers of Apulia
and Sicily

Tancred of Hauteville

Aubrée of = Robert Guiscard = Sigelgaita   Emma = Odobonus   William, Count = Marie, d. of
Buonalbergo   Duke of Apulia   the Marquis   of the Principate   Guy of Salerno

Constance = BOHEMUND I   TANCRED = Cecilia, d. of   d. = Richard of the
d. of Philip I Prince of Antioch   Prince of Galilee   Philip I   Principate and
K. of France   1098–1111   Regent of Antioch K. of France   Lord of Salerno
         (absent 1101–1103 Prince of Antioch
         and after 1105)   d. 1112

BOHEMUND = Alice, d. of   ROGER OF SALERNO
arrived in East in Baldwin II   Prince of Antioch
1126 with title of K. of Jerusalem   1112–1119
Prince of Antioch she was regent
d. 1130   of Antioch between
                1130 and 1136

Raymond of = Constance = Rainold of
Poitiers   Chatillon
Prince of Antioch   Regent of Antioch
1136–1149   with the title of Prince
                  1153–1160

BOHEMUND III

The Norman Rulers of Antioch

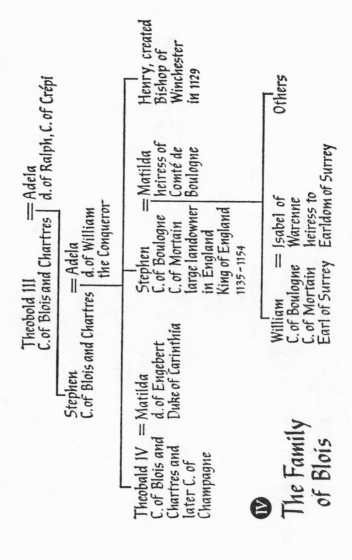

Theobold III
C. of Blois and Chartres $=$ Adela
d. of Ralph, C. of Crépi

Stephen
C. of Blois and Chartres $=$ Adela
d. of William
the Conqueror

Theobald IV $=$ Matilda
C. of Blois and
Chartres and
later C. of
Champagne
d. of Engebert
Duke of Carinthia

Stephen
C. of Boulogne
C. of Mortain
large landowner
in England
King of England
1135–1154 $=$ Matilda
heiress of
Comté de
Boulogne

Henry, created
Bishop of
Winchester
in 1129

William
C. of Boulogne
C. of Mortain
Earl of Surrey $=$ Isabel of
Warenne
heiress to
Earldom of Surrey

Others

Ⅳ

The Family
of Blois

Fulk IV 'le Rechin' = Bertrada of
C. of Anjou   Montfort
C. of Touraine   later
d.1109   Queen of France

Fulk V   = (1)Eremberga
Count of Anjou 1109-1129   d. and heiress
Count of Touraine   of Elias
Count of Maine   C. of Maine
King of Jerusalem
1131-1143   (2)Melisande
                                       d. of Baldwin II   Henry I
                                       K. of Jerusalem   King of England

                        Geoffrey V 'Plantagenet'   =   Matilda
                        C. of Anjou 1129-1151   widow of
                        C. of Touraine   the Emperor
                        C. of Maine   Henry V
                        Duke of Normandy from 1144
                        died 1151

Henry   = Eleanor
Count of Anjou 1151   heiress of Aquitaine
Count of Maine 1151   repudiated wife
Count of Touraine 1151   of King Louis VII
Duke of Normandy 1151
Duke of Aquitaine 1152
King of England 1154

The Counts of Anjou

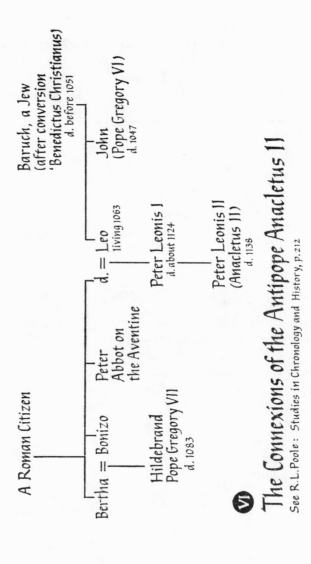

Baruch, a Jew
(after conversion
'Benedictus Christianus)
d. before 1051

A Roman Citizen

```
         ┌───────────────┴───────────────┐
      Peter                           d. = Leo
Bertha = Bonizo    Abbot on                living 1063
                   the Aventine
Hildebrand                         Peter Leonis I
Pope Gregory VII                   d. about 1124
d. 1083
                                   Peter Leonis II
                                   (Anacletus II)
                                   d. 1138
```

John
(Pope Gregory VI)
d. 1047

Ⓥ The Connexions of the Antipope Anacletus II

See R.L.Poole: *Studies in Chronology and History*, p.212

SCHEDULE OF SELECTED DATES

1095 (22 December) Birth of Roger the Great.

1098 Bohemund I, son of Robert Guiscard, becomes prince of Antioch. Kerbogha of Mosul defeated by Bohemund at the Great Battle of Antioch.

1100 (July) Bohemund taken prisoner by the Turks. His nephew Tancred rules Antioch.

(2 August) Death of William Rufus in New Forest.

(5 August) Coronation of Henry I as king of England.

(11 November) Baldwin I becomes king of Jerusalem.

(November) Marriage of Henry I to Matilda, daughter of Malcolm III king of Scotland.

1101 (22 June) Death of Roger 'the Great Count' of Sicily. He is succeeded by his young son Simon.

Robert, eldest son of William the Conqueror, unsuccessfully invades England. He resigns his claim to England but remains duke of Normandy.

1102 Feudal revolt against Henry I led by family of Montgomery.

1103 Capture of Lattakieh by Tancred. Bohemund released by Turks.

1104 Bohemund defeated by Turks at battle of Haran. He departs for the West, leaving Antioch in charge of Tancred.

1105 (28 September) Death of Simon, count of Sicily. He is succeeded as count by his younger brother, Roger, under the regency of their mother, Adelaide.

1106 (5 August) Death of the emperor Henry IV. He is succeeded by his son Henry V.

(August) Battle of Tinchebrai. Robert defeated and taken prisoner by Henry I. England and Normandy reunited.

Marriage of Constance and Cecilia of France respectively to Bohemund I and Tancred.

1107 Submission of Normandy to King Henry I.

1108 Louis VI becomes king of France.

1110 Henry V invades Italy.

1111 Death of Roger Borsa duke of Apulia. He is succeeded by his son William.

Death of Bohemund I.

1111–17 Civil war in Apulia.

1111–13 War between Henry I and Louis VI of France.

1112 Death of Tancred. Roger of Salerno becomes prince of Antioch.
(June) Roger, having come of age, holds a great court at Palermo.

1113 Marriage of Adelaide countess of Sicily, to Baldwin I king of Jerusalem.
Henry I recognized as overlord over Maine and Brittany.

1114 Marriage of Matilda, daughter of Henry I, to the emperor Henry V.

1115 Pope Paschal II proclaims Truce of God in Apulia.

1116–17 Henry V invades Italy.

1117 Adelaide, having been repudiated by Baldwin I, returns to Sicily.
Baldwin II becomes king of Jerusalem.

1118 Jordan II prince of Capua restores Pope Gelasius II to Rome.
(16 April) Death of Adelaide countess of Sicily.
Norman expedition against Gerba in North Africa.

1119 Christian defeat in the battle of the 'Field of Blood' near Sarmeda.
Death of Roger of Salerno.
Louis VI defeated by Henry I at the battle of Brémule.

1120 (25 November) Wreck of the *White Ship*. Death of William, son
of Henry I.

1121 Duke William of Apulia cedes Calabria to Roger, and names Roger
as his heir.

1122 Concordat of Worms between Pope Paschal II and Henry V.

1123 Defeat of the Normans outside Al Mahdia by Hassan.

1125 Death of Henry V. Lothair elected emperor.

1126–30 Bohemund II prince of Antioch.

1127 Marriage of Matilda, widow of Henry V, to Geoffrey count of
Anjou.
(July) Death of William duke of Apulia. Roger invades Apulia
despite opposition of Pope Honorius II and Jordan prince of Capua.

1128 Roger completes conquest of Apulia.
(22 April) Honorius II recognizes Roger as duke of Apulia and as
overlord of Capua.

1129 Roger holds a court of his feudal vassals at Melfi.
Death of the emir Christodoulos.

1130 (14 February) Death of Pope Honorius II. Innocent II and Anacletus II
dispute the papal succession.
A great feudal court held outside Salerno demands that Roger should
assume the dignity of king.

(27 September) Bull of Anacletus recognizing Roger as king. The capital of his realm is to be at Palermo.

(25 December) Coronation of Roger as king at Palermo.

1131–8 Civil war in southern Italy. Confederation of magnates formed against King Roger under the leadership of Pope Innocent II and the emperor Lothair, who invades Italy.

1131 Capture of Amalfi by the emir George of Antioch.
Fulk count of Anjou becomes king of Jerusalem.

1132 The building of the Cappella Palatina in Palermo is begun. George of Antioch takes title of 'Emir of Emirs'.

1135 (1 December) Death of Henry I.
(22 December) Coronation of Stephen of Blois as king of England. Normans capture the island of Gerba. They begin the conquest of the eastern Maghreb.

1137 Death of Louis VI. He is succeeded as king of France by his son Louis VII.
Lothair and Innocent II in possession of Bari.
(December) Death of Lothair. Conrad III becomes emperor.

1139 Death of Anacletus II.
Matilda, wife of Geoffrey count of Anjou, lands in England. Civil war between her and Stephen begins.
(22 July) Defeat of Innocent II and his allies by Roger at the battle on the Garigliano. Innocent recognizes and sanctions all Roger's conquests. He lifts his excommunication of the king.

1140 Great court held by King Roger at Ariano. The royal 'assizes' are drafted and proclaimed.

1141 Battle of Lincoln. King Stephen defeated and taken prisoner.

1143 Building of the Church of the Martorana in Palermo by the emir George of Antioch.

1144 Baldwin III becomes king of Jerusalem.
(December) Capture of Edessa by the Turks.
Geoffrey count of Anjou becomes duke of Normandy.

1145 Eugenius III proclaims the crusade in his bull *Quantum Praedecessores*.

1146 St Bernard preaches the crusade in France and Germany.

1147 Crusade against the Wends.
Eugenius further promotes the crusade in his bull *Divina Dispensione*.

1147–8 Roger attacks, invades and pillages the Eastern empire.

1148 (July) Capture of Al Mahdia by the Normans under the leadership of the emir George of Antioch.

Normans occupy Susa, Sfax and Gabes.

(July) The Christians in the East, having suffered many reverses during the Second Crusade, are finally repelled outside Damascus.

Matilda leaves England and entrusts her cause to her husband Count Geoffrey and her son Henry.

1151 (7 September) Death of Geoffrey count of Anjou. All his possessions and claims pass to his son Henry.

1152 (February) Death of Conrad III.

(March) Election of Frederick Barbarossa as emperor.

(March) Marriage of Count Henry of Anjou to Eleanor, heiress to the duchy of Aquitaine.

Death of the emir George of Antioch.

1153 Capture of Bone for the Normans by the emir Philip of Mahdia. Culmination of the Norman conquests in North Africa.

Treaty between King Stephen and Henry of Blois. Henry is recognized as Stephen's successor to the kingdom of England.

(20 August) Death of St Bernard.

(December) Execution of the emir Philip of Mahdia in Palermo.

1154 (26 February) Death of Roger the Great.

(25 October) Death of King Stephen.

(19 December) Coronation of Henry II as king of England.

CONTEMPORARY RULERS

KINGS OF ENGLAND
Henry I, 1100–35
  (duke of Normandy, 1106–35)
Stephen, 1135–54

KINGS OF FRANCE
Philip I, d. 1108
Louis VI, 1108–37
Louis VII, 1137–80

EMPERORS IN THE WEST
Henry IV, d. 1106
Henry V, 1110–25
Lothair, 1125–37
Conrad III, 1138–52
Frederick Barbarossa, 1152–90

DUKES OF APULIA
Roger Borsa, 1085–1111
William, 1111–27
Roger, count (subsequently king, of Sicily, 1127–54

NORMAN RULERS OF SICILY
Roger I, count, d. 1101
Roger, 'the Great count', 1103–30
  king, 1130–54

EMPERORS IN THE EAST
Alexis I, d. 1118
John II (Comnenus), 1118–43
Manuel I (Comnenus), 1143–80

POPES
Paschal II, 1099–1118
Gelasius II, 1118–24
Calixtus II, 1119–24
Honorius II, 1124–30
Innocent II, 1130–43 (Anacletus II, anti-pope, 1130)
Celestine II, 1143–4
Lucius II, 1144–5
Eugenius III, 1145–53
Anastasius IV, 1153–4

PRINCES OF ANTIOCH
Bohemund I, 1098–1111
Tancred (regent), 1101–3 and after 1105 frequently styled *prince*, d. 1112
Roger of Salerno, 1112–19
King Baldwin (regent), 1126–30
Alice (regent), 1130–6
Raymond of Poitiers, 1136–49
Constance (regent), 1149–53
Rainald of Châtillon, 1153–60

SELECT BIBLIOGRAPHY

The list of publications which here follows is in no way designed to cover the extensive literature which has been devoted to the history of the Norman dominions in the twelfth century. It may serve, however, to indicate my own wide obligations to the work of others. In this matter it might be invidious to discriminate. But all my readers will appreciate what I owe to the magisterial work of such as Erich Caspar, Ferdinand Chalandon, C. H. Haskins, Claude Cahen and Evelyn Jamison; and also to the scholarship of Professor L-R. Ménager, Sir Steven Runciman, Dom. David Knowles and Sir Richard Southern. In this connexion it must also be emphasized that many of the books cited as secondary authorities contain the texts of original documents not available in print elsewhere. Finally, it is hoped that the citation of those works which I have found of particular help to the comparative study that is here attempted may be of service also to those who in due course may extend that comparison both in scope and depth.

A

ORIGINAL AUTHORITIES AND COLLECTIONS OF SOURCES

Albert of Aix, *Liber Christianae Expeditionis*, *Rec. Hist. Crois. Occ.*, IV.

Alexander of Telese, *Liber de Rebus Gestis Rogerii Siciliae Regis*, in Del Re, *Cronisti*, I.

Amari, M., *Bibliotheca Arabo-Sicula*, 2 vols (Turin and Rome, 1880, 1881), contains Italian translations of the chronicles of Al Tigani, Ibn Dinar, Ibn Hamdis, Ibn Khaldun, etc.

Anglo-Saxon Chronicle. A revised translation edited by Dorothy Whitelock, with D. C. Douglas and S. I. Tucker (London, 1961).

Anna Comnena, *Alexiad*, trans. E. A. Dawes (London, 1967).

Annales Barenses, in Migne, *Pat. Lat.*, Vol. 155.

Annales Beneventani, *Mon. Germ. Hist. SS.*, III, pp. 173 et sqq.

Annales Cavenses, *Mon. Germ. Hist. SS.*, III.

Annales Herbipolenses, *Mon. Germ. Hist. SS.*, III.

Select Bibliography

Annalista Saxo, Mon. Germ. Hist. SS., III.

Baudri of Dol, *Historia Hierosolimitana*, Rec. Hist. Crois. Occ., V.

Carmen de Hastingae Proelio, ed. C. Morton and H. Muntz (Oxford, 1970).

Codex Diplomaticus Caietanus, 2 vols (Monte Cassino, 1888–91).

Codice Diplomatica Barese, 18 vols (Bari, 1897–1950).

Codice Diplomatico Brindisiano, Vol. I (Trani, 1940).

Collura, P., *Appendice al Regesto dei Diplomi di re Ruggero compilato da Erich Cypar, Studi Ruggeriani*, pp. 545–629.

Cusa, S., *I Diplomi Greci e Arabi di Sicilia*, 2 vols (Palermo, 1896–8).

Damascus Chronicle of the Crusade, ed. and trans. H. A. R. Gibb (London, 1932).

Delaborde, F. (ed.), *Chartes de Terre Sainte provenants de Notre Dame de Josaphat* (Paris, 1880).

Eadmer, *Historia Novorum*, ed. M. Rule (London, 1884).

——, *Vita Anselmi*, ed. R. W. Southern (London, 1962).

Ekkehart of Aura, *De Expugnatione Hierosolimitana*, ed. Hagenmeyer (Tubingen, 1877).

English Historical Documents, Vol. II, ed. D. C. Douglas and G. W. Greenaway (London, 1953).

España Sagrada (Madrid, 1747–1879).

Falco of Benevento, *Chronicon de Rebus aetate sui gestis* (Del Re, *Cronisti*, I, and Migne, *Pat. Lat.*, Vol. 173).

'Florence of Worcester', *Chronicon*, ed. B. Thorpe, 2 vols (London, 1848, 1849).

Gabrieli, F., *Arab Historians of the Crusades* (London, 1969).

Garufi, C. A., *I Documenti inediti dell epoca Normannia: Documenti per servire alla storia di Sicilia*, Soc. Siciliana di Storia Patria, Ser. Diplomatica, XVIII (Palermo, 1899).

Gerhoh of Reichersberg, *De Investigatione Anti-Christi*, Mon. Germ. Hist. *Libelli de Lite*, III.

Gesta Francorum et aliorum Hierosolimitanorum, ed. R. Hill (London, 1962).

Gesta Stephani, ed. K. R. Potter (London, 1955).

Guibert of Nogent, *Historia Hierosolimitana*, Rec. Hist. Crois. Occ., IV.

Hagenmeyer, H., *Die Kreuzzugsbriefe aus dem Jahren 1088–1100* (Innsbruck, 1902).

Henry of Huntingdon, *Historia Anglorum*, ed. Arnold (London, 1879).

Jaffé, Philip, *Regesta Pontificum Romanorum*, 2nd edition, ed. E. Wattnebach, S. Lowenfeld and others, 2 vols (Leipzig, 1885–8).

John of Salisbury, *Historia Pontificalis*, ed. Chibnall (London, 1956).

——, *ibid.*, ed. R. L. Poole (Oxford, 1927).

Kehr, K. A., *Urkunden der Normannisch-Sicilischen Könige* (Innsbruck, 1902).

Kehr, P. F., see *Regesta Pontificum Romanorum*.

Lawrie, A. C., *Early Scottish Charters* (Glasgow, 1923).

Liber Pontificalis, ed. L. Duchesne, 2 vols (Paris, 1886–92).

Lowenfeld, S. (ed.), *Epistolae Pontificum Romanorum ineditae* (Leipzig, 1885).

Lupus Protospatarius, see *Annales Barenses*.

Mas Latrie, *Traités de Paix et de Commerce: Les Relations des Chrétiens avec les Arabes de l'Afrique septentrionale au Moyen Age* (Paris, 1866).

Ménager, L. R., *Les Actes Latines de S. Maria de Messina* (Palermo, 1961).

Odo of Deuil, *De Profectu Ludovici VII in Orientem*, ed. V. Berry (Columbia U.P., 1948).

Ordericus Vitalis, *Historia Ecclesiastica*, ed. A. Le Prévost and L. Delisle, 5 vols (Paris, 1838–55).

Otto of Freising, *Chronicon* (*Mon. Germ. Hist. SS.*, XX).

——, *ibid.*, translated as *The Two Cities* by C. C. Mierow (Columbia U.P., 1928).

——, *Gesta Friderici*, *Mon. Germ. Hist. SS.*, IX.

Pirro, R., *Sicilia Sacra*, ed. Mongitore (Palermo, 1733).

Ralph of Caen, *Gesta Tancredi*, *Rec. Hist. Crois. Occ.*, III.

Re, G. del, *Cronisti et scrittori sincroni de la dominazione normanna nel regno di Puglia et Sicilia*, 2 vols (Naples, 1868).

Recueil des Historiens des Croisades: Historiens Occidentaux, 5 vols (Paris, 1844–95).

Recueil des Historiens des Gaules et de la France, 24 vols (Paris, 1738–1924).

Regesta Pontificum Romanorum, 8 vols (Berlin, 1911–61). Vol. VIII, with the sub-title *Italia Pontificia*, is edited by P. F. Kehr.

Regesta Regni Hierosolimitani, ed. R. Röhricht (Innsbruck, 1893).

Regesta Regum Anglo-Normannorum, ed. H. W. C. Davis and others, 3 vols (Oxford, 1913–68).

Robert the Monk, *Historia Hierosolimitana*, *Rec. Hist. Crois. Occ.*, III, pp. 717–82.

Robert of Torigni, *Chronicle*, ed. R. Howlett, in *Chronicles . . . of Stephen*, IV (London, 1889).

Röhricht, R., see *Regesta Regni Hierosolimitani*.

Romuald of Salerno, *Chronicon sive Annales*, in Del Re, *Cronisti*, I.

Round, J. H., *Calendar of Documents preserved in France illustrative of the history of Great Britain and Ireland* (London, 1899).

Select Bibliography

Simeon of Durham, *Historia Dunelmensis Ecclesiae* and *Historia Regum*, ed. Arnold, 2 vols (London, 1882–5).

Starrabba, R., *Contributo allo Studio della diplomatica Siciliana dei tempi normani: Diplomi di fondazione delle chiese episcopali di Sicilia* (*Archivio Storico Siciliano*, Nuova Serie, XVIII, Palermo, 1893).

——, *Diplomi della Cathedrale di Messina* (Soc. Siciliana di Storia Patria, Documenti, I, 1876).

Suger, *Gesta Ludovici Regis*, ed. A. Molinier (Paris, 1887).

Taccone Galluci, *Regesti dei Pontifici Romani per le chiese della Calabria* (Rome, 1902).

'Tractatus Eboracenses', *Mon. Germ. Hist. Libelli de Lite*, III. By the 'Norman Anonymous' of Rouen or York.

Ughelli, F., *Italia Sacra*, 2nd edn, 10 vols (Venice, 1717–22).

Watterich, J. M., *Pontificum Romanorum . . . Vitae*, 2 vols (Leipzig, 1862).

William of Malmesbury, *Gesta Regum Anglorum*, ed. W. Stubbs (London, 1870).

——, *Historia Novella*, ed. K. R. Potter (London, 1955).

William of Tyre, *Historia Rerum in partibus transmarinis gestarum*, *Rec. Hist. Crois. Occ.*, III.

B

SECONDARY AUTHORITIES AND WORKS OF REFERENCE

Alphandéry, P., and Dupront, A., *Le Chrétienté et l'idée de Croisade* (Paris, 1935).

Altschul, M., *Anglo-Norman England, 1066–1154* (Cambridge U.P., 1969).

Amari, M., *Storia dei Musulmani de Sicilia*, 3 vols (Catania, 1933–7).

Anastos, M. V., 'Some aspects of Byzantine influence on Latin thought' (see *Twelfth Century Europe*).

Atiya, A., *Crusade, Commerce and Culture* (Indiana U.P., 1962).

Barlow, F., *The Feudal Kingdom of England* (London, 1961).

Barraclough, G., *Medieval Germany*, 2 vols (Oxford, 1948).

——, *Origins of Modern Germany* (Oxford, 1947).

Barrow, G. W. S., 'Les familles normandes d'Ecosse', *Annales de Normandie*, XV (1965).

Bédier, J., *Les Légendes épiques*, 4 vols (Paris, 1908–13).

Bertaux, F., *L'Art dans l'Italie méridionale* (Paris, 1904).

Bishop, E., *Liturgica Historica* (Oxford, 1962).

Bloch, H., 'The Schism of Anacletus and the Glanfeuil forgeries of Peter the Deacon', *Traditio*, VIII (1952).

Bloch, Marc, *Feudal Society* (London, 1961).

———, *Mélanges historiques*, 2 vols (Paris, 1963).

———, *The Royal Touch* (London, 1973).

Boase, T. S. R., 'Recent developments in Crusading historiography', *History*, XXII (1937), pp. 110–25.

Brandileone, F., *Il Diritto romane nelle legge normanne . . . del regno di Sicilia* (Turin, 1884).

Bridery, E., *La condition juridique des Croisés et la privilège de Croix* (Paris, 1909).

Brooke, C. N. L., *Saxon and Norman Kings* (London, 1963).

———, *The Twelfth Century Renaissance* (London, 1970).

Brooke, Z. N., *The English Church and the Papacy* (Cambridge, 1931).

Cahen, C. *La Régime féodale de l'Italie normande* (Paris, 1940).

———, *La Syrie du Nord à l'époque des Croisades, et la principalité franque d'Antioche* (Paris, 1940).

Cambridge Medieval History, Vols III, IV and V (Cambridge, 1922, 1923 and 1926).

Canard, M., 'Une lettre du Calife fatimite al Hafiz à Roger II' (see *Studi Ruggeriani*, I).

Caspar, E., *Roger II und die Gründing der normannisch-sicilischen Monarchie* (Innsbruck, 1904).

Cerone, F., *L'Opera politica e militare di Ruggero II in Africa e in oriente* (Catania, 1910).

Cessi, R., 'Il problema adriatica al tempore de Ruggero II' (see *Studi Ruggeriani*, I).

Chalandon, F., *Histoire de la Domination normande en Italie et en Sicile*, 2 vols (Paris, 1907).

Chartrou, *L'Anjou de 1109 à 1151* (Paris, 1928).

Clagett, M., see *Twelfth Century Europe*.

Cohn, W., *Geschichte des normannische-Sicilische Flotte* (Breslau, 1910).

Complete Peerage of England, Scotland, Ireland, Great Britain and the United Kingdom, by G. E. C., new edition, 13 vols in 14 (London, 1910–59).

Constable, G., 'The Second Crusade as seen by contemporaries', *Traditio*, IX (1953).

Cosack, H., 'Konrad III's Enschluss zum Kreuzzug', *Mittelungen des Instituts für österreichische Geschichtsforschung*, XXXV (1914).

Cottineau, L. H., *Répertoire Topo-bibliographique des abbayes et prieurés*, 2 vols (Macon, 1935, 1937).

Curtis, E., *Roger of Sicily* (New York, 1912).

Daniel, N., *Islam and the West; the Making of an Image* (Edinburgh, 1962).

David, C. W., *Robert Curthose* (Harvard U.P., 1920).

Davis, R. H. C., *King Stephen* (London, 1967).

Dawson, C., *Religion of the Rise of Western Culture* (London, 1948).

———, *The Making of Europe* (London, 1952).

———, *Medieval Essays* (London, 1953).

Deer, J., *Papstum und Normannen* (Cologne, 1972).

Delahaye, H., 'Les lettres d'Indulgence collectives', *Analecta Bollandiana*, XLIV, XLV, XLVI (1926–8).

Demus, O., *The Mosaics of Norman Sicily* (London, 1950).

Dictionary of National Biography.

Diehl, C., *L'art byzantine dans l'Italie meridionale* (Paris, 1894).

Douglas, D. C., 'The development of medieval Europe', *European civilization*, ed. E. Eyre, Vol. III, pp. 1–350.

———, *The Norman Achievement* (London, 1969).

———, 'Les Réussites normandes', *Revue historique* (1967).

Douglas, Norman, *Old Calabria*, 4th edn (London, 1955).

Ducange, C., *Les Familles d'Outre Mer*, ed. E. S. Rey (Paris, 1869).

Duchesne, L., 'Les évêchés de Calabrie', in *Mélanges . . . Paul Fabre* (Paris, 1892).

Edwards, J. G., 'The Normans and the Welsh March', *Proc. Brit. Acad.*, XLII (1956), pp. 155–78.

Erdmann, C., *Die Enstehung des Kreuzzugsgedankens* (Stuttgart, 1935).

Fliche, A., 'La Papauté et les origines de la Croisade', *Rev. Hist. ecclesiastique*, XXXIV (1924).

Folz, R., *The Concept of Empire in Western Europe* (London, 1969).

Freeman, E. A., 'The Normans at Palermo', in *Historical Essays*, III (London, 1879).

Fuiano, M., 'La fondazzione del Regnum Siciliae nella versione di Alessandro da Telese', *Papers Brit. School at Rome*, XXIV (1956).

Gams, B., *Series Episcoporum Ecclesiae Catholicae* (Regensburg, 1873).

Ganshof, F., *Feudalism*, trans. Grierson (London, 1956).

Garufi, C. A., *Censimento e Catasto della populazione servile – Nuovi studi . . . sull' ordinamento administrativo dei Normanni in Sicilia*, *Archivio Storico Siciliano*, n.s. XLIX (1928).

Genicot, L., 'On the evidence of growth of population in the West from the eleventh to the thirteenth century' (see Thrupp *Change in Medieval Society*).

Gibbon, E., *Decline and Fall of the Roman Empire*, ed. J. B. Bury (London, n.d.).

Gieysztor, A., 'The genesis of the Crusades', *Medievalia et Humanistica*, V and VI.

Giunta, F., *Bizantini e Bizantismo nella Sicilia normanni* (Palermo, 1950).

Gleber, H., *Papst Eugen III* (Jena, 1936).

Gottlob, A., *Kreuzablass und Almosenablass* (Stuttgart, 1906).

Gregorovius, F., *The City of Rome in the Middle Ages*, esp. vols IVa and V (London, 1905).

Grousset, R., *Histoire des Croisades*, 3 vols (Paris, 1934–6).

Grunebaum, G. E. von, 'The world of Islam – the face of the antagonist' (see *Twelfth Century Europe*).

Guillaume, P., *Essai historique sur l'abbaye de Cava* (Cava, 1877).

Halecki, O., *The Limits and Divisions of European History* (London, 1950).

Harvey, John H., 'The origins of Gothic architecture: some further thoughts', *Antiquaries Journal*, XLVIII, pt i (1968).

Haskins, C. H., *The Normans in European History* (New York, 1915).

——, *The Renaissance of the Twelfth Century* (Harvard U.P., 1927).

——, 'England and Sicily in the twelfth century', *Eng. Hist. Rev.*, XXVI (1916), pp. 435–47, 641–65.

——, *Studies in the History of Medieval Science* (Harvard U.P., 1927).

Heer, F., *The Medieval World* (London, 1961).

Hefele, C. J., *Histoire des Conciles*, ed. H. Leclerc, 11 vols (Paris, 1907–52).

Herval, R., 'Eclectisme intellectuel à la cour de Roger II', *Studi Ruggeriani*, I.

Holmes, W. T., 'The idea of a twelfth century renaissance', *Speculum*, XXVI, 1953.

Holtzmann, W., 'Il regno di Ruggero e gli inizi di una sistema di stati europei, *Studi Ruggeriani*, I.

——, 'Die altesten Urkunden des Kloster S. Maris del Patir', *Byzantina Zeitschrift*, XXVI (1926).

Jamison, E., *Admiral Eugenius of Sicily* (London, 1957).

——, 'Some notes on the *Anonymi Gesta Francorum* . . ., in *Studies Presented to . . . M. K. Pope* (Manchester, 1939).

——, 'The Sicilian Norman kingdom in the minds of Anglo-Norman contemporaries', *Proc. Brit. Acad.*, XXIV (1938).

——, 'The Norman administration of Apulia and Capua', *Papers Brit. School at Rome*, VI (1913), pp. 221–481.

——, 'Norman feudalism in southern Italy', *Congrés des Sciences historiques*, I (1938).

Kantorowicz, E. H., *Laudes Regiae* (California U.P., 1946).

——, *The King's Two Bodies* (Princeton U.P., 1957).

——, 'Kingship under the impact of secular jurisprudence' (see *Twelfth Century Europe*).

Kitzinger, E., *The Mosaics of Monreale* (Oxford, 1966).

Knowles, M. D., *The Monastic Order in England* (Cambridge U.P., 1940).

——, *The Historian and Character* (Cambridge U.P., 1963).

Kugler, B., *Bohemund und Tankred* (Tubingen, 1862).

La Monte, J. L., 'Some problems of Crusading historiography', *Speculum*, XV (1940).

——, 'To what extent was the Byzantine Empire the suzerain of the Crusading states?', *Byzantion* (1936).

Latourette, K. S., *A History of the Expansion of Christianity*, Vol. II (London, 1939).

La Torre, A. de, 'Ruggero y Alphonzo VII', *Studi Ruggeriani*, I.

Lenormant, F., *La Grande Grèce*, 3 vols (Paris, 1881–4).

Le Patourel, J., 'The Norman colonization of Britain', in *Normanni et la loro espansione.*

Leyser, K., 'England and the Empire in the early twelfth century', *Trans. R. Hist. Soc.*, Ser. 5, Vol. X (1960).

Lloyd, J. E., *History of Wales* (London, 1911).

Lopez, R. S., *Birth of Europe* (London, 1965).

Lopez, R. S., and Raymond, I. W., *Medieval Trade in the Mediterranean World* (Oxford, 1953).

Loyd, L. C., *The Origins of some Anglo-Norman Families* (Harleian Society, CIII, 1951).

Luchaire, A., *Louis VI, le Gros* (Paris, 1890).

Marongiu, A., 'Consezione della Sovranitá di Ruggero II', *Studi Ruggeriani*, I.

Ménager, L. R., 'L'Institution monarchique dans les états normands d'Italie', *Cahiers de Civilization medievale*, II (1959).

——, 'La legislation sud-Italienne sous le domination normande', in *Normanni et la loro espansione.*

——, 'Le Byzantinisation religieuse de l'Italie meridionale et la politique monastique des Normande d'Italie', *Rev. Hist. ecclesiastique*, LIII (1958) and LIV (1959).

——, *Amiratus, l'Emirat et les origines de l'amirauté* (Paris, 1960).

Monti, G. M., *L'Italia e la crociàta; l'espansione mediterranea della Sicilia* (Bologna, 1940).

Mor, C. G., 'Roger II et les assemblés du royaume normande', *Rev. Hist. de Droit français et étranger*, Ser. 4, vol. 56 (1958).

Munro, D. C., 'The western attitude to Islam during the Crusades', *Speculum*, VI (1931).

——, *The Kingdom of the Crusaders* (New York, 1936).

Nicholson, R. L., *Tancred: a study of his life and work* (Chicago, 1940).

Normanni (I) et la loro espansione in Europa nel alto medievo (in *Centro di Studi medieve*, XVI (Spoleto, 1969).

Norwich, J. J. Lord, *The Normans in the South*, 2 vols (London, 1966).

——, *The Kingdom in the Sun* (London, 1970).

Pacaut, M., *Louis VII et son Royaume* (Paris, 1964).

Paratore, E., 'Observazioni sugli scrittori di Ruggero II' (see, *Studi Ruggeriani*, I).

Pollock, F., and Maitland, F. W., *History of English Law before the time of Edward IV*, 2 vols (Cambridge, 1898).

Pontieri, E., 'La Madre di Re Ruggero' (see *Studi Ruggeriani*, II).

——, *Tra in Normanni nel Italia meridionali* (Naples, 1964).

Poole, A. L., *From Domesday Book to Magna Carta* (Oxford, 1951).

Poole, R. L., *The Exchequer in the Twelfth Century* (Oxford, 1915).

——, *Lectures on the History of the Papal Chancery* (Cambridge, 1915).

——, *Studies in Chronology and History* (Oxford, 1934).

Prestwich, J. O., 'War and finance in the Anglo-Norman State', R. Hist. Soc. Trans., Ser. 5, IV (1954).

Ritchie, R. L. G., *The Normans in Scotland* (Edinburgh, 1954).

Round, J. H., *Feudal England* (London, 1895).

——, *Geoffrey de Mandeville* (London, 1892).

——, *Studies in Peerage and Family History* (1901).

Rousset, P., *Les Origines et les caractères de la première Croisade* (Neufchatel 1945).

Runciman, S., *History of the Crusades*, 3 vols (Cambridge, 1951–4).

——, 'The Holy Lance found at Antioch', *Analecta Bollandiana*, LXVII (1950).

Rupp, Jean, *L'idée de Chrétienté dans la pensée pontificale des origines à Innocent III* (Paris, 1939).

Saunders, J. J., *Aspects of the Crusades* (Canterbury, N.Z., 1962).

Schramm, P., *History of the English Coronation* (Oxford, 1937).

Setton, K. M., and Baldwin, M. W. (eds.), *A History of the Crusades*, Vol. I (1955), Vol. II (1962) (Pennsylvania U.P.).

Smail, R. C., *Crusading Warfare* (Cambridge, 1956).

Southern, R. W., 'The renaissance of the twelfth century', *History*, XLV (1959).

——, *The Making of the Middle Ages* (London, 1953).

——, *St Anselm and his Biographer* (Cambridge, 1963).

——, 'The place of Henry I in English history', *Proc. British Academy*, XLVIII (1962).

Stefano, A. de, *La Cultura in Sicilia nel periodo normanno* (Bologna, 1954).

Stenton, F. M., *The First Century of English Feudalism* (Oxford, 1952).

Stevenson, W. B., *Crusaders in the East* (Cambridge, 1907).

Studi Ruggeriani – *Atti del Convegno internationale di Studi Ruggeriani, Scc. Siciliana di Storia Patria* (Palermo, 1955).

Thrupp, S., *Change in Medieval Society* (London, 1965).

Twelfth Century Europe and the Foundation of Modern Society, ed. M. Clagett and others (Madison, 1961).

Ullmann, W., *Medieval Papalism: the political theories of Medieval Canonists* (London, 1949).

——, *Principles of Government and Politics in the Middle Ages* (London, 1961).

——, *History of the Papacy in the Middle Ages* (London, 1972).

——, *The Growth of Papal Government in the Middle Ages* (London, 1969).

Vacandard, E., *Vie de S. Bernard* (Paris, 1920).

——, 'Saint Bernard et la seconde Croisade', *Revue des Questions historiques*, XXVIII (1885).

Vasiliev, A. A., 'Medieval ideas of the end of the world', *Byzantion*, XVI (1942).

Villars, J. B., *Les Normands en Mediterranée* (Paris, 1951).

Walzer, R., 'The Arabic transmission of Greek thought to medieval Europe', *Bull. John Rylands Library*, XXIX (1945).

Ward, P. L., 'The coronation ceremony on medieval England', *Speculum*, XIV (1939).

West, F. J., *The justiciarship in England* (Cambridge, 1960).

White, L. T., *Latin Monasticism in Norman Sicily* (Harvard U.P., 1938).

Wieruszowski, H., 'Roger II of Sicily – Rex Tyrannus – in twelfth century thought', *Speculum*, XXXVIII (1965).

Williams, G. H., *The Norman Anonymous of 1100 A.D.* (Harvard U.P., 1951).

Williams, W., *St Bernard of Clairvaux* (Manchester, 1935).

Yewdale, R. B., *Bohemund the First* (New York, 1917).

INDEX